's

4/23

Britain, Ireland and the Second World War

Titles available and forthcoming in the *Societies at War* series

War Damage in Western Europe
Nicola Lambourne

War Aims in the Second World War
Victor Rothwell

The Battle of Britain on Screen:
'The Few' in British Film and Television Drama
S. P. MacKenzie

British Children's Fiction in the Second World War
Owen Dudley Edwards

The Second World War and Forced Migration Movements in Europe
Rainer Schulze

Britain, Ireland and the Second World War
Ian S. Wood

Sweden, the Swastika and Stalin:
The Swedish Experience in the Second World War
John Gilmour

Britain, Ireland and the Second World War

Ian S. Wood

Edinburgh University Press

With love to Helen, Ben, David, Robbie and Julie

© Ian S. Wood, 2010

Edinburgh University Press Ltd
22 George Square, Edinburgh
www.euppublishing.com

Typeset in Melior by
Iolaire Typesetting, Newtonmore, and
printed and bound in Great Britain by
CPI Antony Rowe, Chippenham and Eastbourne

A CIP record for this book is available from the British Library

ISBN 978 0 7486 2327 3 (hardback)

The right of Ian S. Wood
to be identified as author of this work
has been asserted in accordance with
the Copyright, Designs and Patents Act 1988.

Published with the support of the Edinburgh University
Scholarly Publishing Initiatives Fund.

Contents

Acknowledgements

Writing this book and drawing together some of my thoughts on the history of the Irish state, of Northern Ireland and of Britain's relationship to them during the period which, in Irish scholarship, is still called 'the Emergency' has been a wholly enjoyable task. It has also been a challenge because of the sheer quality of work published on this area over the last three decades.

Some of it, inevitably because of a combination of a word limit and deadlines for publication, has come too late for me. A case in point is the Royal Irish Academy's new collection of documents on Irish foreign policy, covering a crucial seventeen-month period between 1939 and 1941. Its editors have done a superb job casting important light on the sensitive subject of highly secret defence co-operation initiatives between the London and Dublin governments. They also reveal the extent to which, from fear of a possible German invasion, de Valera sanctioned the destruction of many classified files.

This has left a tantalising gap in our knowledge, as has the loss of many papers covering Eire's relations with Germany after 1938. These were destroyed by fires at the Irish embassy in Berlin caused by allied air attacks on the city.

Professor Eunan O'Halpin's new book, *Spying on Ireland: British Intelligence and Irish Neutrality during the Second World War* was also published after my work went to press but this is the place to acknowledge his superlative work on the Irish state's military and security policy before and during the Emergency.

Robert Fisk should also be saluted here for giving us his path-breaking work *In Time of War: Ireland, Ulster and the Price of Neutrality 1939–1945*. It is still as readable as it is informative nearly twenty-five years after it was first published. Clair Wills, in *That Neutral Island: a Cultural History of Ireland During the Second World War*, has given us a work of equal quality which will surely stand the test of time just as well. My good friends, Professor Graham Walker and Dr Brian Barton, are historians of Ulster Unionism and of Northern Ireland, from whom I have learned much. I always look forward to their excellent company in Belfast and I am especially indebted to Brian for lending me his own copy of Moya Woodside's Mass Observation diary.

Kevin Kenny gave me access to his stimulating dissertation and to a useful back run of articles from the *Irish Press*. He and his wife Celia also gave me generous hospitality both in Edinburgh and at their home in Dublin, and this is a good place to thank them again.

I must pay tribute here to Dr Eamon Phoenix. His 'On This Day' column in the *Irish News*, in which he reruns items in that paper from fifty years back, is an endlessly vivid source of which I have made extensive use in this book.

The help I have received from the staff of the National Library of Scotland, Edinburgh University Library and the Public Record Office of Northern Ireland has been indispensable. So, too, has been that of Commandant Victor Laing and his colleagues at the Irish Military Archive at Cathal Brugha barracks in Dublin. Former sergeant Paddy Cremin was a knowledgeable and genial guide to the army museum at Michael Collins barracks in Cork and made material available to me which I have used in this book.

I must also thank the Carnegie Trust for Scotland which gave me generous financial support that has covered travel and other expenses. Blackstaff Press in Belfast has given me permission to quote from *John Hewitt, the Selected Poems*, Michael Longley and Frank Ormsby (eds), 2007. The Curtis Brown Group Ltd, London, has agreed, on behalf of the Trustees of the Mass Observation Archive, that I may quote extracts from Moya Woodside's diary.

J. Tyler-Copper worked tirelessly to convert my manuscript into a form that was acceptable to a publisher. She, indeed, made significant improvements to it and I want to thank her, as I also want to thank Esmé Watson and Eddie Clark from Edinburgh University Press for their support and patience. My thanks go, too, to my son David who gave me invaluable assistance with the final typescript. So too did Anne Loughnane with Irish names used here.

Sean McKeown in Belfast has been unfailing in his hospitality and welcome company there, and I also want to mention, in no special order, Hugh Jordan, Jim McDowell, Andrew Sanders, John Brown, Ian Budge, Henry Cowper, Mario Relich, Paul Addison, Jeremy Crang, George Hewitt, Ian Donnachie and Gerry Douds. They have kept me on course and all have my gratitude.

1

The Origins of Éire's Neutrality

When, on the evening of Sunday, 3 September 1939, Éamon de Valera broadcast to the people of Éire, as the Irish state had been renamed two years earlier, Britain and France had already declared war on Germany. His wholly predictable message was that his government would stay out of the conflict, adhering, it has been said, to a stance of non-belligerency rather than one of neutrality in the sense in which that word had been used and refined over many years by jurists and writers on interstate relations.[1]

'With our history,' the Taioseach told his listeners, 'with our experience of the last war and with part of our country still unjustly severed from us, we felt that no other decision and no other policy was possible.'[2]

De Valera's statement was a product not only of a dramatic shift of political power which had brought him to office in 1932 but also of the 1921 treaty itself. This settlement, if such it was, was seen by optimists at the time on both sides of the Irish Sea as the basis for ending an ancient quarrel. Others, like Michael Collins, saw it as a necessary compromise. It offered, he famously claimed, 'the freedom to achieve freedom'.[3] Churchill, one of the principal British negotiators of the treaty, saw it as a way of securing essential British interests. Arguably, it could not have been both but he and Collins, for very different reasons, needed to 'talk up' the case for the treaty.

Two critical developments lay behind the 1921 treaty and the Government of Ireland Act a year earlier which had made partition a reality. These were the extraordinary transformation of both Irish nationalism and Irish Unionism over the previous three decades.

Until the split within his party, brought about by the O'Shea divorce case and his involvement in it, Charles Parnell had dominated the politics of Irish nationalism with his own charisma as well as with the formidable political machine he and his supporters had created to press the case for constitutional Home Rule. Parnell's supreme skill lay in linking that cause to both agrarian militancy and Fenian insurrectionism while never letting these elements take control of the Home Rule party.

The Achilles heel of the Home Rule movement may, however, have lain in its very success in mobilising so much nationalist support within the enlarged electorate resulting from the 1885 Reform Act. This success, it has been argued, served to arouse expectations of social mobility and personal fulfilment which could not be satisfied in an Ireland where growing numbers of educated lower-middle-class Roman Catholics found career advancement blocked off both by Protestants and by Englishmen. Their frustration made many of them ready converts to a cultural and literary revival in the late nineteenth century which aspired to go beyond constitutional Home Rule.[4]

This revival's most celebrated adherent and contributor was William Butler Yeats. He was motivated by his belief in a national literature under threat from Anglicising forces as well as from the advent of mass society. Writing in English, not Irish, but immersing himself in the ancient legends and folk tales of County Sligo where his mother came from, he created an idealised vision of a peasant Ireland. In this he was little different from an intelligentsia elsewhere in late nineteenth- and early twentieth-century Europe who identified themselves with what they wanted to think of as national cultures defined in pre-industrial and indeed pre-modernist forms.[5]

Yeats may have briefly joined the Irish Republican Brotherhood, or the Fenians, as they are more often known,[6] but his heart was never in it. He did it to impress his great love Maude Gonne and to convince her that he was a man of action, not just a dreamer. For others, espousing the cause of cultural revival, especially in the form of the Irish language movement, was a vital step towards political commitment. The Gaelic League, which grew rapidly after its formation in 1893, was a powerful influence upon many of those who joined the 1916 rising. Yet some of its founders, such as Douglas Hyde, an Ulster Protestant and League president from its inception to 1915, worked hard to keep it non-political. By as early as 1900, however, his essentially pluralist vision of the role of a revived national language was on the defensive against a much more narrowly Catholic view of Irishness.

This seismic shift within nationalism was in part a product of British policy in Ireland. Thirty years after the legislative union of 1801 the Dublin administration set up a National Schools system which, while it allowed regular access by clergy of all denominations, rigorously excluded Irish culture and history from its syllabus. Increasingly for Catholic parents who wanted something for their children closer to their own values and who could not afford the fees charged by the Jesuits, an alternative was the schools provided by the Christian Brothers, founded by Edmund Rice in 1808. These offered strict discipline, Irish language and culture, and patriotic history taught from some very simplistic texts. The Brothers' nationalism, like that of the Church as a whole, was a conservative one. It sought to marginalise the secular and radical rhetoric of the Protestant leaders of the 1798 rising or later the Irish Republican Brotherhood (IRB), whose bombings and social radicalism was condemned by the Irish bishops.[7]

Cardinal Paul Cullen, an archbishop for thirty years, personified the fear of what nationalism could become and concern with how the Church could control it. As Dr Conor Cruise O'Brien has put it, 'Cullen and the Hierarchy and the (Christian) Brothers with their approval, were aiming to supplant irreligious nationalists with religious ones, meaning obedient Catholics, and they were singularly successful in this'.[8] The truth of this may be measured by the extent to which the Catholic Church achieved a strategic place within Home Rule nationalism, even under the Protestant leadership of Parnell. Since his fall there have been no non-Catholic leaders of either constitutional or insurrectionist Irish nationalism.

This Church, it must be stressed, was a militant and confident one at the start of the twentieth century, seeking new converts, intervening in education and feeling able, through the Vatican, to decree in 1908 that in any mixed-marriage children should be raised as Roman Catholics. The message to Protestant Ireland and Ulster could not have been much clearer. Sinn Féin, when it emerged in 1905, not yet as a republican movement but as a militant alternative to constitutional nationalism, was led by Catholics such as Arthur Griffith who saw the Christian Brothers' schools as the model for education in an independent Irish state.

In 1916 Sinn Féin would throw its weight behind armed rebels such as Patrick Pearse, president of the republic, proclaimed in Dublin on Easter Monday. Shaped by his part in the language movement, the conspiratorial politics of the IRB and his own intense Catholicism, Pearse foretold his own death and that of many others when, in response to the carnage of European war, he wrote in December 1915:

> It is good for the world that such things should be done. The old heart of the earth needed to be warmed with the red wine of the battlefields. Such august homage was never before offered to God as this, the homage of millions of lives gladly given for love of country.[9]

By then the concept of blood sacrifice had taken hold of Pearse but much Irish blood had already been offered in Britain's cause in a conflict which divided Irish nationalism as deeply as the 1912–14 Home Rule crisis. With Home Rule enacted but on hold after Britain's declaration of war on Germany, John Redmond, the nationalist leader in Westminster, had little to offer the party's support other than the call to enlist in the Crown forces to secure the deferred reward of Home Rule. Politically it was a high-risk strategy which split the Volunteer movement to whose formation in November 1913 Redmond had given guarded support as an answer to Loyalist Ulster's arming and drilling in response to the threat of Home Rule.[10] Redmond's party still held seventy-three Westminster seats from the two general elections of 1910. Events unleashed by the war, such as the Easter Rising, the executions of its leaders and the threat of conscription in Ireland, brought Sinn Féin to centre stage and, in the December 1918 elections, the old Home Rule party was left with just six seats.

For Irish Unionism war in 1914 made possible a closing of ranks which came as a relief to some of its leaders, above all to Sir Edward Carson. 'King Carson', his Loyalist nickname after 1912, had begun to entertain his own doubts about the emergence of a paramilitary Unionism in the form of the Ulster Volunteer Force and the collision course with Britain it had embarked upon. Carson used luridly uncompromising language in his excoriations of Home Rule but recent work on him has stressed the limits he privately accepted as to what extraconstitutional militancy could accomplish: 'He was no proto-Fascist leading armed men against lawful authority', one biographer has argued. 'Despite his grand strategic design of defeating Home Rule for the whole of Ireland, he knew that his duty lay in making whatever reasonable settlement could be achieved.'[11]

Carson's career is often cited as proof of the 'Ulsterisation' of Irish Unionism before 1914, yet he himself was the product of a relatively liberal Unionism which, outside Dublin, drew much of its strength from the 'big house' influence of ascendancy landowners. Carson's own upbringing was a middle-class and urban one though his mother's family was of the gentry and had an estate in Galway. He made his name at the Dublin Bar in a period after the 1886 Home Rule crisis when southern Unionism still had a predominance which Ulster was slow to challenge.

The necessary conditions for an Ulster-based Unionism were there, however. The two Home Rule crises of 1886 and 1893 gave it a more confident voice, as suggested by the formation, in the former year, of an Ulster Loyalist and Anti-Repeal Union and in 1892 the calling of an Ulster Convention to oppose Home Rule. The emergence of the latter body has been called a key moment in the 'Ulsterisation' of opposition to Home Rule. The Belfast pavilion where it met may have displayed a banner with '*Erin go Bragh*' [God Save Ireland] emblazoned on it, but Presbyterians and Orangemen were strongly represented at the Convention.[12] At the general election that year, nineteen of the twenty-three seats won by Unionists were in Ulster and, in 1905, the formation of an Ulster Unionist Council formalised a growing division within Unionism, even though the South had some representation on it.[13]

For some, more profound forces underlay these changes in party political structures: 'The North of Ireland', it has been claimed, 'was becoming during the nineteenth century an ethnic frontier between the British and Irish nations. As the settlement colonial structure decayed the two communities became opposed national peoples in conflict for the same land.'[14] Not everyone saw it in these terms at the same time but a significant transformation was at work, especially in the Ulster counties that would later become Northern Ireland.

What drove the process was economic growth in north-east Ulster, especially in Belfast and the Lagan valley with their close trading links to mainland Britain. Gladstonian land reform had taken the rent issue out of Ulster politics and, on the eve of World War I, nearly 70 per cent of Ulster farmers owned their holdings, a higher figure than that for Ireland as a whole.[15] Out of this grew an increasingly confident Ulster identity reinforced by ongoing debates on the merits of federalism and 'Home Rule all round', the latter cause espoused by Winston Churchill in 1911, even as a new Home Rule crisis became imminent.[16]

Defining an Ulster which could be fitted into any constitutional package arising from this debate was overtaken by the crisis brought on by the 1912 Home Rule Bill. Separate status for Ulster had been given rather more consideration by Gladstone than by Parnell in the

1886 debates but, by 1912, the situation was dramatically different. As the Liberal government presented their bill that year, they did so with the certainty of being able to enact it because their legislation the previous year had removed the veto powers of the House of Lords. In the tempestuous struggle which the bill unleashed, any separate Ulster settlement was deployed not on its own merits but as a weapon with which to block Home Rule and, indeed, to bring down Asquith's government. This latter concern was certainly the priority of the English constitutional lawyer A. V. Dicey, a deeply reactionary opponent of Liberal social reform for whom Irish Home Rule was final proof of the party's perfidy.

Dicey wrote of the bill as showing the tyranny of which democracy was capable[17] and, in language comparable to that of Margaret Thatcher, John Major and some Labour leaders decades later in their response to Scottish devolution, he argued that any Dublin legislature once in being would open the way to a separate Irish state. For this reason, he told his readers in 1912, they 'must resist Home Rule with the undivided zeal which enabled the Republicans of the Northern States during the war of Secession to withstand, in Congress and on the field of battle, every attempt of the South to break up the great American Republic'.[18]

'There may exist,' Dicey also wrote, 'acts of oppression on the part of a democracy, no less than of a king, which justify resistance to the law, or in other words, rebellion.'[19] Language like this fuelled the fire of Loyalist opposition to Home Rule and much debate has centred on the issue of whether this opposition, spearheaded by the Ulster Volunteer Force, ever really had the capacity or the will to confront the British state militarily. Carson's oratory at the UVF's initial parades, and the huge publicity operation set up by Sir James Craig to maximise its impact, helped to provide the mini-state of Northern Ireland after 1921 with what has been called its 'creation myth'.[20] Orange lodge banners and Loyalist murals remain as visual testimony to this, yet even as he 'mesmerised the Protestant masses in a rich Dublin brogue' Carson saw the need for compromise.[21]

It had to be a compromise that secured optimum terms for Protestant Ulster, though he clung to the hope that Loyalist mobilisation could unnerve London and still block Home Rule. When the government's legislation passed its last parliamentary hurdle on 25 May 1914, it was clear to Carson that Unionism's political strategy had failed. Furthermore, a few weeks beforehand, the UVF claimed to have dramatically increased its firepower with the Larne arms landings. There was little choice for Carson but to accept the Larne operation and acclaim it as a victory. Yet the 25,000 rifles and three million rounds of ammunition for weapons of three different makes were never really going to arm a body which claimed 100,000 members. The UVF also had only a few machine guns and no artillery while the military competence of its enlisted members and its command structure varied widely from area to area.[22]

These questions, it should be noted, have continued to be asked about the many UVF units which were incorporated into the 36th Ulster Division, raised and designated with Kitchener's approval in the autumn of 1914. Unionist leaders overestimated the rate at which UVF members would enlist in the army. Many were wary of the British government's intentions and wary, too, of the fate of their jobs and farms if they left them to join up. Enlistment levels were slow to peak, especially in rural Ulster, and were not in general much higher than elsewhere in Ireland in 1914 and 1915.[23]

The 36th Division's dreadful losses at the Somme in July 1916 gave it an enduring and iconic place in the self-image of Loyalist Ulster. There were, however, some who thought that the scale of these losses could have been reduced by more careful officer selection and better training. James B. Armour, a Presbyterian minister in Ballymoney, County Antrim, who was a Liberal Home Ruler, certainly took this view. He had never been impressed by Carson and, in a letter to his son in September 1913, Armour had called his campaign against the government's Irish policy 'a compound of bluff and bunkum'.[24]

As to the carnage on the Somme, he wrote:

> Carson is largely to blame for the debacle as he insisted that the rank and file would select their own officers with the result that the officers chosen were addressed by their names, discipline there was little and training for war was entirely absent.[25]

This, of course, was not the whole story as other divisions of Kitchener's New Army were also ill-prepared for what they would meet on the Somme. By late 1916, the Division's Ulster composition was being diluted by drafts from elsewhere in Ireland and beyond and, in October of the same year, the officer in command of it was even making the case for it to merge with the 16th Irish Division, which was recruited from outside Ulster.[26]

The slaughter on the Somme and the mourning for it which spread across Ulster did not deter Carson, in a 1916 Christmas message, from urging the need for further sacrifice.[27] He would soon take office in Lloyd George's new coalition, having been one of the architects of Asquith's downfall, but the distance between him and his Ulster Unionist support base was beginning to widen. In June 1916 he had told the Ulster Unionist Council that Home Rule was 'a legislative reality if not yet an institutional one'[28] and that the definite exclusion of six Ulster counties from it was going to be the best bargain on offer from London. This had been at the core of his negotiating strategy since 1914 but he needed all his eloquence to carry the Council with him.

When Lloyd George responded to the Home Rule party's increasing loss of electoral ground to Sinn Féin by calling an Irish Convention in July 1917, Carson supported it. Its main outcome was the agreement of nationalist and southern Unionist delegates to a plan for immediate domestic self-government on an all-Ireland basis though there was no agreement on whether this package should include fiscal autonomy. The convention failed and its proposals split both the southern Unionists and the nationalists. Redmond, close to the end of his life, left it with the words: 'I have no cards. I am a leader without a party.'[29] and its fate was sealed by Sinn Féin's decision to boycott it and the Ulster Unionists' refusal to give any ground on the exclusion of at least six of the northern counties from any form of Home Rule.

Even as the die was cast, Carson began to talk in more conciliatory terms about federalism in the British Isles, reviving briefly a debate which had been current before 1914. The signs of his disengagement form Irish politics were growing even though he accepted nomination for a North Belfast seat at Westminster in 1918 and held it until he was made a Lord of Appeal in May 1921. He lived in the south of England for the rest of his life but used his membership of the Lords to denounce in vitriolic terms the partitionist Irish settlement negotiated by Lloyd George and Churchill with the Sinn Féin and Irish Republican Army (IRA) leadership.

This speech has been called 'the authentic cry of Irish (as distinct from Ulster) Unionism at the last with only oblivion before it'.[30] When Carson delivered his philippic Sinn Féin, its support, galvanised by the events of 1916 and by Britain's abortive attempt to apply conscription to Ireland, had won seventy-three of Ireland's Westminster seats at the 1918 general election. Its successful candidates refused to occupy them, setting up a rebel Dáil in Dublin as the IRA began its war against the Crown forces. This led to Britain's ultimate move to what it hoped would be disengagement in the form of the 1920 Government of Ireland Act.

This was an attempt to enact a partitionist settlement in which a six-county northern statelet, along with the rest of the island, would each be accorded purely internal self-government, with bicameral legislatures and separate judicial systems. Each would be bound to the other by a forty-member Council for Ireland picked from the two parliaments and endowed with limited legislative powers but with the ultimate right to vote for a unitary Irish state. British sovereignty would remain unabridged. As Article 75 of the Act put it:

> Notwithstanding the establishment of the Parliaments of Southern and Northern Ireland, or the Parliament of Ireland, or anything contained in this Act, the supreme authority of the Parliament of the United Kingdom shall remain unaffected and undiminished over all persons, matters and things in Ireland and every part thereof.[31]

Outside Northern Ireland this Act never became operative and the Anglo-Irish Treaty of 6 December 1921 gave Ireland a constitution modelled largely on that of Canada. Northern Ireland was given the right to opt out of this within one month of the Royal Assent being given to the legislation needed to ratify the treaty. Its Unionist government, led by Sir James Craig, was prompt in availing itself of this right.

For a British negotiator like Churchill, who had come to see the limits to what military force, often brutally used, could achieve in Ireland, this settlement was one which would secure essential national interests. It would leave the Royal Navy strategic anchorages in an Irish state within the British Empire. To him this involved no infringement of the new Free State's sovereignty. The treaty also provided for a Boundary Commission to keep the new interstate border under review, and Ulster Unionists had to be reassured that this body would not cause their fledgling mini-state unsustainable loss of territory.

Predictable IRA attacks were launched along the new border and spread to Belfast where pitiless sectarian carnage had raged since 1920. In March 1922, Churchill, who had moved from being Secretary of State for War to the Colonial Office, appealed to Collins, with whom he had formed a degree of personal rapport during the treaty negotiations, and to Arthur Griffith, president of the Dáil, to use their influence along with Ulster Unionist leaders to bring under control the terrible killing north of the border. Collins met Craig and agreed to an end to IRA operations in the north as well as tougher security measures to protect Roman Catholics there. In correspondence with Collins, Churchill strove to convince him of the need for the Free State to coexist with Ulster Unionists. 'They are your countrymen,' he had written earlier, 'and require from you at least as careful and disciplined handling as you bestow on the extremists who defy you in the South.' [32]

He could hardly say otherwise to Collins for, throughout the treaty negotiations, one of his priorities was to secure Northern Ireland's separate status. If maintaining this meant military action on the border in support of the Unionist government, Churchill was ready for it though Lloyd George feared his propensity for recklessness. This was, indeed, how he saw Churchill's use of troops in early June 1922 in the Pettigo-Belleek area on the County Fermanagh border. It was in response to Free State army movements on their side of the border and also some limited IRA activity. This narrow triangle of disputed territory was just the sort of area Dublin hoped might be ceded to it if the Boundary Commission began its adjudications. Churchill's action inflamed the situation but it was resolved by the Free State forces' withdrawal, and the episode strengthened his relations with the Ulster Unionists.

It soon fell to Collins to order the Free State army into action against the anti-treaty IRA in a brutal internecine struggle which cost him his life but from which the new state emerged intact. So, too, did Northern Ireland despite the sectarian bloodbath amid which it had been brought to birth. The border also survived though Collins had left the treaty negotiations under the impression that significant concessions would, in due course, be made to the Free State. Churchill always denied any complicity in leading the Irish delegation at the treaty talks to believe in such an outcome and, in late 1925, when the commission finally reported, it offered no more than minor two-way transfers of territory.[33]

William Cosgrave, president of the Executive Council of the Free State, saw this as, in effect, an abrogation of Articles 11 and 12 of the treaty. His rage was also, however, a product of his fear for his own survival of the political fallout from the commission's ruling.[34] He received scant sympathy from the Baldwin government in London and was rebuffed by the Unionist government in Belfast when he pressed for some concessions on the rights of the Catholic minority under its jurisdiction. There was, however, a conciliatory offering to Dublin when London allowed that the Free State's payment of its already agreed share of Britain's National Debt be phased out over a sixty-year period.

Land annuity repayments were a different matter. They were due to the Crown for loans advanced to Irish tenant farmers who wanted to purchase their farms under land legislation from 1891 to 1909. The 1920 Government of Ireland Act provided the right of northern and southern administrations to retain the revenue from land annuities. For the Free State, this was replaced by the 1921 treaty, and a 1923 Anglo-Irish financial agreement required the Dublin government to collect the annuities from tenants and repay them to Britain. Two years later the IRA launched a campaign to abolish these payments and it was taken up as an issue by Fianna Fáil, the party formed by de Valera, after his decision to recognise the Free State's institutions. Once he took office as Taoiseach in 1932, the annuities became central to a bitter economic war in which Irish refusal to make the payments was answered by special restrictive British duties on Irish imports.

These episodes demonstrated the initial and continuing weakness of the Free State in its relationship with Britain. Even in the first troubled year of its existence, as battle raged over Dublin's Four Courts with the anti-treaty IRA, the Ulster Unionists finalised their plans to end proportional representation in local council elections. It was a clear signal to the nationalist community that government policy was to minimise their presence in the administration of local services. Collins claimed that this both violated and jeopardised the 1921 treaty and, for a time, it seemed that the Royal Assent would be withheld which, indeed, it could have been under Article 75 of the 1920 Government of Ireland Act.

Craig and his ministers made it clear, on 27 July 1922, that they would resign if the royal veto was used. Taoiseach William Cosgrave argued that this legislation should be at least delayed until the Boundary Commission reported but Royal Assent was granted on 11 September though the Unionist government accepted a one-year delay in implementing the new voting system as well as an equally controversial redrawing of local electoral boundaries which was part of the package. Nothing could have illustrated more clearly the reality of London's limited control over the government of Northern Ireland, despite the wording of the 1920 act.[35]

At the height of the crisis one adviser to the London government had claimed that the powers of its Northern Ireland counterpart were akin to those of a British dominion.[36] They were never intended to be that even if the Stormont buildings, opened in 1932, had a grandiose style commensurate with such status. The Northern Ireland government could raise only local taxation and was in the position, where it remained until direct government was imposed by Britain in March 1972, of handling spending decisions over revenues, most of which it had no say in raising. The parliament which finally moved to Stormont was not a sovereign assembly because a Lord-Lieutenant could, in theory, exercise a Crown veto over its legislation.[37] The 1922 crisis over local council voting and electoral boundaries signalled that this was unlikely to happen, least of all over the exercise of internal security powers or when proportional representation in elections to the province's parliament itself was abolished in 1929.

 Northern Ireland's relationship to Britain was occasionally described by Unionists as a federal one but this was inaccurate as there was no shared sovereignty. Ultimate constitutional authority, hardly used for half a century to address the province's communal tensions, lay with Westminster, and it was finally used in 1972 to suspend the institutions created in 1920 and replace them with direct rule. The relationship was the product of a settlement which Irish nationalists for long found hard to see as anything other than a Machiavellian British strategy to abort the dream of uniting their island's 'four green fields'.[38] Others came to see it as the logical outcome of a culture of imperial control rooted in Anglo-Saxon racial stereotyping of the Irish and committed to conceding the minimum to their national aspirations.[39] The reality of 1920–1 was, however, one in which the basis for any workable and non-violent unitary Irish state was as tenuous as that for the continued existence of.

 Yugoslavia after 1990. After Sinn Féin's victory in the 1918 Westminster Irish nationalists elections, could not accept this, holding to the view, as Conor Cruise O'Brien has put it, 'that they had a right to secede from the United Kingdom but that Unionists did not have the right to secede from the entity they sought to create'.[40]

 Northern Ireland's survival as a devolved entity within the United Kingdom served to redefine the Irish question even as its bitter internal divisions hardened, while being simultaneously masked by the rhetoric of Unionist leaders or late converts to their cause such as Churchill. Writing of it in a newspaper in 1933, and in response to de Valera taking power in Dublin, he declared: 'We would no more allow hostile hands to be laid on the liberties of the Protestant North than we would allow the Isle of Wight or the castles of Caernarvon or Edinburgh to fall into the hands of the Germans or the French.'[41]

For the new Irish state dominion status was a reality from the moment of its creation. As elsewhere in the burgeoning British Commonwealth, this involved the Crown being represented by a Governor General through whom an oath of allegiance had to be sworn by all who served the new state. This oath, rather than a partition of the island which many republicans thought would soon prove unsustainable, was what divided most bitterly pro- and anti-treaty republicans in the civil war which started in the summer of 1922.

The Governor General had power to 'reserve' legislation by the Dáil or parliament but the state's constitution declared that its sovereignty was derived from the people, and the parliament was given constituent power over an eight-year period to alter the constitution. Thereafter, constitutional changes would be subject to referendum votes. The authority of the Crown was declared in the constitution to be derived from the voluntary association of the Free State with the British Commonwealth of Nations, and the state would not join in any wars affecting Britain except by the authority of its own parliament.[42]

Events would show that the new state would stretch to its limits the autonomy granted it via dominion status under the 1921 Treaty. However, Cumann na nGaedheal, a party formed in 1923 out of an assortment of pro-treaty political groupings, concerned itself initially with the imperatives of state building, retaining for the purpose nearly all the personnel of the former British administration. It also created a new police force, the Garda Síochána and a National Army of nearly 50,000 men. Discontent among the latter's officers, many of them former pro-treaty IRA men, brought some to the point of mutiny in March 1924 over proposed financial cuts and manpower reductions.

Good intelligence work neutralised the danger and civil power was upheld, a crucial victory for a government whose priority was to create and maintain democratic structures.[43] The issue of partition was a potential distraction from this priority but the Cosgrave government moved increasingly to a position of pragmatism where relations with the northern state were concerned. Civil war and the death of Collins served to undermine the northern IRA's offensive capability, and Cosgrave felt safe in abandoning the Sinn Féin demand for the boycott of industry across the border. He also backed away from his government's decision to fund the salaries of Roman Catholic teachers who refused to recognise the authority of Northern Ireland.[44] The border itself was given an appearance of durability with the erection along it of a string of Free State customs posts, yet this had little bearing on Dublin's acceptance, under protest, of the 1925 findings of the Boundary Commission.

Free State policy towards Northern Ireland has been aptly described as

> a self-defeating mixture of consensual rhetoric, petty coercion and
> an increasingly passive sympathy with Ulster Catholics: the
> symbolism suggested a commitment to an inclusivist unitary state,
> but the programme of action riled northern Unionists without
> bringing much benefit to northern nationalists.[45]

On the international stage, ministers like Kevin O'Higgins were able
to develop the concept of dominion status to Éire's advantage both at
the League of Nations after joining it in 1923 and at gatherings such
as the 1926 Imperial Conference. Contacts made there led, five years
later, to what has been called 'the crowning glory of the party's (i.e.
Cumann na nGaedheal's) diplomatic offensive within the Commonwealth – the Statute of Westminster'.[46]

For all practical purposes, this dismantled Westminster's remaining legislative authority over the dominions. Nonetheless, the party
of Cosgrave and O'Higgins remained vulnerable to nationalist and
republican initiatives with which opponents could outflank it. Sinn
Féin's continued policy of abstention from taking seats in the Dáil
left it on the margins of political debate and manoeuvre. In 1926 de
Valera finally came out against abstentionism. Narrowly defeated
over it within Sinn Féin, he left the party to form Fianna Fáil, and the
next year led it to a major success in a general election, winning
forty-four seats, only two fewer than the governing party. What
followed, in the highly charged aftermath of the IRA's assassination
of O'Higgins, vice-president of the Executive Council or cabinet, was
high drama.

De Valera led his successful candidates into the Dáil and wrote his
name in the ceremonial book containing the Oath of Allegiance to the
Crown, while declaring that he was doing it only as an empty but
necessary gesture without 'binding significance in conscience or in
law'.[47] Five years later he and his colleagues were in power, having
built up a powerful support base across the twenty-six counties.
Leaving their predecessors little credit for their part in securing the
1931 Statute of Westminster, they went to work quickly to remove
the Oath of Allegiance from the constitution and to curtail the
Governor General's powers prior to their later abolition.

De Valera was forced to restore the military tribunals he had
denounced in opposition in order to curb a resurgent and vengeful
IRA as well as the paramilitary 'Blueshirt' movement led by General

Eoin O'Duffy. Amid the heightening political turbulence, work began on a new constitution. This retained much of what had been agreed in 1922 but there were important changes too. Article 2 defined the national territory as 'the whole island of Ireland' but, in Article 3, the state's actual jurisdiction was limited to the twenty-six counties. The president of the Executive Council became the Taoiseach, and a presidential head of state was created to be elected by the people. Articles 40 to 45 reflected Catholic social teaching on fundamental rights concerning family law, marriage, education and property. Article 44, setting out the 'special position' to be accorded to the Roman Catholic Church, was repealed by a referendum in 1972, as were Articles 2 and 3, in 1998.

As a clear majority endorsed the new constitution in the November 1937 referendum, the mounting threat of war in Europe and how the Irish state should respond to it confronted de Valera and his government with the ultimate test of what sovereignty meant. Neutrality was not, either as a word or a concept, enshrined in that year's Éire constitution, yet important signals had already been given by the Taoiseach as to what the state's stance would be. Addressing the League of Nations assembly at Geneva on 2 July 1936, he gave to an audience, respectful of the then Free State's support for the League, a fairly clear view of his response to the possibility of renewed war in Europe.

> Peace is dependent upon the will of the great states. All the small states can do, if the statesmen of the greater states fail in their duty, is resolutely to determine that they will not become the tools of any great power, and that they will resist with whatever strength that they may possess any attempt to force them into a war against their will.[48]

In the previous year de Valera had backed sanctions against Italy over Asbyssinia but their failure had diminished his faith in the League, and his July 1936 speech was meant as a clear indication of the Irish State's stance if and when war came.

Tension with Britain was still high at this time because of the so-called economic war. Since taking office, de Valera had refused to pay any land annuities arising from earlier British loans to assist land purchases by Irish farmers. London had hit back with special duties on Irish imports, especially cattle and dairy produce and, in turn, de Valera's government retaliated with emergency charges on British coal, machinery, and iron and steel goods. Serious damage to

British–Irish trade and real hardship to Irish farmers had resulted but the appointment of Malcolm MacDonald as British Dominions Secretary in 1935 began a process by which this futile trade war was ended.

At the time of MacDonald's appointment, the Cabinet Committee on Ireland had not met for a full ten months but the personal rapport he quickly formed with de Valera helped to bring Britain's relations with it back to centre stage. In May 1936 MacDonald wrote a paper for the cabinet setting out in a sympathetic way de Valera's problems with militant republicanism. It has been called 'a turning point in Anglo-Irish relations'[49] because its author, who grew to like the Taoiseach and put up with his jokes about mean Scots, argued that de Valera's position on the border was essentially a gradualist one, despite his often uncompromising public language, and that he would be open to a negotiated end to the ongoing trade war with Britain.

Talks to this end between the two governments began in early 1938 but de Valera, with some discreet encouragement from Mac-Donald, made sure that any calling off of the trade war would be conditional upon the return to full Irish jurisdiction of the 'treaty ports'. These were Cóbh, known prior to 1921 as Queenstown, Berehaven in Bantry Bay on the south-west and Lough Swilly in County Donegal. All were deep-water anchorages with ageing coastal gun batteries. Their peacetime maintenance and use in time of war or the threat of it were entrusted to Britain under two articles of the December 1921 Treaty. From the start of the 1938 talks, Chamberlain, the British prime minister, gave strong signals that he was prepared to move on the issue of the ports and also to end duties on Irish imports but that no imposed end to partition could be entertained by his government against the will of a majority in Northern Ireland. Privately, however, he agreed that the border was an anachronism.

Nearly twenty years earlier, de Valera had conceded the principle of Britain having access to the ports. He incorporated this in his so-called 'Document No. 2' which he drafted for a secret session of the Dáil as an alternative to what became the Anglo-Irish Treaty. His concern was to define 'external association' with Britain and its dominions as a relationship for Irish republicans much preferable to one based on any oath of allegiance to the Crown. In 1938, however, the treaty ports were a prize worth grasping once it became clear that Chamberlain saw their status as negotiable.

De Valera held out for as long as he could on the partition issue prior to agreement on the ports being reached in April. These were returned unconditionally to Irish control and the trade war was brought to an end with Britain's land annuity claims for payments from the Irish state of £100 million reduced to a lump sum payment of one tenth of it. British duties on Irish imports were also ended, while Éire was obliged only to review its own retaliatory charges. De Valera was disappointed over having made no progress on partition though he did his best to maintain its status as an issue in the 1938 talks.[50] Even so, the return of the ports as war loomed again over Europe was a huge victory on which de Valera capitalised in a general election that gave his party a decisive victory.

Most of nationalist Ireland applauded what de Valera had achieved. The *Irish News*, read predominantly by Catholics in Northern Ireland, echoed the mood in its editorial. The agreement, it declared, 'wipes out barriers which for years have embittered relations between the two countries and opens the way for a new friendship, confidence and cooperation'.[51] It went on to argue that with regard to defence 'Britain will have nothing to fear from a free and independent Ireland but everything to gain by having a good neighbour'.[52] After the signing, a lunch was hosted at Downing Street by Chamberlain and his wife. During it the prime minister returned to his guest a pair of field glasses which he had had to surrender to a British officer on 30 April 1916 when he became a prisoner at the end of the Easter Rising in Dublin.

For Churchill, however, Chamberlain's agreement with de Valera was hard to forgive, 'a gratuitous surrender' he later wrote of it in his great history of World War II.

> A more feckless act can hardly be imagined – and at such a time. It is true that in the end we survived without the ports. It is also true that if we had not been able to do without them we should have retaken them by force rather than perish by famine. But this is no excuse. Many a ship, many a life were soon to be lost as a result of this improvident example of appeasement.[53]

Churchill distrusted de Valera's intentions from the moment he took office in 1932 and could never take MacDonald's more nuanced view of him. Interviewed in 1981, MacDonald reflected on Churchill's inability to understand the Irish leader, though they did eventually have a friendly meeting, albeit not until 1953.[54]

> These old colonialists thought that those who wanted to be independent were wild men. He didn't attempt to understand

Dev because Dev wanted to get away from the Empire. Churchill thought he should be regarded as an enemy of Britain. This dictated his attitude before the war, during the war and for some time afterwards.[55]

In reality agreement on the treaty ports was followed by an observable softening in de Valera's expressed attitudes towards Britain. Indeed, even during the 1938 talks, in so far as he had stressed the issue of Ulster, it had been to state that, if Britain could use its influence to resolve it, then any Irish government would allow it whatever wartime facilities it might need. There was, it has been forcefully argued, a real continuity here with the position de Valera had taken as far back as 1920, when he declared:

An independent Ireland would see its own independence in jeopardy the moment it saw the independence of Britain seriously threatened. Mutual self-interest would make the people of these two islands, if both independent, the closest possible allies in a moment of real national danger to either.[56]

Others also took a pragmatic view of the Irish state's relations with Britain in time of war. Kevin O'Higgins, a bitter opponent of de Valera during and after the 1921 Treaty, addressed the Dáil in February 1927 on the subject of neutrality which he called 'a consummation devoutly to be wished for but we are unable to alter the geographical relations between this state and Great Britain and we are unable to alter the strategical aspects of the matter.'[57]

In September 1938, as Hitler's demands on Czechoslovakia over the Sudeten territory grew more menacing, Britain's delegation at the League of Nations in Geneva supported de Valera's candidature for presidency of the League Assembly. He used his election to this position to call for a settlement based on the rights, as he saw them, of ethnic Germans in the Sudetenland. The League had no part in the Munich Agreement which effectively met Hitler's demands but de Valera, on his way home, stopped in London to call on Chamberlain. Without success, he argued that there were analogies between the Sudeten situation and the plight of the nationalist minority in Northern Ireland.

After his return to Dublin, he spoke publicly of a possible alliance with Britain in exchange for an end to partition and, in an interview with the London Evening Standard, he urged that it was 'possible to visualise a critical situation arising in the future in which a united free Ireland would be willing to co-operate with Britain to resist a common attack'[58] He felt, however, the need to add that 'no Irish leader will ever be able to get the Irish people to co-operate with Great Britain while partition remains. I wouldn't attempt it myself, for I know I should fail.'[59]

This, in its essentials, remained de Valera's position a year later when Britain and France finally declared war on Germany. When he addressed the Dáil on 2 September 1939, the day after Germany invaded Poland, he was less concerned to speak of neutrality as an end in itself than as a means of asserting the state's full sovereignty in the form of an independent foreign policy. He also introduced a constitutional amendment to allow draconian emergency legislation. This originated the use of the antiseptic word 'emergency' to describe the Second World War for the official purposes of the Irish state.

Even as he spoke, Hitler's U-boat crews were making ready to leave their bases to begin a relentless hunt for any ships carrying the British flag or which might give aid in any form to Britain. They would take a dreadful toll and could have tipped the scales of war in Hitler's favour. It was this that prompted the poet, Louis MacNeice (1907–63), to make an emotional appeal to his compatriots in his poem 'Neutrality'. In it he tried in vain to convince them that it was British naval and aircrew members who, in the cold waters of the Atlantic, would pay the real price of Irish neutrality.

Notes

1. T. Salmon, *Unneutral Ireland: an Ambivalent and Unique Security Policy* (Oxford: Clarendon Press, 1989), pp. 121–5.
2. J. T. Carrol, *Ireland In the War Years* (Newton Abbot: David and Charles, 1975), p. 112.
3. T. P. Coogan, *Michael Collins* (London: Arrow Books, 1991), p. 301.
4. A. Jackson, *Ireland 1798–1998* (Oxford: Blackwell, 1999), p. 170; also J. Hutchinson, *The Dynamics of Cultural Nationalism: the Gaelic Revival and the Creation of the Irish Nation State* (London: Allen and Unwin, 1987), pp. 255–85.
5. P. Alter, *Nationalism* (London: Arnold, 1989), pp. 41–6.
6. R. Foster, *W. B. Yeats: a Life*, Vol 1, *The Apprentice Mage* (Oxford: Oxford University Press, 1998), p. 112.
7. C. C. O'Brien, *Ancestral Voices: Religion and Nationalism in Ireland* (Dublin: Poolbeg, 1994), pp. 24–7.
8. Ibid., p. 25.
9. R. Dudley Edwards, *Patrick Pearse: the Triumph of Failure* (London: Faber, 1977), p. 245.
10. A. Jackson, *Ireland 1798–1998*, pp. 167–8.
11. D. George Boyce, 'Edward Carson', in *Oxford Dictionary of National Biography:*

From the Earliest Times to the Year 2000, Vol. 10 (Oxford: Oxford University Press, 2000), p. 309. See also H Montgomery Hyde, The *Life of Sir Edward Carson, Lord Carson of Duncairn* (London: Heinemann, 1953), pp. 339–40 and p. 368, and A. Jackson, *Sir Edward Carson* (Dublin: Historical Association of Ireland/Dundalgan Press, 1993), pp. 35–41.

12. G Walker, *A History of the Ulster Unionist Party: Protest, Pragmatism and Pessimism* (Manchester: Manchester University Press, 2004), p. 13.
13. Ibid., pp. 22–4.
14. F. Wright, *'Two Lands on One Soil' – Ulster Politics Before Home Rule* (Dublin: Gill and Macmillan, 1996), p. 510.
15. G. Martin, 'The Origins of Partition', in M. Anderson and E. Bort (eds), *The Irish Border: History, Politics, Culture* (Liverpool: Liverpool University Press, 1999), pp. 57–113.
16. R. S. Churchill, *Young Statesman: Winston S. Churchill 1901–1914* (London: Heinemann, 1967), pp. 456–7.
17. A. V. Dicey, *A Fool's Paradise: Being a Constitutionalist's Criticism of the Home Rule Bill of 1912* (London: John Murray, 1913), pp. 113–23.
18. Ibid., pp. xxx–xxxi.
19. Ibid. See also D. George Boyce, 'The State and the Citizen: Unionists, Home Rule and the British Constitution 1886–1920', in D. George Boyce and A. O'Day, *The Ulster Crisis* (London: Palgrave Macmillan, 2005), pp. 47–63.
20. A. Jackson, 'Unionist Myths 1912–1985', *Past and Present* 136, August 1992, pp. 164–85.
21. A. Gailey, 'King Carson: An Essay on the Invention of Leadership', *Irish Historical Studies*, XXX, No. 117, May 1996, pp. 66–8.
22. T. Bowman, 'The Ulster Volunteer Force 1910–1922: New Perspectives', in D. George Boyce and A. O'Day (eds), *The Ulster Crisis*, pp. 247–59. Also, 'The Ulster Volunteers 1913–14: Force or Farce?' *History Ireland*, Vol. 10, No. 1, spring 2002, pp. 43–7 and C. Townshend, *Political Violence in Ireland: Government and Resistance Since 1848* (Oxford: Clarendon Press, 1983), pp. 249–55.
23. T. Bowman, 'The Ulster Volunteer Force and the Formation of the 36th Ulster Division', *Irish Historical Studies*, XXXII, No. 125, May 2000, pp. 498–515.
24. J. R. B. McMinn, *Against the Tide: a Calendar of the Papers of the Reverend J. B. Armour, Irish Presbyterian Minister and Home Ruler*, Public Record Office of Northern Ireland, 1985, p. 129.
25. Ibid., p. 168.
26. Y. McEwen, 'What Have you done for Ireland? The 36th Ulster Division in the Great War: Politics, Propaganda and the Demography of Deaths', *The Irish Sword*, Vol. XXIV, No. 96, 2004, pp. 194–218.
27. Ibid.
28. Jackson, *Sir Edward Carson*, p. 53.
29. A. T. Q. Stewart, *Edward Carson* (Dublin: Gill and Macmillan, 1981), p. 114.
30. N. Mansergh, *The Unresolved Question: the Anglo-Irish Settlement and its Undoing, 1912–1972* (New Haven and London: Yale University Press, 1991), pp. 197–8.
31. J. Magee, *Northern Ireland: Crisis and Conflict* (London: Routledge, 1974), p. 54.
32. M. Gilbert, *World in Torment: Winston S. Churchill, 1917–1922* (London: Heinmann, 1975), p. 712.
33. E. Staunton, 'The Boundary Commission Debacle 1925: Aftermath and Implications', *History Ireland*, Vol. 4, No. 2 1996, pp. 42–6.
34. Ibid. See also Staunton, *The Nationalists of Northern Ireland* (Dublin: Columba Press, 2001), pp. 79–101.

35. B. Barton, 'Northern Ireland 1920–25', in J. R. Hill (ed.), *A New History of Ireland* Vol. VII, *Ireland 1921–1984* (Oxford: Oxford University Press, 2003), pp. 189–93.
36. Ibid.
37. D. L. Keir, *A Constitutional History of Modern Britain* (London: Adam and Charles Black, 1938), p. 527.
38. Walker, *A History of the Ulster Unionist Party*, pp. 58–9.
39. R. N. Lebow, *White Britain and Black Ireland: The Influence of Stereotypes on Colonial Policy* (Philadelphia: Institute for the Study of Human Issues, 1976). See also, B. O'Shea, *Myth and Reality: Propaganda and Censorship in the Creation of the Irish Free State, January 1919–June 1922* (Unpublished PhD thesis, Open University, 2002).
40. C. C. O'Brien, *Memoir: My Life and Themes* (London: Profile Books, 1998), p. 6.
41. *Daily Mail*, 15 February 1933; see also R. Fisk, *In Time of War: Ireland, Ulster and the Price of Neutrality* (London: Deutsch, 1983), pp. 64–5.
42. D. L. Keir, *Constitutional History of Modern Britain*, pp. 540–1.
43. E. O'Halpin, *Defending Ireland: the Irish State and its Enemies Since 1922* (Oxford: Oxford University Press, 1999), pp. 46–51.
44. D. H. Akenson, S. Farren and J. Coolahan, 'Pre-University Education 1921–1984', in J. R. Hill (ed.), *A New History of Ireland 1921–1984*, p. 712.
45. A. Jackson, *Ireland 1798–1998*, p. 280.
46. Ibid., p. 282.
47. T. Ryle Dwyer, *Eamon de Valera* (Dublin: Gill and Macmillan, 1980), p. 75.
48. Ibid., p. 102.
49. J. Bowman, *De Valera and the Ulster Question 1917–1973* (Oxford: Oxford University Press, 1982), p. 137.
50. Ibid., pp. 174–81.
51. *Irish News*, 26 April 1938.
52. Ibid.
53. W. S. Churchill, *The Second World War*, Vol. 1: *the Gathering Storm* (London: Cassell, 1948), p. 216.
54. Lord Moran, *Winston Churchill: the Struggle for Survival 1940–65* (London: Constable, 1966), p. 473.
55. Fisk, *In Time of War: Ireland, Ulster and the Price of Neutrality*, pp. 43–4.
56. R. Fanning, *Independent Ireland* (Dublin: Helicon, 1983), p. 121.
57. T. Salmon, *Unneutral Ireland*, p. 119.
58. Ryle Dwyer, *Eamon de Valera*, p. 110.
59. Ibid.

2

Éire's Emergency, Britain's War

There are several thousand British war graves on Irish soil. In many of them, on lonely headlands from the windswept coast of Donegal and Sligo to Kerry, are buried victims of the Battle of the Atlantic, Royal and Merchant Navy crew members whose ships were sunk by German U-boats and aircraft without the protection Éire's ports might have provided had Dublin not closed them to British forces. The bitterness this caused lasted for many decades over which Irish neutrality in the war against Hitler's Reich remained a contentious and divisive subject.

Whether the Treaty Ports would have been decisive if available to Britain has been much debated. Churchill, out of office at the time, had vociferously opposed the Chamberlain government's decision to hand them back to Éire. Only days into his appointment, in September 1939, as First Lord of the Admiralty he made his views clear on the issue, urging Cabinet colleagues to take stock of whatever means of coercion might be available to secure the use of the ports. He went further, asking the Crown's law officers to report on the legality of Éire's non-belligerent status. Chamberlain, naturally cautious and influenced by Malcolm MacDonald's and his own contacts with de Valera over the 1937–8 negotiations, took a more flexible view of the intentions of Éire and its leader than Churchill ever managed to do.[1]

On 5 November 1940, Churchill used the House of Commons to go public with his thoughts on the Treaty Ports, calling their loss 'a most heavy and grievous burden which should never have been placed on our shoulders, broad though they be'.[2] Severe sanctions against Éire were considered at Cabinet level though any decision was inhibited by the fear of what Irish reactions might be.[3] Even as the matter was being debated, intensive work was under way to upgrade and enlarge anchorage, fuelling and supply facilities at Londonderry and on Lough Foyle which would soon become crucial to the brutal and attritional war to keep open Britain's Atlantic lifeline. Equally important for convoy protection was the parallel expansion of Royal Air Force bases in Northern Ireland.

All this helped to counterbalance the loss of the ports and, in January 1941, Churchill gave a qualified view of their importance to Lord Cranborne, the Secretary of State for the Dominions:

> I do not consider that it is at present true to say that possession of these bases is vital to our survival. The lack of them is a grievous injury and impediment to us. More than that it would not at present be true to say.[4]

He went on to argue that, in altered circumstances, action over the ports might become necessary.

> I do not personally regard Irish neutrality as a legal act, and we having not recognized Southern Ireland as a sovereign state, that country is now in an anomalous position. Should the danger to our war effort through the denial of the Irish bases threaten to become mortal, which is not the case at present, we should have to act in accordance with our own self-preservation and that of our cause.[5]

The following month, however, provided a tacit acknowledgement by the Admiralty and by the Royal Navy that the Irish ports were not going to be retrieved for operational use. This took the form of a decision to move the Western Approaches Command from Plymouth to Liverpool. It has been called 'the beginning of the end of a period of strategic delusion by naval planners and a recognition that the battle of the Atlantic would have to be fought without the geo-political unity of the British Isles'.[6]

That geopolitical unity might have survived partition but, once de Valera had announced Éire's non-belligerency, he could not compromise it over the issue of the ports. Temperamentally, Churchill could never accept this. Some have attributed his attitude to an essentially imperialist mindset which made it difficult for him to recognise Irish political nationhood, especially if it was interpreted in ways that seemed at variance with British interests.[7] Malcolm

MacDonald, the key figure in negotiating the return of the ports to
Éire, certainly took this view of Churchill:

> He didn't attempt to understand Dev because Dev wanted to get
> away from the Empire. Churchill thought he should be regarded as
> an enemy of Britain. This dictated his attitude before the war,
> during the war and for some time afterwards.[8]

A succession of emissaries to Dublin tried and failed to shift de
Valera on the ports issue. Early in 1941 Wendell Wilkie, who had been
the Republican candidate for the American presidency the previous
year, told the Member of Parliament and diarist, Harold Nicolson, how
he had raised the question with the Taoiseach, accusing him at a
meeting in Dublin of being inconsistent in his professed desire for
Britain and its allies to win the war, yet making that outcome harder.
'So in the end', he reported, 'that fine and obstinate Spaniard was
obliged to say that he was afraid that if he leased the bases, Dublin
might be bombed.'[9] Wilkie, who had seen the German Blitz at first
hand in London, Coventry and elsewhere, told de Valera he was not
impressed any more than American opinion would be.

The Australian prime minister, Robert Menzies, visited de Valera
soon after Wilkie, much against Churchill's wishes. Like others, he
warmed to the Taoiseach as a person and returned certain of his
political authority over Éire and of his preference for a British
victory. On his policy over the ports, however, Menzies

> found it difficult to convince him that the results for Great Britain
> were disastrous. He would stand in front of the map and puzzle as
> to why bases in Éire could be of the slightest importance. I waxed
> eloquent on the vital battle of the Western Approaches and on the
> immense importance of air bases for fighter squadrons if the
> hellish combination of the Focke-Wulf and the German U-boat
> were to be defeated. But I spoke in vain. These considerations were
> alien to his mind.[10]

De Valera's position on the ports was abundantly clear and he was
thereafter unlikely to give any ground over operational facilities to
the RAF on Éire's soil.

Well ahead of these representations to de Valera, all major convoys
to Britain were, in consequence of German possession of bases in
occupied France, being directed away from routes passing south of
Éire to the North West approaches where protection was guaranteed

from air and naval forces operating out of Northern Ireland.[11] The strategic urgency of access to the Treaty Ports proved in reality to be a transient matter though the symbolism remained potent. At the war's end the Admiralty, under pressure from the Dominions office to quantify the cost to Britain of Éire's neutrality, drew up figures claiming that 368 ships and 5,070 crew members had been lost in Luftwaffe attacks and U-boat sinkings which might have been averted if the southern ports had been available for convoy protection.

How accurate these figures could be remains debatable but bitterness over the war at sea and the impact on it of Éire's neutrality was heightened by the reality of its very obvious economic dependence upon Britain and its dominions during the years of Emergency. Éire had merchant vessels of its own to bring in essential supplies but, to sail at all, they needed allocations of coal in British ports. Necessarily, much of what was vital to Éire was carried to its ports in British ships because its own merchant fleet was small. As the U-boats' toll on British shipping mounted, there was pressure in London for severe reduction on space for Éire-bound cargo.[13] In truth, Churchill never applied such reductions in a spirit of revenge for Irish neutrality but the imperative of survival in the Battle of the Atlantic made it unavoidable.

By 1941 reductions in supplies to Éire of petrol, oil, coal and fertiliser began to bite, and de Valera's government set up Irish Shipping Lines, a state-backed company which, in its first operational year, bought eight cargo ships and chartered five more. This did not resolve Éire's supply crisis because, to use British port facilities, all Irish ships required special certification.[14] Without this they could be stopped at any time by the Royal Navy or denied coal-bunkering or repair facilities. Once at sea, even flying the Irish tricolour and with 'Éire' printed on their hulls, they could be, and were, subject to U-boat attack. Demands from ships' officers and crews to have their vessels armed were pressed in the Dáil by opposition speakers in February 1941 but de Valera and his ministers refused to depart from their view that this could compromise the country's neutral status.[15]

All of this influenced one hugely successful autobiographical account of the war on the Atlantic. Nicholas Monsarrat (1910–79) served on convoy escorts as a naval lieutenant and, in his novel The Cruel Sea, he recalled the anger of some of his shipmates.

They saw Ireland as a safe haven under the British umbrella, fed by her convoys and protected by her air force, her very neutrality guaranteed by the British armed forces: they saw no return for this protection save a continued sabotage of the Allied war effort.[16]

If this was their view, then it took little account of the bravery of Irish seamen also running the gauntlet of Admiral Doenitz's 'wolf-packs' and saving British survivors from sinkings by them in the Irish Sea and the Atlantic. It also ignored Irishmen in the Royal Navy, such as Commander Fogarty Fegen from Tipperary who captained an armed merchant ship, HMS *Jervis Bay*, in a heroic action against the German battleship *Admiral Scheer* in mid-October 1940. This saved most of a convoy and earned Fegen a posthumous Victoria Cross.

The status of the Treaty Ports nagged at Britain's relations with Éire at least until Northern Ireland built up the infrastructure to meet the needs of a decisive number of ships and aircraft for convoy protection on the sea lanes north of Donegal and Malin Head. America's entry into the war was also crucial to the outcome of the struggle for the Atlantic but, two months prior to that, Malcolm MacDonald was still convinced that the 1938 agreement on the ports had been the right course of action. 'He contends that he was right to give up the Irish bases,' Harold Nicolson wrote in his diaries after meeting him on 6 October 1941.

> Had we kept them, we might be at war with Éire today and American help would be more distant than it is. Besides, if we get through the war without breaking Irish neutrality, we shall have a grievance against Éire, instead of Éire having her dull, unending grievance against us.'[17]

David Gray, Roosevelt's often abrasive minister in Dublin, who deplored de Valera's position on the Treaty Ports, had already said as much almost a year earlier, in correspondence with his Secretary of State: 'As we see it here any attempt by Churchill to negotiate for the ports will be hopeless. He has the choice between seizing them and paying the price in possible bloodshed and certain hostility and doing without.'[18] Churchill himself could not forgive de Valera, as he was to make clear very publicly at the war's end but, at the December 1943 Cairo conference, the old warrior felt obliged to tell Roosevelt that the ports issue was best dropped for, if it was reopened, de Valera would use it as an excuse to revive the issue of Northern Ireland's future status.

De Valera's uncompromising stance on the ports was for him an affirmation of Éire's full sovereignty as, indeed, was the policy of neutrality itself. Yet it was a policy which has been called 'Janus-faced'[19] in that it involved conflict, mostly at a political level and notably over the ports issue, but also a high degree of co-operation with Britain on matters military and related to intelligence operations.

Militarily, and also in relation to intelligence operations, that co-operation dated back to Britain's declaration of war on Germany but, for Churchill, bringing the Irish state into the war seemed an attainable objective as Hitler's armies swept into the Low Countries and France in the early summer of 1940. Lord Moran. Churchill's doctor even made the dubious claim after the war, and in rather overblown language, that he had never given up the hope of this: 'He thought if he had gone on he would have been able to bring Ireland back into the fold. Anyway, as far as he was concerned, there would always be a candle burning in the window for the wandering daughter.'[20]

Bringing Ireland, or at least Éire, 'back into the fold' was, of course, precisely what Churchill did attempt in June 1940, as Britain's military situation worsened by the day, and reports which have been described as 'sometimes fanciful'[21] were reaching the Cabinet about the strength of the IRA and a pro-German 'fifth column' in Éire. Some of the more eccentric of these came form Charles Tegart, an Ulster Unionist who had spent much of his career in imperial policing in India and Palestine as well as doing undercover work against the IRA between 1919 and 1923.[22]

Once again, Malcolm Macdonald, who had just taken over the Health Ministry under Churchill, was seen as the necessary man for negotiations with de Valera. Between 17 and 27 June 1940 he made three secret visits to Dublin on what his biographer has described as 'clearly an impossible mission'.[23] At his first interview with the Taoiseach, MacDonald sounded him out about the chances of Éire either ending its neutrality or inviting in British forces to defend it against a possible German invation. Rebuffed on this, he then suggested that de Valera and Lord Craigavon, the prime minister of Northern Ireland, form a joint all-Ireland defence council which, he argued, would be a significant step to a united Ireland.

At a third meeting, having made no headway, MacDonald was authorised to give to de Valera a document that would commit Britain to a declaration accepting the principle of Irish unity. In return for this Éire was asked to join in the work of a North–South body to study the constitutional practicalities of unification and to accept British forces in the Treaty Ports and on its territory as a

whole to forestall any German invasion. Éire would also have to act
to suppress the IRA, already an illegal body there since 1936, and
deport German and Italian nationals. From de Valera's point of view,
the document contained one large loophole, namely that, if his
government did accept it, London would then 'seek to obtain the
consent of Northern Ireland'.[24]

Lord Craigavon's reaction was predictable. He called the offer
'treachery to Loyal Ulster'[25] to which he would never be a party.
Churchill had, indeed, appeared to agree to a phasing out of partition
without any formal declaration of war being asked of Éire in return.
One historian who has been committed to denigrating Churchill's
wartime role as one of simply presiding over British decline, is John
Charmley yet, surprisingly, in a lengthy biography,[26] he makes no
reference to the June 1940 talks. Clive Ponting, however, does so in a
tendentious study of that year. In it he incorporates a reference to the
talks in a chapter entitled 'Impotence'.[27]

One major recent history of modern Ireland has called the June
1940 offer 'the high watermark of British tractability'.[28] Yet de
Velera's rejection of it was no surprise. Some have argued that he
was influenced by what may have appeared to him the likelihood of a
British defeat which would render the offer meaningless. Such a
prospect was not unwelcome to some of those close to him, such as
Joseph Walshe, the permanent secretary at the Department of External Affairs. He was exhilarated by Hitler's victories in 1940 and
what he saw as Éire's role in a German New Order in Europe.[29] His
views were similar to those of Cardinal Joseph MacRory, Archbishop
of Armagh and Primate of All Ireland since 1928, and also of Dan
Breen, a former IRA hero of the War of Independence who had
become a party colleague of de Valera in the Dáil. For him the war
was not a fight against Fascist barbarism but simply 'a re-run of the
old imperial conflict of 1914 to 1918 which Britain had regrettably
won'.[30]

In fact, de Valera always wanted Britain and its allies to triumph
but without Éire's neutrality being compromised. MacDonald certainly believed this. 'Far from being content to sit happy and see us
strangled'[31] de Valera, in his view, conceived of the state's neutrality
as benevolent to Britain's cause. As to the June 1940 offer, he wrote
later that the Taoiseach.

> dismissed the suggestion about a United Ireland as a promise
> which, however sincere, might produce no effective result. At the
> same time, he said emphatically that he and his colleagues wanted

us to win the war, and he argued that one reason why Éire should remain neutral was that this would reduce the danger of us being defeated in the struggle.[32]

Departing from neutrality to a point that provoked Germany could lead to an invasion which would then increase the threat to Britain.

This was a benign and also fairly accurate reading of de Valera's position. It was broadly accepted by Sir John Maffey, Britain's representative in wartime Dublin, who proved his value to both countries throughout the 'Emergency'. Churchill had not taken Maffey into his confidence over the June 1940 talks though Mac-Donald did, it seems, consult him. Maffey's role was to carry out a damage-limitation exercise after the initiative had clearly failed.[33]

Most accounts of these events see Britain's offer to de Valera as arising from desperation and based on a promise which could not have been delivered, one which he had no choice but to reject.[34] There are, however, some who have raised the issue of whether opinion in Éire may possibly have been less of an obstacle than has usually been assumed to some form of alliance or open military co-operation with Britain.[35]

The authors of a semi-official biography of de Valera also posed the question of whether an abridgement of neutrality in a context clearly linked to Irish unification might, in fact, have been acceptable to the electorate: 'the whole atmosphere would have been so completely transformed', they suggest, 'that one can only speculate as to what path Ireland would or would not have chosen'.[36] It should, however, also be recalled that, among those who espoused the case against neutrality, there was acceptance that de Valera, given the still bitter divisions within the Irish state, had little choice in the matter. A case in point was James Dillon, the opposition Fine Gael party leader who, in February 1942, resigned from his position over the issue.

The other factor in any assessment of the June 1940 offer's prospect of acceptance has to be the Unionist government of Northern Ireland. Sir Wilfrid Spender, the head of the Stormont civil service, confided to his diary his premonitions about the talks before they had started, doubting whether de Valera would bring Éire into the war even 'if he got some eyewash concessions'.[37] In a note to a colleague, Robert Gransden, he quoted an unnamed contact just back from the United States, whose view he himself endorsed, that 'Great Britain had entirely the whip-hand over Éire'[38] if it wanted to use it but he offered, too, the thought that the Dominions Office might oppose this. He may well have had in mind what he saw as Malcolm MacDonald's influence, though he was no longer Secretary of State there, unsurprisingly given Churchill's suspicions of him.

Not all the Unionist cabinet shared Spender's belief in the 'whip-hand', though an ill and elderly Lord Craigavon certainly did. From late May 1940 onwards he was under intense pressure from London to make constructive proposals for drawing Dublin into talks about all-Ireland defence issues. His reaction was as inflexible as it had always been, refusing to take part until Éire gave up its neutrality. By June a split developed within his cabinet. His administration had been less than dynamic in its conduct of Northern Ireland's war effort. Two of his younger colleagues, Sir Basil Brooke, agricultural minister and John McDermott, in charge of public security, were ready, in the dire crisis of 1940, to consider a change in the province's constitutional position if Éire joined the war: 'For them, loyalty to the king and empire and the defeat of the Axis powers transcended commitment to the maintenance of the Union.'[39]

This potential crisis for Unionism passed with de Valera's refusal of Churchill's offer but it had left a faltering leadership open to a charge of 'little Ulsterism' being put above the needs of Britain fighting for its life. Brooke's son later claimed that his father had told him that maintaining partition would have had to give precedence to saving 'western civilization' if that had become the choice.[40]

Such a choice looked as if it might be imminent in June and July 1940 as the Germans prepared to implement Operation Sea Lion for the invasion of Britain and the Luftwaffe began its attempt to destroy the RAF's fighter defences. Although most of a defeated army had been rescued from Dunkirk, the need to rebuild and expand it, as well as gearing the economy to full war production, created an incipient manpower crisis. In anticipation of such a crisis and ahead of actual hostilities, conscription had been introduced by the Chamberlain government in April 1939 but it was not extended to Northern Ireland for fear of what was thought likely to be the hostile reaction of the minority community. This was despite the urgings of Lord Craigavon who saw its acceptance as a badge of the province's loyalty to the Crown.

Craigavon's wife, who was in London at the time of this decision, saw it as simple appeasement of de Valera. In her diary she claimed that Chamberlain put it to Lord Craigavon in stark terms: 'if you really want to help, don't press for conscription. It will only be an embarrassment. What else could James do than say very well, I won't.'[41] She drew from Chamberlain's stance the conclusion that appeasement would go beyond conscription to the issue of the border itself. One of her husband's colleagues, Sir Basil Brooke, writing in his Fermanagh constituency newspaper, attributed the government's weakness to.

> the presence in our midst of a minority who, whilst prepared to share in the benefits of empire . . . were either afraid or too despicable to take a hand in the defence of the country who defended them and were prepared to go to any length to prevent loyal and brave men from doing their duty.[42]

In reality, there was little appetite for conscription in either community. Indeed, a populist element within the majority had signalled opposition well before the war. At the Ulster Hall in Belfast in May 1935, what a newspaper called 'amazing statements' were made by an independent Unionist Councillor Gallagher from Londonderry. He told an audience of the Ulster Protestant Society that in any future war they should stay at home: 'Why should they go out to help Roman Catholic France and Fenian Belgium to smash Protestant Germany? We have played the Pope's game too long.'[43]

The Northern Ireland Labour Party, which represented a mainly Protestant electorate though eschewing sectarianism, also opposed conscription. When, in a Stormont debate in March 1938, Lord Craigavon seemed to be preparing the ground for it in a speech in which he expressed confidence that he 'could rely on the Ulster people sharing their responsibilities with their kith and kin of every part of the Empire',[44] he was challenged by a Labour member, Jack Beattie, who denied Northern Ireland's right 'to commit the people to the foreign policy of another nation'.[45] A year later, at Belfast's May Day rally, one of the party's leading figures, Harry Midgley, who had in fact fought in World War I, came out strongly against conscription.[46]

There was further evidence that there was little appetite for conscription. Proof of this came quickly when a scheme of national registration, planned before the war, was launched in Northern Ireland as it was in Britain as a whole. In the latter, its purpose, of course, was to provide a basis for military and, if needed, industrial conscription. In Northern Ireland its purpose was merely to provide an administrative framework for food rationing. Every household was required to fill up a ration book application form setting out the details of everyone in the house as well as those temporarily absent. Some 320,000 copies were issued but Craigavon himself felt he had to explain to the Stormont parliament that the scheme was not intended as a way of preparing the ground for conscription.[47]

In some years prior to the war, voluntary enlistment in the province had yielded better results than in the rest of the United Kingdom but, since September 1939, recruitment there, after an initial surge in the first few weeks of the war, had been a disappointment to the government. It picked up again in the weeks after Dunkirk only to fall off once more and surpassed the 1,000-a-month mark only three times in 1941 and never once in 1942.[48] This was in spite of vigorous recruitment publicity, much of it co-ordinated initially by Sir Basil Brooke, someone whose appeals for volunteers were unlikely to have much resonance within the nationalist community.

Within that community even wearing the uniform of the Air Raid Precaution service (ARP) could cause family frictions, as Brian Moore recalled in an autobiographical novel set in wartime Belfast,[49] while the republican movement and the IRA were in friendly contact with the Third Reich and sought to oppose and obstruct Britain's war effort in Northern Ireland. When Churchill's government authorised Stormont in the 'invasion summer' of 1940 to follow its example by raising a force of Local Defence Volunteers (LDV), which became known as the Home Guard, Craigavon insisted that, in Northern Ireland, it should be based on the Royal Ulster Constabulary's (RUC) B Special reservists, a body deeply distrusted by the nationalist community. This and the decision to place it under overall police authority made it seem a sectarian force, as the Mass Observation diarist Moya Woodside stated, remarking that it recruited few Catholics.[50]

She, in fact, claimed that even the Queen's University LDV unit was discouraging Catholics who wanted to join though there was criticism in the local press of what was happening. Moya Woodside blamed it on the Unionist government: 'Craigavon and co prefer to play the party game and continue to cold-shoulder Catholics, many of whom are anxious and willing to undertake National Service, while at the same time reproaching them with lack of interest and non-cooperation.'[51]

When this became apparent to the government in London, the War Office investigated the matter, as did the Home Secretary, Sir John Anderson, whose knowledge of Ireland and its internecine divisions went back to his time as a joint undersecretary at Dublin Castle during the War of Independence. His bleak conclusion was that no action from Whitehall was worth attempting and that most of the minority community in Northern Ireland would distrust the Home Guard whatever the basis of its formation and recruitment.

When the Orange Order announced in the early summer of 1940 that it would call off its traditional July parades, there were cynics whose immediate reaction was that this was to conceal from the public gaze the number of brethren of military age who had opted out of joining up.[52] Even in what was still the Unionist stronghold of Queen's University, its vice chancellor, Sir David Lindsay Keir, felt compelled to circulate a letter to all undergraduates and staff of military age urging them to enlist. Moya Woodside reported that this appeal was resented by many of her friends who taught at Queen's. She quotes one of them as saying that 'if the Vice-Chancellor wished to turn the University into a recruiting station, it would have been better to have closed the place down altogether and refused to accept male students for the duration'.[53]

There was a certain 1ogic to this view but she also quoted undergraduates voicing a preference for conscription which would at least place Queen's on the same footing as universities in the United Kingdom as a whole. There students could either volunteer for an early call-up or pursue their courses over a period of deferment until their call-up came. This, Moya Woodside put it, would at least 'free them from the present invidious position'.[54]

Recruitment within Northern Ireland's majority community, it was clear early on in the war, suffered from the long shadow of the Somme and the sour memory of sacrifices ill-rewarded by the unemployment and poverty of the interwar years. Indeed, doubts had been there even a generation earlier among Loyalists with visceral fears of 'the other side taking over' if they gave up secure jobs for enlistment and possible overseas service. This was a fear accepted even quite late on in the war by the Ulster Unionist Party. [55]

Some men, perhaps many, of military age within the Unionist population, it would appear, did not even consider joining up. Brian Faulkner, later to become the province's last prime minister prior to the imposition of direct rule by Britain in March 1972, gave up his law degree at Queen's University in 1940. He became a manager in his father's successful shirt factory which went over to seven-day working because of extra wartime contracts. Much later, and a trifle cynically, he would justify this decision to himself and in print:

> It was of course, my own decision to stay in the family factory, and in retrospect, it was a foolish one. The only service to the country

that many people recognised was service in the armed force. So medals and military rank were valuable assets for political advancement in the post-war world and lack of either was a serious obstacle to overcome. This has been specially true in Northern Ireland, where the practice of using one's wartime rank has persisted among many politicians until recently. But I regarded my task as a particularly useful and important part of the country's war effort. It was also important for the family business that my father had created.[56]

No such self-serving calculations figured in the decision to enlist made by the Belfast-born writer Sam McAughtry. He grew up in the fiercely Loyalist and working-class Tiger Bay area in the north of the city where there was a strong tradition of service in the British forces and in the merchant navy. 'There were no pacifists in Cosgrave Street,' he wrote later.

> We thought highly of the Crown forces. When World War Two was more than a year off the men of my district joined the Territorial Army in hundreds. The annual bounty of eight pounds or so helped, of course, but the men would have joined anyway.[57]

This enthusiasm, as recruitment figures continued to show, was not typical of the Protestant community as a whole, and conscription remained an issue in the minds of Unionists. Whether enlistment levels without conscription would have been any higher in the rest of Britain must, of course, remain a matter of conjecture.

When John Andrews became prime minister after the death of Lord Craigavon in November 1940, he was soon under pressure to reopen the case for conscription. A decisive factor in this was the Luftwaffe's Blitz on Belfast during April and early May of 1941. The city's defences and emergency services were ill-prepared for this, and a chaotic and large-scale exodus of population resulted, imposing huge strains on adjacent areas. For John McDermott, the Public Security minister, this clinched the case for conscription in the province.

'This country has suffered and is suffering from being only half in the war,' he minuted to the Cabinet.

> There is a general feeling that we are neither one thing nor the other and I think this has contributed to the unsettling effect of the raids. There is no feeling, as above noted, of equality of sacrifice

throughout the country. The willing horse is bearing the brunt and we are in danger of working him to death.[58]

Conscription, he went on to argue, would create this equality:

> Its introduction would cause difficulties with the minority but I doubt if they would be as great as they were at the beginning of the war and I feel that such difficulties will be more than offset by the benefits gained.[59.]

Both Ernest Bevin, the Minister of Labour, and Churchill himself were enthusiastic for another bid to extend conscription to Northern Ireland. On Saturday, 24 May, they met a deputation to London led by Prime Minister Andrews and four of his ministers. It was also joined by Sir Charles Wickham, the inspector-general of the RUC. He proved to be a key figure in the talks because of his knowledge of the security situation. Against estimates of the 50,000 additional men who could be raised by a call-up in Northern Ireland, he stressed the way an intermittently active IRA would gain support in response to conscription. De Valera had already condemned it, as had Cardinal MacRory.

The cardinal's statement, issued from the Archbishop's Palace in Armagh two days before the London meeting, declared that Ireland was 'an ancient land, made one by God, partitioned by a foreign power, against the vehement protests of its people. Conscription would now seek to compel those who writhe under this grievous wrong to fight on the side of its perpetrators.'[60] As protest rallies increased in nationalist areas of the province, Andrews began to have second thoughts, and these eventually outweighed the optimism of colleagues as well as that of Harry Midgley of the Northern Ireland Labour Party who believed that the recent Blitz had begun to bring the working-class population closer together.[61] Wickham was not so sure, fearing that conscription would not have the full support of the Protestant community either.

Irish American and de Valera's influence was always going to have a bearing on the outcome. John Winant, the United States ambassador to London, who had replaced the pro-appeasement Joseph Kennedy, took up the matter with Roosevelt once he was aware of what was afoot. 'I cabled the facts to the President,' he later wrote. 'He replied at once saying he hoped no action would be taken. I took the matter up with the Prime Minister. He did not carry out the recommendation made by the Government of Northern Ireland.'[62]

Someone else who may also have helped to change Churchill's mind was Malcolm MacDonald who had been sent by him to Canada as British high commissioner. W. L. Mackenzie King, the dominion's prime minister, told him on 24 May that he had just received a massage from de Valera expressing his anger and alarm over conscription being extended to Northern Ireland. King told MacDonald that he was thinking of writing to Churchill himself 'to speak of the possible effect of this step on Irish-American opinion and of its repercussions in Canada'.[63] He did so, with MacDonald's support, and three days later Churchill informed parliament that he did not intend to press the issue of conscription.

Hardliners within the Stormont administration were less than impressed by the way both governments seemed to them to have retreated. Spender felt that the security situation in the province had improved over the last few months yet, 'in spite of these advantages timorous whisperings were allowed to have influence and the final decision was to give way to the representations of the Éire government'.[64] He was particularly dismayed by what he saw as the degree of support in Westminster for a decision that would be a 'bad signal'[65] to the United States that Britain could not get all its people to play their part in the war.

David Gray, Franklin D. Roosevelt's minister in Dublin, certainly took a dim view of the inevitable decision to back way from conscription in Northern Ireland. This was also the president's view but Churchill, after Pearl Harbor and the arrival of a substantial American force in the province, returned to the issue and wrote to Roosevelt about it on 11 April 1943. 'The situation is now changed,' he argued.

The United States forces are in Northern Ireland in considerable numbers and we have the spectacle of young Americans taken by compulsion form their homes to defend an area where young fellows of the locality loaf about with their hands in their pockets. This affects not only recruiting but the work of the important Belfast shipyards which are less active than the British yards.[66]

Churchill was certainly right on the last point but there was little support for him from Washington when he went on to declare that 'I am thinking therefore of reopening the question and asking the Northern Ireland government whether they would like me to have another try. A loud caterwaul may be expected from de Valera.'[67] Andrews, in Belfast, was no more convinced of the case than

Roosevelt and had earlier written to Robert Gordon, a Unionist colleague, that it 'did not belong to the realm of practical politics'.[68]

Bizarrely, conscription was brought back to centre stage in the final months of the conflict by Sir Basil Brooke who replaced Andrews as prime minister in late April 1943. Early in 1945 London had made it known to Brooke that compulsory military service would have to be maintained even when hostilities finished. Brooke wanted Northern Ireland to reap the benefits of any post-war consensus on social welfare policy and felt that, in return, his government should yet again signal its willingness for conscription to be extended to the province. He also believed it would help to secure its position within the union and help to counteract possible post-war unemployment as industry's order books became less full with the winding down of military contracts.

Unsurprisingly, Churchill's government was unimpressed with a proposal which seemed to be a way of using conscription, at a time of greatly decreased danger to those called up, to cushion Northern Ireland at British taxpayers' expense against possible post-war problems. Brooke was so keen on the idea that he even approached the Catholic hierarchy to see whether more funding for their church schools might soften their innate hostility to conscription. He made it known he would be ready to negotiate on the issue with nationalist politicians[69] but, in the face of the London government's opposition, the matter went no further.

Conscription in Northern Ireland, like the issue of the Treaty Ports, nagged at Éire's relations with Britain during the war years and always had the potential to destabilise them. An additional irritant to them during this time and afterwards was the reality that, through-out the 'Emergency', as one recent study of the period has put it, 'The real defenders of Irish neutrality against a threat from Germany were the Royal Navy and the British forces in Northern Ireland, who would have been expected to cross the border to expel any invaders from the Third Reich.'[70] Indeed, pre-1939 debates in the Irish state on sustainable levels of defence expenditure were influenced by the thought that this would be the case.

This contributed decisively to what Professor J. J. Lee has de-scribed as the Irish state's 'astonishing achievement'[71] in actually reducing public expenditure as a proportion of its gross domestic product (GDP) between 1939 and 1945. The fact that the burden of making a reality of Éire's neutral status fell on British shoulders should not be taken to mean that the state was indifferent to the military implications of its neutrality. How it responded to them must now be examined.

Article 8 of the treaty of 1922 limited the size of the new Irish state's defence forces as a proportion of the population to the strength at any given time of Britain's forces in relation to its population. The Dáil debates on the treaty made little or no reference to defence issues or, indeed, to neutrality. In the Free State's constitution, however, there was a clause setting out, that except in the case of any actual invasion, the defence forces would not be committed to 'active participation' in any war without the consent of the Oireachtas, which at that time meant the king, the Dáil and the Senate.

The creation of the Irish state and the civil war which followed saw a rapid expansion of its armed forces. By April 1923 there were 3,600 officers and more than 44,000 other ranks, and over the financial year which ended in March 1924, defence expenditure exceeded £11 million.[72] The mutiny of that year (see Chapter 1) was a watershed for the Free State's relationship with the army, and large-scale demobilisation followed it. Within a year its strength was reduced by two-thirds and expenditure was cut back to £4 million.[73]

In July 1925 the general staff asked for directions on defence policy from the Free State government, and three alternative policies were considered. One was the creation of an independent defence force; the second the organisation of a force which would be an integral part of the British 'imperial forces'; and the third option was the abandonment to Britain of all responsibility for defence against external enemies. Much of the debate was taken up with possible internal threats from the anti-treaty IRA, from ex-army men dismissed after the 1924 mutiny, as well as from labour unrest or renewed sectarian conflict in Northern Ireland.[74]

The government finally, in October 1925, set out a defence policy which, in its essentials, remained unchanged until after the Second World War. This involved limiting the army to 12,000 men but organised in a way that would make rapid expansion possible. It was stressed that, while it would remain an autonomous force, it would have to be able to co-operate in any emergency with Britain's armed services. In the ensuing bitter clashes with the Ministry of Finance, the relative youth and inexperience of the general staff told against it on the issue of funding.[75] Training and equipment suffered badly. So, too, did recruitment which was not helped by the fact that Free State citizens could still enlist in Ulster-based regiments which had been kept in being at the end of 1921 while several other famous Irish regiments had been disbanded.

In 1938, the Armagh-based Royal Irish Fusiliers conducted a

regimental census which showed that 34 per cent of their recruitment had been from across the border.[76] Pay and conditions of service were significantly better in the British army, and other regiments took their share of recruits from the Free State, as did the Irish Guards which, from its creation in 1900, had recruited strongly from nationalist Ireland.[77]

The economic crisis of the 1930s led to further stringent cuts in defence expenditure, and the army's strength fell far below the 12,000 figure set out in the 1925 agreement. A National Defence Association of serving and former officers had little success in its representations on the army's behalf and failed totally to halt what has been called 'the systematic attenuation'[78] of the state's capacity for defence. In 1938 the army had reached its lowest point, with under 6,000 regulars and a reserve of around 14,500 men.

At least the army maintained high standards of drill and ceremonial, and was much applauded for its part in military tattoos and pageants staged in Dublin in 1927 and 1929. Its school of music was particularly successful, especially when Fritz Brase, a former German officer, took over as its director.[80] He was, however, a Nazi and a member of that party's Auslandsorganisation which was active beyond Germany's border. When the army discovered this, they, with de Valera's support, requested him to choose between the party and the school of music. He opted for the latter but, until 1939, continued to mix socially with Dublin's expatriate German community in which many Nazis were prominent.[81]

As its numbers dwindled, the army's ethos also became more conspicuously Roman Catholic. Masses, pilgrimages and other public devotional acts became common. Even so, the morality of serving soldiers remained suspect and, in 1926, the Catholic press accused the army of, in effect, encouraging contraception by limiting its cash allowances and accommodation to enlisted men with four children only. [82]

One significant decision made in this period came with Fianna Fáil's arrival in power after the 1932 Dáil elections. It announced the formation of a part-time volunteer force which IRA sympathisers could join without compromising their beliefs. When this army reserve force was finally set up two years later, it proved, in fact, to be a means of luring young men away from paramilitary activism. The chance to get basic military training under the national flag, as well as to earn a modest cash allowance, drew in more than 11,000 men within a year and, when war came in 1939 the Volunteer Force played an important part in the army's rapid expansion.[83]

Over the period between the return of the Treaty Ports to Éire and the actual outbreak of war, there was only a modest increase in defence expenditure but the Irish military historian J. P. Duggan probably understated things when he wrote that 'the country was almost defenceless when the Second World War broke out'.[84]

Debates on military expenditure in the 1930s outside the Irish state were dominated by the issue of air power, how best to develop it and whether there was any effective defence against its offensive deployment. An Irish Air Corps was created after the Free State's formation, albeit under the overall jurisdiction of the army, and there were a few serving officers who grasped air power's importance. One of them was Colonel Michael J. Costello whose call, in 1930, for a clear policy to be set out on the Air Corps and its role was blocked on financial grounds. He tried again in 1938 and once more had to admit to failure.[85]

When war came, only a few hundred men were serving in the Air Corps. 'Air defence during the Emergency was conspicuous by its absence,' one authority on the Irish state's armed forces has written.[86] A handful of ageing Avro Anson and Gloucester Gladiator fighter aircraft took to the air in patrol flights in the first days of the Emergency but the strain was acute on manpower services and on the aircraft themselves. They would have stood little or no chance against the Luftwaffe had there been even a thought of using them in response to its accidental bombing of Dublin in late May of 1941.

None of this stopped some of these aircraft being used in state-funded propaganda films designed to impress audiences with the message that Éire's neutrality was being backed up by a real military effort. In one such film, given general release in late 1940 as part of the 'Step Together' campaign to boost recruitment to the defence forces, five aircraft, a significant part of the Air Corps' total strength, were shown flying in formation as the final credits rolled.[87]

An attempt was made in 1940, with the support of the defence minister, Frank Aiken, to buy American aircraft. This, however, was effectively opposed by the Air Corps itself. Its preference was for British aircraft which were never forthcoming and, in the event, it had to make do with salvaging aircraft which crashed on Irish territory. Even when these were repaired, there was never enough fuel or ammunition for them to assume an operational role. Twenty years earlier W. B. Yeats had written unforgettably, in *An Irish Airman Foresees His Death*, of the lure of aerial combat. In 1939 and 1940 young Irishmen who felt that same lure joined the RAF.

Yeats had written his poem in memory of Robert, the son of his literary agent and personal friend, Lady Gregory, but had portrayed him as someone without ideals or belief in the war which claimed his life in 1918.[88] This, in fact, was no more true of him than of many of the Irish volunteers who flew with the RAF a generation later. One of them was Eugene Esmond, who was killed in action over the English Channel in 1942 and awarded a posthumous Victoria Cross. Among his Tipperary ancestors was one executed for his part in the 1798 United Irish rising and another who also won a VC in the Crimea. Two years before his death, he had written to his family: 'I can think of no greater honour, nor a better way of passing into Eternity than in the cause for which the Allies are fighting this war.'[89]

The Air Corps may have had no military role that it was equipped to play but it nonetheless made a significant contribution to Éire's defence and to the Allies' cause by its constant work on aircraft identification and plotting. This work was done by a network of ground observers whom it recruited and trained. From 1939 onwards, they monitored all violations of Éire's air space but they pursued a policy of active liaison, authorised by the government, with the RAF and, after December 1941, with the United States Air Force, on all matters relating to Luftwaffe activity off Ireland's coast as well as forced landings and aircraft and aircrew recovery within Éire.[90]

As has been stated earlier in this chapter, Éire's wartime economic survival depended largely upon British shipping and its Royal Navy escorts, though Irish seamen did pay with their lives for helping to maintain, through their state's limited cargo fleet, the flow of essential supplies from ports such as Liverpool, Bristol and Glasgow. Even so, their sacrifice was overshadowed by the sea war's cost to Britain. At the height of the battle of the Atlantic, villagers and fishermen on the storm-swept coasts of Mayo, Donegal and Kerry became hardened to the awful task of retrieving the often badly decomposed bodies of naval and aircrew members who had been victims of U-boats and of the Luftwaffe.

The national, Dublin-based press reported little of this but newspapers circulating in coastal areas of the west could scarcely avoid it, given the demands on local people, police and clergy involved in bringing ashore, identifying if possible, and burying the victims.[91] Peadar O'Donnell wrote a moving short story about cheerful Donegal fishermen rowing out to strip a stricken vessel of whatever they could take away, only to find, under a swarm of seagulls, the floating body of a young sailor. After that, one of them said: 'No man now stands on the cliff-top and looks out, without dread, over the wide wastes of the bay for sign of things floating.'[92]

Apart from the Treaty Ports, with their poorly maintained guns and fortifications, Éire in 1939 was without any resources to defend its coasts and territorial waters. Neutral Norway, it has been pointed out, in September 1939 had placed orders for 129 aircraft and had a navy of sixty-three ships, though forty-four of these had been built before 1918; Éire had just two. Few outside the Defence Forces had queried the wisdom or the morality of this situation: 'God would provide for his children through the Royal Navy and the Royal Air Force, hitherto unlikely agents of the divine will, but now constrained to protect Ireland in Britain's self-interest'[93] was the cynical view of one Irish historian of this period.

British Admiralty urgings that the Dublin government should at least begin to develop a coastal patrol and minesweeping force had not been acted upon so, when hostilities in Europe became imminent, a marine service had to be created from scratch. Like the Air Corps, it was placed under the overall command of the army and, at the outbreak of war, it had just one motor torpedo boat on order from Britain. Six more were ordered and two vessels used for fisheries protection duty were incorporated within the new service and fitted with 12–pounder guns and some lighter armaments. They were tasked with patrolling Irish coastal waters as well as with improvised minesweeping work. Initially crew members often used rifles to destroy floating mines.

When they finally arrived, the motor torpedo boats were, because of their age, of limited operational value though they and their crews were used in publicity films and photographs funded by the defence department. This was the navy which Patrick Campbell (1913–80), the writer and humorist, decided to join when he returned to Dublin in 1939 after failing to make his mark with the Beaverbrook press in London. Campbell, a scion of the Protestant ascendancy and heir to a title, later recalled telling of his decision to a friend in a bar. The predictable reply was: 'The Irish Navy, Bejasus, I didn't know we had one.'[94]

Campbell in fact joined the Port Control Service's Dublin unit and, after some very basic training, spent much of his time on what he described, in a hilarious account of his experience, as a malodorous and grease-encrusted tugboat stationed in Dublin Bay. It was the crew's duty to intercept and board foreign ships, which they often did in order to acquire extra tea to supplement their own very limited rations. The sense and the sound of an all-too-real war, however, was not far away from them. As the German Blitz intensified, Campbell recalled: 'Some nights we'd hear the sounds of airplane engines coming up from the south and turning east over the lights of Dublin. Those were the nights when Liverpool got it again.'[95]

Campbell came to feel guilty about his own essentially safe and sometimes farcical service. 'The only way I can counter my own feelings about this when people start talking about the war,' he later wrote, 'is to say, "You don't know what suffering is until you've been the one Protestant among thirty-two Catholics in the Dublin Bay Port Control."' But it isn't nearly funny enough, in the light of Buchenwald, Belsen and the London Blitz in which his sister was killed.[96]

His sense of unease grew in later years even as his reminiscences delighted readers and television viewers.

> In fact I didn't want to talk about the war at all. It's an uncomfortable feeling, to say the least, to have missed a fearful experience that millions of other people endured – or failed to survive, including my own sister . . . Some people gain a life-long inferiority complex from not having been to a public school or a university. Not having been in a war that nearly all one's contemporaries endured is a great deal worse.[97]

As with the Air Corps, the Marine service did prove highly effective in its coastal surveillance and intelligence-gathering operations. Ultimately, it maintained over eighty observation posts around the Irish coast where its monitoring of all German air and naval movement, especially once it was equipped adequately with radio transmitters, proved immensely valuable to Britain and its allies. It was also one of their tasks to alert lifeboat crews to any sinkings off the Irish coast and to help survivors ashore as well as retrieving, and where possible identifying, bodies.

For the Irish army, even the ever-closer approach of war failed to strengthen its case for increased funding. In the summer of 1938 it asked for an extra ten million pounds for equipment to bring it up to a minimal level of military readiness. Yet again, the Finance ministry proved an immovable opponent. The army was authorised to spend just £600,000 which, owing to slow-moving purchasing procedures, it would not be able to use fully within the existing financial year. At the height of the Munich crisis a desperate general staff told the government that the defence forces as a whole were fit for little more than an internal security role.[98]

A few weeks later, de Valera chaired a lengthy Cabinet meeting on defence and a scheme of re-equipment was agreed upon. Even then the Finance ministry held out, arguing that British self-interest would ensure that Ireland would not be invaded and therefore radical increases in defence expenditure were not justified.[99] When Britain declared war on Germany and de Valera announced the existence of the 'Emergency' army, mobilisation began with a target figure of 37,000 men, but this quickly outran the resources needed for it and, in December 1939, the government ordered the goal to be cut back to 29,000.

This was a serious blow to army morale, as was the IRA's Magazine Fort raid in December 1939. In this coolly planned and executed operation, an IRA unit took over the army's main armoury and ammunition store in Dublin's Phoenix Park, removing from it weapons, explosives and more than a million rounds of ammunition. Nearly all the stolen material was quickly recovered but army security had been poor and its Chief of Staff, General Michael Brennan, resigned. Some later accounts of this episode even grandiosely described it as 'Ireland's Pearl Harbor'.

To replace Brennan the government went well down the hierarchy of possible candidates before selecting Colonel Dan McKenna. This highly competent officer would later be described by the Chief of Britain's Imperial General Staff, Sir Alan Brooke, as 'a pretty rough diamond'[100] after they dined together in Belfast in 1942, but McKenna had energy and military knowledge which Brooke also recognised. From the outset he made it clear that Éire's army must do its job with the weapons it had, not the weapons it would like to have. He put a premium on intensive infantry training, insofar as this could compensate for the shortage of equipment. 'Rifle marksmanship became a religion and McKenna its high priest as he rode roughshod over resistance to his demands and at least 20,000 American army surplus rifles had been shipped over after the fall of France.'[101]

Notes

1. I. S. Wood, *Churchill* (Basingstoke: Macmillan, 2000), pp. 151–2.
2. R. Fisk, *In Time of War: Ireland, Ulster and the Price of Neutrality 1939–45* (London: Deutsch, 1983), p. 242, but all references henceforth are from the 1985 Paladin edition.
3. J. Colvile, *The Fringes of Power: Downing Street Dairies 1939–45* (London: Hodder and Stoughton, 1968), pp. 305–6.
4. W. S. Churchill, *The Second World War*, Vol. III, *The Grand Alliance* (London: Cassell, 1950), p. 641.
5. Ibid.
6. G. R. Sloan, *The Geo-Politics of Anglo-Irish Relations in the 20th Century* (London and Washington, DC: Leicester University Press, 1977), p. 210.

7. Fisk, *In Time of War*, pp. 546–7.
8. Ibid.
9. H. Nicolson, *Diaries and Letters, 1939–45* (London: Collins, 1967), pp. 139–40.
10. R. Menzies, *Afternoon Light: Some Memories of Men and Events* (London: Cassell, 1967), p. 41.
11. S. W. Roskill, *The War at Sea*, Vol. I, *1939–45* (London: HMSO, 1954), p. 263.
12. Sloan, *The Geo-Politics of Anglo-Irish Relations in the 20th Century*, pp. 226–7.
13. J. T. Carroll, *Ireland in the War Years, 1939–1945* (Newton Abbot: David and Charles, 1975), p. 80. Also, M. Gilbert, *Finest Hour, Winston S. Churchill 1939–1941* (London: Heinemann, 1983), p. 938.
14. Fisk, *In Time of War*, p. 315.
15. Ibid., pp. 316–18.
16. N. Monsarrat, *The Cruel Sea* (London: Cassell, 1951), pp. 151–2.
17. Nicolson, *Diaries and Letters, 1939–45*, p. 185.
18. Sloan, *The Geo-Politics of Anglo-Irish Relations in the 20th Century*, p. 211.
19. Ibid., p. 197.
20. Lord Moran, *Winston Churchill: the Struggle for Survival* (London: Constable, 1966), p. 330.
21. J. P. Duggan, *Neutral Ireland and the Third Reich* (Dublin: Gill and Macmillan, 1975, p. 100.
22. Fisk, *In Time of War*, p. 207.
23. C. Sanger, *Malcolm MacDonald: Bringing an End to Empire* (Liverpool: Liverpool University Press, 1995), p. 198.
24. Ibid.
25. Fisk, *In Time of War*, p. 207.
26. J. Charmley, *Churchill: the End of Glory* (London: Hodder and Stoughton, 1993).
27. C. Ponting, *1940: Myth and Reality* (London: Cardinal, 1990), pp. 189–94.
28. A. Jackson, *Ireland 1798–1998*, p. 302. See also T. P. Coogan, *De Valera: Long Fellow, Long Shadow* (London: Hutchinson, 1993), pp. 549–54.
29. C. C. O'Brien, *My Life and Themes* (London: Profile, 1999), pp. 99–103; also D. Keogh, *Twentieth Century Ireland: Nation and State* (Dublin: Gill and Macmillan, 1994), p. 115.
30. E. O'Halpin, *Defending Ireland: the Irish State and its Enemies Since 1922* (Oxford: Oxford University Press, 2000), pp. 151–3.
31. Sanger, *Malcolm MacDonald: Bringing an End to Empire*, p. 199.
32. Ibid. See also M. MacDonald, *Titans and Others* (London: Collins, 1972), pp. 84–5.
33. K. Kenny, *Sir John Maffey and Anglo-Irish Relations During the Second World War*, MSc dissertation, Centre for Second World War Studies, Edinburgh University (1998), p. 10.
34. B. Girvin, 'Politics in Wartime: Governing Neutrality and Elections', in B. Girvin and G. Roberts (eds), *Ireland and the Second World War: Politics, Society and Remembrance* (Dublin: Four Courts, 2000), pp. 30–1; also R. Fisk, *In Time of War*, pp. 212–16.
35. H. Patterson, *Ireland Since 1939: the Persistence of Conflict* (Dublin: Penguin, 2006), pp. 58–9.
36. Earl of Longford and T. P. O'Neill, *Eamon de Valera* (Dublin: Gill and Macmillan, 1970), p. 349.
37. Public Record Office of Northern Ireland, henceforth PRONI, D. 559, Sir W. Spender, Diary, 20–5 May 1940.
38. Ibid., 2 May 1940, W. Spender to R. Gransden.
39. B. Barton, 'Northern Ireland, 1939–45', in J. R. Hill (ed.), *A New History of Ireland*, VII, pp. 238–9.

40. Fisk, *In Time of War*, p. 186.
41. J. Bowman, *de Valera and the Ulster Question*, pp. 203–5.
42. B. Barton, *Northern Ireland in the Second World War* (Belfast: Ulster Historical Foundation, 1995), pp. 118–19.
43. *Irish News*, 25 May 1935.
44. Ibid., 23 March 1938.
45. Ibid.
46. G. Walker, *The Politics of Frustration: Harry Midgley and the Failure of Labour in Northern Ireland* (Manchester: Manchester University Press, 1985), p. 117.
47. J. W. Blake, *Northern Ireland in the Second World War* (Belfast: HMSO, 1956), pp. 93–4.
48. Ibid., pp. 199–200.
49. B. Moore, *The Emperor of Ice-Cream* (London: André Deutsch, 1956). This reference is to the London Flamingo edition, 1994, p. 15.
50. Tom Harrisson, Mass Observation Archive, University of Sussex, Diary of Moya Woodside, 20 October 1940; henceforth M. Woodside, Diaries.
51. Ibid.
52. Barton, *Northern Ireland in the Second World War*, p. 13.
53. M. Woodside, Diaries, 10 March 1940.
54. Ibid.
55. PRONI, DL327/7, Minutes of Ulster Unionist Party Standing Committee, 11 April and 10 November 1944; also 9 February 1945.
56. B. Faulkner, *Memoirs of a Statesman*, edited by John Houston (London: Weidenfeld and Nicolson, 1978), pp. 13–14.
57. S. McAughtry, *McAughtry's War* (Belfast: Blackstaff, 1985), p. 3.
58. PRONI, CAB 4/473/10, J. McDermott to the Cabinet, 12 May 1941.
59. Ibid.
60. *Irish Independent*, 23 May 1941.
61. Barton, *Northern Ireland in the Second World War*, p. 52.
62. J. Winant, *A letter from Grosvenor Square* (London: Hodder and Stoughton, 1947), p. 187.
63. Sanger, *Malcolm MacDonald*: Bringing an End to Empire, p. 217.
64. PRONI, D 559, W. Spender Diaries, 30 May 1941.
65. Ibid.
66. W. Kimball, *Churchill and Roosevelt: an Alliance Forged*, Vol. II (Princeton: Princeton University Press, 1984), pp. 186–7.
67. Ibid.
68. PRONI, CAB 9C/22/1, Andrews to Gordon, 4 November 1942.
69. PRONI, CAB 4/622. Cabinet Papers, 19 April 1945; also B. Barton, *Northern Ireland in the Second World War*, pp. 76–7.
70. H. Patterson, *Ireland Since 1939: the Persistence of Conflict*, p. 52.
71. Lee, *Ireland 1912–1985: Politics and Society*, p. 234.
72. A. E. C. Bredin, *A History of the Irish Soldier* (Belfast: Century Books, 1978), pp. 542–3.
73. E. O'Halpin, 'Politics, the State and the Armed Forces', in J. R. Hill (ed.), *A New History of Ireland 1921–1984*, p. 103.
74. P. Young, 'Defence and the New Irish State 1919–39', *The Irish Sword*, 1993–94, Vol. XIX, pp. 1–11.
75. Ibid.
76. K. Jeffrey, 'The British Army and Ireland Since 1922', in T. Bartlett and K. Jeffrey (eds), *A Military History of Ireland*, (Cambridge: Cambridge University Press, 1996), p. 433.

77. P. Verney, *The Micks: the Story of the Irish Guards*, (London: Peter Davies, 1970, p. 15).

78. O'Halpin, 'Politics the State and the Armed Forces', in J. R. Hill (ed.), *A New History of Ireland*, pp. 12–22.

79. D. Parsons, 'Mobilisation and Expansion 1939–40', *The Irish Sword*, 1993–94, Vol. XIX, pp. 96–7.

80. O'Haplin, *Defending Ireland*, p. 96.

81. D. O'Donghue, 'State Within a State: the Nazis in Neutral Ireland', *History Ireland*, November/December 2006, Vol. 14, No. 6, pp. 134–5.

82. Ibid., pp. 96–7.

83. O'Haplin, *Defending Ireland*, pp. 134–5.

84. J. P. Duggan, *A History of the Irish Army* (Dublin: Gill and Macmillan, 1991), p. 180. See also D. Keogh, *Twentieth Century Ireland: Nation and State* (Dublin: Gill and Macmillan, 1994), p. 108.

85. P. Young, 'Defence and the New Irish State 1919–39', *The Irish Sword*, 1993–94, Vol. XIX, pp. 67–8.

86. O'Haplin, *Defending Ireland*, p. 154.

87. C. Wills, *That Neutral Island: a Cultural History of Ireland During the Second World War* (London: Faber and Faber, 2007), pp. 67–8.

88. R. F. Doherty, *Irish Men and Women in the Second World War* (Dublin: Four Courts Press, 1999), p. 96.

89. R. F. Foster *Irish Story: Telling Tales and Making It Up in Ireland* (London: Penguin, 2001), pp. 67–8.

90. O'Haplin, *Defending Ireland*, p. 155.

91. Wills, *That Neutral Island*, pp. 136–44.

92. Ibid.

93. Lee, *Ireland 1912–1985: Politics and Society*, p. 265.

94. P. Campbell, *My Life and Easy Times* (London: Anthony Blond, 1967), p. 163.

95. Ibid., p. 171.

96. Ibid., p. 166.

97. Ibid., p. 164.

98. O'Halpin, *Defending Ireland*, pp. 142–3.

99. Ibid.

100. A. Danchev and D. Todman (eds), *War Diaries 1939–1945: Field Marshal Alanbrooke* (London: Weidenfeld and Nicolson, 2001), p. 277.

101. Duggan, *Neutral Ireland and the Third Reich*, p. 195.

3

Éire: Crisis and Survival

Colonel Dan McKenna confessed to being shocked at the state of the army when he took over as Chief of Staff in 1940 but as the war in Europe rapidly moved into a more menacing phase, he was soon guaranteed the manpower and funding increases he hoped for. By the end of the year he had over 40,000 men under arms. This mobilisation effort was one geared to the concept of neutrality as something which, in the last resort, might have to be fought for. 'It was backed up by a rigorous, if at times simplistic publicity campaign involving theatre productions, local pageants, film footage, photographic displays and the army's ubiquitous school for music.'[1]

The speed and brutality with which the German Reich had crushed neutral states in Scandinavia and the Low Countries posed all too clearly the question of Éire's capacity for self-defence, even as its defence forces began to undergo expansion. The related issue of accepting British help against any German invasion also had to be faced though, in talks in June 1940 with Malcolm MacDonald, de Valera declined to enter into any overtly defensive arrangements with Britain. What seemed, in that year's fevered summer and autumn, to be an increasingly imminent German move against Ireland had been prefaced by highly secret talks, in late May, between British officials and Joseph Walshe of the External Affairs Department as well as senior officers in G2, the Irish army's intelligence unit.

These contacts can, in fact, be traced back to the period after the 1938 agreement on the Treaty Ports when Walshe had approached the Dominions Office on the question of Anglo-Irish security liaison. This laid the foundations for an important degree of wartime co-operation between specialised British agencies and their Irish counterparts. This joint effort, it has been said, from its inception 'enjoyed de Valera's personal benediction'.[2]

Colonel Liam Archer of G2 took part in these 'invasion summer' talks with British intelligence officers, as did General McKenna. It fell to him, as the new Chief of Staff, while having to acknowledge Éire's military weakness, to agree to some basic principles of co-operation in the event of a German attack. He was, however, authorised to make it clear that any supportive British troop movements into Éire could come only after its forces had first engaged the invaders. He, Archer and Walshe were also authorised to accept a British proposal for immediate action to expedite the co-ordination of defence measures, and a young staff officer, Lieutenant Colonel Dudley Clarke, was ordered to travel to Dublin for this purpose.[3]

Clarke, who had personal experience of the German blitzkrieg in Norway, flew to Belfast with Walshe and Archer and, wearing civilian clothes, travelled on to Dublin. His remit was to impress upon his hosts that Britain was building up its forces in Northern Ireland and that armoured units with supporting infantry were ready to cross the border to help the Irish army if the Germans landed. Irish officers in return presented him with details of weapons and equipment they would need. General McKenna also emphasised, for Clarke's benefit, that there could be no question of calling for a British presence until a German invasion had started. This was a blow to Clarke who had been instructed to secure agreement if he could on a pre-emptive movement of British troops into Éire.

Clarke's visit concluded with a tour of Irish army defensive positions, and he returned to London convinced that at least the groundwork for defence co-ordination had been achieved. He had also been left clear in his own mind about Éire's position on any British troop movements across the border ahead of an actual German landing. A few weeks later de Valera would reiterate this position in his talks with MacDonald. .

One advocate of a pre-emptive British move across the border was the northern prime minister, Lord Craigavon. In late June 1940, Neville Chamberlain, who had remained in Churchill's war cabinet as Lord President of the Council, sent a telegram to Craigavon advising him that there was little chance of any further progress in talks with de Valera about bringing Éire into the war. Craigavon's

reply was prompt: 'Your telegram confirms my confidential information and conviction that de Valera is under German dictation and is
far past reasoning with.' He went on to urge the case for British
seizure of the Treaty Ports and a 'military advance south'.[4]

Craigavon followed this up with a memorandum to Churchill
which, it has been rightly said, 'betrayed the ingenious attention
to detail of a truly eccentric mind'.[5] An occupation of the Irish state,
he urged, would need the appointment of a military governor,
preferably Scottish or Welsh. These also should be the nationalities
of the occupying military forces, and one of their responsibilities
would be a leafleting campaign, in English and Irish, explaining the
benign intentions of the occupiers.

Craigavon, with barely three weeks to live, met Churchill in
London on 7 July 1940. Some of what was in his memorandum
was not so far removed from Churchill's own more intemperate
observations at the start of the war. No record survives of their
conversation, and Lord Craigavon's thoughts did not feature in
subsequent debates on British policy towards Éire.

Given that Churchill did not finally rule out naval or military
moves to retake the Irish ports until late 1943, Éire's military
planners had to allow for the contingency of a British invasion. In
the late summer of 1940 Major General Bernard Montgomery, later
Field Marshal Montgomery, was in command of 3 Infantry Division.
They were based in the south of England and he had orders to work
on plans for possible operations to capture the Azores and the Cape
Verde Islands. 'Then, after much work,' he later recalled,

> I was told to prepare plans for the seizure of Cork and Queens-
> town in Southern Ireland, so that the harbours there could be used
> as naval bases for anti-submarine war in the Atlantic. I had
> already fought the Southern Irish once, in 1921 and 1922, and
> it looked as if this renewed contest might be quite a party – with
> one division.[6]

The plans, he stressed, came to nothing. 'It seemed curious to me,'
he went on, 'that anyone in his senses could imagine that, at a time
when England was almost defenceless, the Prime Minister would
allow to leave England the only division which was fully equipped
and ready to fight.'[7] In reality, if operations against Éire had ever
been sanctioned by Churchill, they would have involved other units
operating from out of Northern Ireland. Irish army defences against

an attack from there centred on the valleys of the Boyne and Blackwater rivers where all crossings were covered by rapidly constructed blockhouses and machine gun positions. These, like strongpoints close to the Treaty Ports, were to be backed with mobile units including motorcycle troops as well as cavalry and members of the Local Defence Force.

This last body had originated in 1940 as the Local Security Force, a part-time body under Garda control to act essentially as a police auxiliary force. Some of its units were issued with arms and others were limited to observation and surveillance duties. By October 1940 it had recruited 180,000 men, mainly those unable or unwilling to enlist for full-time service. In early 1941 it became the Local Defence Force and recruited as wide a cross-section of the community as did the Home Guard in Britain.

One of those who joined it was Garret FitzGerald, later a Taoiseach and co-signatory with Margaret Thatcher of the 1985 Anglo-Irish Agreement. This was in January 1942 when he was just fifteen years old. He joined a signals unit to escape what he imagined would be the rigours of infantry service. Decades later he recalled some rudimentary and unclear sex education lectures from an officer at a training exercise in the country outside Dublin. During this he caught dysentery and spent much of his time trudging through muddy fields to the unit latrines. Above all, he warmed to the memory of a unique array of Dublin characters whom he might not otherwise have met without doing his wartime service, even though, as he put it, he had joined up 'on the somewhat dubious grounds that experience in the Netherlands during the Nazi invasion had shown that the armed forces suffered less casualties than the civilian population'.[8]

The writer John de Courcy Ireland was living in the small village of Muff on Donegal's border with Northern Ireland when war came. He joined a local LDF unit and also reminisced about it many years later.

We patrolled up and down the Inishowen peninsula keeping a lookout for U-boats and such like. I remember one patrol when our unit reached the border late at night. Suddenly we heard aeroplanes overhead. My second-in-command remarked that they sounded very different from those which we were accustomed to hear. He had hardly said it when bombs started falling on Derry. Four of our unit vamoosed, I have to admit, leaving just the two of us. There weren't many bombs, but they did make an awful clatter. Within half an hour, half the population of Derry – or so it seemed

– poured across the border. Then we had to go and knock up the parish priest, the rector, the doctor and everybody else in the neighbourhood to put them up. The refugees from Derry were terrified.[9]

Another former member of the LDF who had served in one of its medical units later met a former regular army officer who told him: 'Most of us regarded most of you as a bloody hindrance rather than a help.'[10] His response was that this, if true, was perhaps a reflection of the quality of training offered and he admitted that the ultimate test of invasion never came. If it had, he was adamant that he and his comrades would have done their duty:

No doubt we would have fought hard and even if the government capitulated guerrilla warfare would have gone on, but the strength of guerrilla resistance depends almost entirely upon the support to be obtained from a civilian population living in fear of savage reprisals. There is no doubt too that, just as happened elsewhere, some who would risk everything against enemy A might play the Quisling for enemy B and vice versa.[11]

He, in fact, took a very positive view of what the Irish state had achieved militarily during the Emergency years. For him they were

times of belief and a certain quiet appreciation that we had our freedom, at least, if incomplete. A British occupation could well have put the clock back; there was a feeling that our manumission was fragile. There were certainly threats being made to it.[12]

Had these perceived threats become reality, it has to remain debatable how much resistance the Irish forces could have offered. Even with the Soviet Union and the United States in the war as its allies, Britain's defence planners were still allowing for the possibility of having to deploy troops in Éire. Sir Alan Brooke, later Field Marshal Alan Brooke, who became Chief of the Imperial General Staff in 1941, made a diary entry early in 1942 concerning 'a new plan for Ulster Force to move into Éire in the event of an invasion'.[13]

Others who served in the defence forces took the view, at least in retrospect, that they would have had a chance of halting a German airborne invasion whereas a cross-border operation by British forces would have been much harder to contain. All were only too aware of the rapid cave-in of small armies in neutral states in 1940 when Hitler's troops invaded.

> Whatever our superiors thought, and they knew our capabilities against an armoured thrust better than we did, and whatever our politicians thought, the ordinary soldier who might survive such a blitzkrieg would be hoping for the leadership which should give him an alternative to stacking arms and the quiet march to the prisoner-of-war cages which was the fate of the small continental armies.[14]

These were the thoughts many years later of E. D. Doyle who had been an enthusiastic volunteer in 1940.

Given the greater likelihood of the invader being Germany, it made sense for the army to withdraw from use its very Gemanic-looking helmets which, at the start of the war, became the subject of much mocking comment from the British press and newsreel film commentaries. This was prompted in part by the sometimes jaunty and eccentric angles at which the helmets were worn. They had nearly all been bought in a bulk purchase from the British company Vickers in 1927 since the Weimar republic was forbidden under the Versailles treaty from exporting military equipment. In late 1940 the helmets were phased out and replaced by a British model. Thereafter, whether on increasingly large-scale training exercises or on parade, the Irish army at least looked little different from its British counterpart.

Whether its appearance on parade or field exercises simply served to mask the reality of its military weakness is something that nobody writing on this period of Irish history can afford to ignore. It remains difficult to disagree with J. J. Lee's verdict that 'the Irish policy of resisting to the last gasp but failing to provide remotely adequate means to sustain resistance against a determined enemy hardly deserved its good luck, however astutely de Valera played his diplomatic cards'.[15] The state was rather better prepared to confront an enemy within its borders, the IRA.

Once in office in 1932 the Taoiseach had been quick to repeal the previous government's legislation and also to release all IRA prisoners. These were all anti-treaty hardliners who, unlike de Valera and his ministers , still refused to recognise or compromise with the Free State. These decisions by Fianna Fáil were calculated risks but IRA violence after 1932 was directed away from the state to angry confrontations in the streets with General Eoin O'Duffy's Army Comrades Association, or the Blueshirts as they were also known. As chief of police in the Free State's early days, he had taken severe measures against anti-treaty republicans, and the paramilitary movement he formed in 1933 echoed his clericalist and authoritarian views as well as his admiration for Mussolini's regime in Italy.

IRA violence, however, went beyond attacks on O'Duffy's men, and an increasingly militant element within the IRA was ready to justify renewed attacks on Free State forces. This led de Valera, in an address to Fianna Fáil's national executive in late March 1935, to appeal in vain for a halt to actions by the IRA which, he argued, could only 'bring comfort and encouragement to the enemies of this country'.[16] His chance to act decisively, however, came on 24 March 1936 when IRA gunmen shot dead a retired British Vice Admiral, Henry Boyle Somerville, at his home at Castletownshend in County Cork.

This elderly victim's offence was to have given help and advice to young men from an area where jobs were scarce about how to enlist in the Royal Navy. Only a few weeks earlier the organisation had also murdered an alleged informer at Dungarvan in County Waterford. A series of arrests followed and, in mid-June, the Justice Department declared the IRA to be an illegal body.

As war in Europe drew closer, the government took an even tougher line against the IRA with its Offences Against the State legislation enacted in June 1939. This created a new type of criminal court with military judges presiding who could try and sentence people charged with 'special category offences'. These covered a whole range of seditious activities: membership of proscribed bodies; possession of treasonable documents; obstruction of government servants; the holding of meetings designated under the Act, which also hugely increased the state's powers of search, arrest and detention without trial or internment. So, in September 1939, Éire was formidably equipped to respond to IRA activity or to any other internal threat but more legislation followed to enlarge sweepingly government control of every aspect of national life. Existing law, some of it dating back to British rule, allowed for the interception of mail, cables and telephone calls, while the state already had control of radio transmissions.

When, on 3 September, de Valera proclaimed Éire's non-belligerent status to the Dáil, the IRA was already at war and had been since the start of the year. De Valera's response was to reinforce his existing legislative armoury in early 1940 with the Offences against the State (Amendment) Act which gave summary powers to military tribunals to try designated cases and pass death sentences. Large-scale arrests of suspected republicans and IRA men had already taken place, and an internment camp was reopened close to the Irish army base at the Curragh in County Kildare.

As these draconian measures began to be activated against the IRA, its leadership was already in contact with Berlin. Seán Russell, its Chief of Staff, had been on a fund-raising visit to the United States and, when war came, he was under surveillance and his visa was about to expire. He thus faced the prospect of deportation and the Curragh internment camp so he made contact with Nazi German circles in New York. Their links with Admiral Canaris, head of the *Abwehr* or German intelligence service, made it possible for him to travel to Genoa in Italy and from there to Germany. He reached Berlin in May 1940, his safe arrival masterminded by Edmund Vessenmayer a Foreign ministry official whose remit was to co-ordinate subversion both in enemy and non-aligned states. Russell at once began to train for a secret mission to Éire which he never accomplished owing to his death in transit to the west of Ireland in a U-boat in August 1940.

Whether his abortive mission could have accomplished anything of military significance must remain open to doubt, given how hard the IRA had been hit by the state's measures against it. Yet, since 1933, the Nazis had invested a significant effort in using the influence they had in Ireland to cultivate contacts with the IRA. This influence owed much to the Irish state's readiness to look beyond its own borders and Britain, too, in order to fill appointments to major positions. Brase, the army's director of music, was one of these and an active Nazi. A more important figure, however, was Adolf Mahr, an Austrian archaeologist who, in 1934, with de Valera's approval, was made director of the Irish National Museum in Dublin.[17]

Mahr worked hard in his professional capacity but was also an anti-Semite and active Nazi who took charge of the party's Auslandsorganisation or foreign department in Éire, recruiting young Germans with an interest in Irish history and ethnography. His influence ran to having those who declined to join the party sent home in disgrace and also to the vetting of appointments to the Germen legation in Dublin. Others who were part of what has been called a 'State within a state',[18] held senior appointments in engineering, forestry and turf development in which they were well placed to carry out map work and photographic reconnaissance of potential military use.

In January 1939, as the IRA began its bombing campaign in England, Mahr would have known of the arrival in Éire of Oskar Pfaus, an *Abwehr* agent posing as a writer. His task was to seek contacts with the IRA but he had not been well enough briefed for it, making one of his first approaches to General O'Duffy, still one of the organisation's most bitter opponents. O'Duffy gave him no help but neither did he report his presence to the authorities. Pfaus did make some contacts, notably with Jim O'Donovan, the IRA's engineering and explosives specialist, and these helped prepare the ground for the German Foreign Office's readiness to back Russell's mission to Ireland the following year.[19]

All this activity was monitored by British Intelligence services well ahead of their underfunded Irish counterparts.[20] Their relative slowness to recognise the possibility of the IRA actively seeking German help or of German nationals within Éire pursuing covert activities on behalf of Berlin have been described as 'significant intelligence failures'.[21] The Treaty Ports Agreement of 1938, however, and de Valera's affirmation that Éire would not let its territory be used to harm British interests, compensated for this and, indeed, laid the basis for seven years of security and intelligence co-operation between the two states.

In late August 1938, the Irish Department of External Affairs approached the Dominions Office in London on the matter of co-operative security arrangements. The Garda and the Justice Department had set aside their doubts about the army intelligence service, G2, taking on a domestic security role, and its head, Colonel Liam Archer, met in secret with MI5 and MI6 operatives in London. The fruits of this co-operation have started to emerge in new releases of material from the British national archives in London. They reveal how MI5 referred to G2 as its 'Dublin link' and also how the Garda Special Branch regularly shared intelligence with the RUC in Northern Ireland.[22]

The RUC officer who passed on to MI5 the information which came to him from Dublin was a Captain Roger Moore. His Dublin sources were so good that MI5 admitted that, on occasions, it received better information from the RUC than through its 'Dublin link'. The MI5 officer with overall responsibility for Dublin contacts was Guy Liddell who had joined the service in 1931 and become deputy director of its counter-espionage work. His published diaries clearly show the regularity of his and his brother Cecil's contacts with Archer and G2, especially over the matter of German agents who landed in Éire.

Oskar Pfaus, the first agent, had landed before the outbreak of war but was quickly put under surveillance. A succession of others followed, one of whom was Hans Marschner who was captured soon after parachuting into County Wexford in March 1941. He was in possession of a powerful radio transmitter to maintain contact with the Luftwaffe. Cecil Liddell was interested enough in Marschner, also known as Guenther Schutz, to fly to Dublin for a briefing from G2 and Liam Archer. His diary entry recorded that 'He [i.e. Archer] seemed to have reached the same conclusions as ourselves about the German intelligence service. His experience so far of all the agents who landed in Éire is that their plans were singularly ill-conceived and badly carried out.'[23]

Of the twelve agents who landed in Éire during the period of the Emergency, nearly all were apprehended within weeks, or in some cases, days. They were a good deal more fortunate than their colleagues who landed in Britain, seeing out the rest of their war in Dublin's Mountjoy prison or in the detention block of an army barracks in Athlone. The exception among them was Herman Goertz who landed on 12 May 1940 and remained at large until November 1941. He committed suicide in May 1947 while still in captivity, having long since recognised the futility of his mission to wartime Éire. A swastika flag covered his coffin and he was buried in a Dublin cemetery in his Luftwaffe uniform.

He was a captain in the *Abwehr* which he had joined from the Luftwaffe, and his mission was to link up with the IRA for acts of sabotage in Northern Ireland. After landing safely in County Meath he was lucky to escape arrest while staying with Stephen Held, a Dublin contact. In his hasty departure from the latter's home, he had to abandon German codes, money and his radio transmitter. More important was a document called Plan Kathleen, drawn up by the IRA but regarded as facile by the Germans. It covered major German troop landings in Northern Ireland and IRA attacks to help them against British forces and communications there.

While on the run, Goertz made some contacts with the Irish army and, in particular, with Major Niall MacNeill, an intelligence officer in the Northern division commanded by his brother Hugo and based along the border. Niall MacNeill was a Nazi sympathiser who had contacts with the German legation in Dublin.[24] Nothing of significance came from these approaches by Goertz and, when the IRA's Jim O'Donovan was arrested and interned, he lost his best contact with the organisation and, through him, with the *Abwehr*.

News of Plan Kathleen caused real alarm to de Valera and his ministers. They were not in an immediate position to know of the Germans' dismissive view of it, and it did seem to signal some intent by them to use the IRA for their own purposes. This, for de Valera, could only compromise Éire's neutrality because it might have the effect of tempting Churchill to seize the Treaty Ports as a pre-emptive measure against any cross-border troop movements by German forces who might land in the north with IRA support.

Of course, none of this happened and the crisis passed but G2 sent copies of Plan Kathleen to MI5 in London, and the RUC, through their Dublin contact, also acquired a copy. The episode was a delicate one for British Intelligence because it was all-important for Guy and Cecil Liddell to maintain the secrecy of their contacts with G2 and the Garda Special Branch. Sir Charles Wickham, inspector general of the RUC, had underestimated the importance of this, and Guy Liddell, in a testy correspondence, had to impress it upon him.[25] A related danger also was that some elements in the Garda might leak G2–MI5 contacts to the Germans who could treat them as a breach of Éire's neutrality.

Notwithstanding risks like these, the intelligence war against both the IRA and German agents hoping to work with it was one which Éire's security forces helped to win. This was of no small importance to Britain and its allies, and was indeed the hidden side of the Irish state's neutrality. So, too, were the co-operative contacts between the British and Irish armies during and after the 'invasion summer' of 1940, and also the agreement which provided a safe air corridor across Donegal to the Atlantic from the RAF's seaplane base on Lough Erne in County Fermanagh. The Irish maritime and coastal services made their contribution by the readiness with which they shared with the Royal Navy and RAF weather reports and data on German movements by sea or in the air.

On 24 May 1941 Maurice Moynihan, a civil servant and secretary to the Department of the Taoiseach set out a document which enumerated these and others areas of co-operation with Britain. He incorporated figures on estimated numbers of Irish citizens serving in the Defence Forces and, unimpeded by the Irish state, in the British forces too. His conclusion was that 'We could not do more if we were in the war.'[26]

One man who would not have been convinced by this claim was David Gray who had arrived as American minister in Dublin in April 1940. Seventy years old at the time of his appointment, Gray had put in many years in journalism and in public service and had the ear of

President Roosevelt whose wife Eleanor was his own wife's niece. He was of Scottish Presbyterian pedigree on his mother's side. Possibly this, as well as an often irritable personal style, soon created problems, injecting an element of tension into what was never going to be an easy wartime relationship between the United States and Éire.

Gray showed himself to be increasingly intolerant of Éire's neutrality, especially after his president's decisive re-election to a third term in November 1940 made him less dependent on the Irish American lobby. He has been compared unfavourably with Britain's representative in wartime Dublin, the former colonial civil servant, Sir John Maffey, a stylish and patrician figure who made a real effort to understand de Valera and his priorities. 'The policy of neutrality', he wrote to Anthony Eden in October 1939,

> commands widespread approval in Éire. It is remarkable how even the pro-British group, men who have fought for the Crown and are anxious to be called-up again, men whose sons are at the front today, loyalists in the old sense of the word, agree generally in supporting the neutrality of Éire.[27]

Maffey was never anything less than determined in representing Britain's interests to de Valera and his ministers but, at the same time, his view of Irish state policy was a more flexible one than Gray could ever have arrived at.[28] The latter, into his retirement and after the war, remained unforgiving of Éire's policy. In an introduction he was asked to write to a strongly Unionist view of the Irish question, he accused de Valera of having 'maintained a neutrality which served only Hitler's objectives'[29] and keeping Dublin 'a lighted city, serving as a beacon to guide German bombers proceeding north to attack Belfast'[30] while Éire lived off British supplies and ultimate protection.

Late in 1940 Gray had begun to press the case for Éire to reconsider its position on British naval access to the Treaty Ports. He did this not just in private talks with ministers and civil servants but also at social gatherings where opposition politicians were present. He may well also have briefed the British embassy in Washington that Frank Aiken, de Valera's minister for the co-ordination of defensive measures, was pro-German. Aiken was not, though he was never less than tenacious in presenting the case for neutrality or using his extensive censorship powers to prevent any undermining of it. These leaks to Washington about Aiken came ahead of a visit by him to the United States in March 1941 which he hoped might result in American arms and equipment being made available to Éire. His 7 April meeting with Roosevelt was an angry fiasco at the height of which the president sent crockery flying off his Oval Office desk in the White House, so incensed was he at Aiken's insistence that there was still as much a possibility of Britain invading his country as of Germany doing it.

This encounter negated any chance of significant American military aid to Éire, and Cordell Hull, the American Secretary of State, wrote of how, 'in his conversations with leading members of Government, Aiken showed himself to be strongly anti-British'.[31] This outcome was what Gray had wanted, given his view that any aid to Éire had to be conditional on de Valera at the very least rethinking state policy on the Treaty Ports. Hull authorised Gray to put it to de Valera

> that, in accordance with our policy, we would continue to make available to Britain and the empire and other countries resisting aggression, all our production of military and naval material not required for our own rearmament programme. We could not therefore make it available to Éire until that Government was ready to show a more cooperative attitude toward the war efforts of these nations.[32]

Éire, in fact, continued to request American arms and munitions, without success but, in September 1941, two cargo ships of the United States merchant marine service were made available to carry food supplies to Irish ports. Both were, in due course, sunk by U-boats. Aiken toured the United States for some weeks, reiterating to Irish American audiences the case for his country's neutrality, which simply served to add to the tension of Gray's dealings with de Valera. At least, however, on the issue of Britain extending conscription to Northern Ireland, Gray was able to find some temporary common ground with the Taoiseach by identifying himself strongly with his president's view that it would be impractical and politically counter-productive.[33]

Japan's attack on Pearl Harbor on 7 December 1941 raised Gray's hopes of de Valera moving perhaps some way from neutrality once America finally entered the war as an ally of Britain. Roosevelt shared these hopes but did not go so far as Churchill who sent a telegram to de Valera after the news of Pearl Harbor came. With typical flamboyance he declared: 'Now's your chance. Now or never: a Nation once again. Am ready to meet you at any time.'[34] This was vintage Churchill, right down to borrowing the title of an old Irish Home Rule anthem. He meant that Éire could now in good conscience enter the war as an ally of America but Lord Cranborne, the new Dominions Secretary of State, had to point out how easily the message might be misinterpreted in Dublin. De Valera later recalled receiving it. 'I conclude that it was Mr Churchill's way of intimating 'now is the chance for taking action which would ultimately lead to the unification of the country'. I indicated to Sir John Maffey that I did not see the thing in that light.'[35]

Proof of de Valera's political authority is that, despite America's entry into the war, he came under no real pressure because of it to re-examine neutrality as a policy. Indeed, James Dillon, leader of the major opposition party Fine Gael, as it had become in 1933, achieved little more than his own isolation after openly challenging neutrality in a speech in the Dáil after America had joined the war, and he resigned from the party in February 1942.

One immediate outcome of Pearl Harbor was the arrival of American troops in Northern Ireland early in 1942. American 'technicians' had for some time been making preparations on the ground for this in co-operation with British forces. It came as no surprise to de Valera but he resented not being consulted. In the protest which he made public soon after the Americans began to land, he stressed that he and the people of Éire had no hostility to the United States but added: 'it is our duty to make it clearly understood that no matter what troops occupy the Six Counties, the Irish people's claim for the union of the whole of the national territory and for supreme jurisdiction over it will remain unabated'.[36]

De Valera, it has been said, thought he was responding to this development in as moderate a way as possible[37] but he had given much offence to American opinion. Michael Brennan, Éire's minister in Washington, gave the full text of the Taoiseach's speech to the State Department, adding that the arrival of American troops in the north had signalled to Irish people that they might be used in hostile cross-border operations. Rooselvelt offered assurances that this would not happen but was privately angered by the way de Valera had reacted.[38] His country's goodwill towards the ending of partition diminished as a result: 'Whatever sporadic interest may have remained was rooted in strategic self-interest; empathy for Dublin's course faded as the war progressed.'[39]

All this was part of the build-up to Operation Overlord, the invasion of Normandy scheduled for June of 1944, and Gray used it unsuccessfully to try to re-open the issue of the Treaty Ports, arguing the case for an ultimatum to Éire if de Valera once again refused access to Britain and its allies. Strategically, the ports had receded in importance. Winant, Roosevelt's ambassador in London, was among those who argued that to resurrect the issue would give de Valera a pretext for reviving partition as a bargaining counter at a point in the war at which the border issue had become quiescent.[40]

Relations between Washington and Dublin remained cool for much of 1942 and into the following year, and the American press ran numerous stories claiming that the Irish capital was full of German agents. In autumn of 1942, however, the Office of Strategic Services, later to become the Central Intelligence Agency, sent a representative to Dublin to monitor the performance of Éire's intelligence services. Gray resented his presence, feeling that, as minister, he should be the sole source of information to Washington. These initial OSS contacts were positive and prepared the ground for the organisation's head to visit Éire in March 1943. His mission was to talk to G2 and the Garda and to secure access to their data on Axis agents in Ireland and the codes they were using.[41]

As D-Day drew nearer, the Allies' greatest priority was the absolute security of the entire operation. This brought to centre stage in Irish–American relations the role of the diplomatic missions still maintained in Dublin by Germany and Japan. Hempel, the German minister, had maintained the most correct of relations with the Irish government and regarded its continuing neutrality as Germany's best option. British intelligence and their American counterparts, however, had growing fears of the use to which the German legation's radio transmitter might be put. As far back as 1941, Hempel had been warned about its use by de Valera's government, and in February 1942 British intelligence attributed to it meteorological signals which had helped the escape of the battleships *Scharnhorst* and *Gneisenau* from Brest through the Channel to the North Sea.[42] But such signals might just as easily have been relayed to the German navy by Luftwaffe aircrews operating over the Channel.

The following year saw suspicions growing about the use of the legation's transmitter though, by this time, virtually everything it sent out was being intercepted and decoded by both British intelligence and G2. Even so, the transmitter was still a provocation and, in December 1943, the capture by the Irish security forces of two more German agents brought the issue to a head.[43]

The Irish government responded to the Allies' concern that the transmitter was being used for more than sending weather reports to

Berlin, and issued a demand to Germany that it be handed over to them. Hempel finally agreed at the end of 1943 to surrender it to a Dublin bank where it could be kept under joint custody. For Gray this was not enough, and his continuous representations to Washington bore fruit in his government's message to de Valera on 21 February 1944 which it fell to him as minister in Dublin to present to the Taoiseach.

This became known as the 'American Note'. Its principal demand was that de Valera and his government took appropriate action to close down the German and Japanese legations in Dublin. The note read:

> We should be lacking in candour if we did not state our hope that this action will take the form of severance of all diplomatic relationships between Ireland and these two countries. You will, of course, readily understand the compelling reasons why we ask as an absolute minimum, the removal of these Axis representatives, whose presence in Ireland must inevitably be regarded as constituting a danger to the lives of American soldiers and to the success of Allied military operations.[44]

The note did incorporate assurances to Éire that there would be no invasion or violation of its neutrality. One aide's account of de Valera's reaction to Gray's presentation of it was that he showed no outward anger but 'merely looked sour and grim'.[45] If anything, his reaction was more hostile when, the following day, Maffey presented him with a much shorter note, simply stating Churchill's agreement with the American request. On 7 March, Brennan, the Irish minister in Washington, handed over the Taoiseach's reply which was, of course, a rejection of the note, calling it a demand that Éire take a 'first step towards war'.[46]

De Valera wanted the note withdrawn and sought the help of Canada with whom Éire had maintained a good relationship during the war. Canada had not been consulted about the note but, while still sympathetic to de Valera's position, did not feel itself to be able to call for its withdrawal even when, on 10 March, the American State Department gave it public release along with confirmation of Éire's rejection of the note. Twelve days prior to this, John Hearne, Éire's high Commissioner in Ottawa, presented to the Canadian government an eloquent memorandum in which he called the note an attempt to make people outside Éire believe of de Valera that 'he alone stood between the Irish people and their entry into the war.'[47]

'The fact was,' Hearne continued, 'that Mr de Valera's leadership was unbreakable because at this moment he most fully and unequivocally represented the mind and heart of the whole people. He would never yield to the pressure now applied and, should he do so, he would not hold office for ten minutes after his surrender.'[48] This put the Irish case as strongly as the Taoiseach himself could have done but, not for the last time, intervention by Churchill worked to strengthen de Valera's position. On 14 March he told the House of Commons of his government's support for America's stance and of the need to 'isolate Southern Ireland from the outer world during the critical period which is now approaching'.[49]

He did not specify economic sanctions as a way of making a reality of this isolation but he regarded with equanimity Éire's fear that they might follow. On 19 March 1944, he wrote to Roosevelt:

> It is early days to start reassuring de Valera. There is not much sense in a doctor telling a patient that the medicine he has just prescribed for his nerve troubles is only coloured water. I think it would be much better to keep him guessing for a while.[50]

There was no need, he stressed, to stop necessary trade but Éire's fear of this happening was a weapon for all that, while the controls over movement and communication were vital to save the lives of British and American soldiers. Churchill went on:

> It seems to me that so far from allaying alarm in de Valera's circles we should let fear work its healthy process. Thereby we shall get behind the scenes a continued stiffening-up of the Irish measures to prevent leakages, which even now are not so bad.[51]

These last words were at least an acknowledgement that Éire's intelligence services had worked with the Allies and not against them. The danger remained that prohibitions on Irish shipping sailing to designated ports in Spain and Portugal would be interpreted in Dublin as economic sanctions but, to Churchill, it was a risk worth taking. In this he had the backing of Cordell Hull who cabled him from Washington: 'I am inclined to believe that for the time being at least we should not make any statement to the Press or commit ourselves to the Irish Government that we have no intention of instituting economic sanctions.'[52]

The day before Churchill's statement to parliament, Britain suspended all travel between its shores and Éire's ports as well as all cross-border traffic. Aer Lingus flights to Britain were halted, and

Irish travellers were forbidden from using British or American civil flights out of Éire. More restrictions followed on telephone calls and the importing of British newspapers. De Valera was able to use an atmosphere of heightened fear, exacerbated by Churchill's 14 March statement, to his own political advantage by calling a general election in May 1944. Fianna Fáil, which had lost overall control in the Dáil at elections the previous autumn, gained fourteen seats to remain in office with a comfortable majority.

The Normandy invasion was successfully launched and Irishmen – Catholic and Protestant – from both sides of the border and from the Irish community in Britain were part of it: infantry who crossed fire-swept beaches; airborne units dropped inland ahead of the sea landings; and more who served with the Royal Navy and the RAF. Under Éire's oppressive wartime censorship they were non-persons but their sacrifices and the victory to which they contributed allowed the state to emerge from the crisis created by the American Note. The isolation of Éire prior to D-Day was rapidly wound down but de Valera, his political position secured, had work to do, especially in rebuilding relations with the United States. Peace was still nearly a year away and testing moments were ahead for him in his dealings with Britain and its western ally.

Notes

1. Wills, *That Neutral Island*, pp. 95–100.
2. O'Halpin, *Defending Ireland*, p. 143. See also F. H. Hinsley and C. A. G. Simkins, *British Intelligence in the Second World War*, Vol. 4: *Security and Counter-Intelligence* (London: HMSO, 1990), pp. 16–17.
3. O'Halpin, *Defending Ireland*, pp. 174–5. See also J. T. Carroll, *Ireland in the War Years 1939–1945*.
4. Fisk, *In the Time of War*, pp. 210–11.
5. Ibid., p. 211.
6. B. Montgomery, *Memories of Field Marshal the Viscount Montgomery of Alamein* (London: Collins, 1958), p. 70.
7. Ibid.
8. *Irish Times*, 8 May 1985.
9. *History Ireland*, Vol. 5, No. 4, winter 1997, pp. 12–14.
10. Ibid. See also E. D. Doyle, 'Soldier and Officer: the Army in Two Perspectives in the 1940s', *The Irish Sword*, Vol. XVIII, No. 72, winter 1991, pp. 1165–83.
11. Doyle, *Soldier and Officer*.
12. Ibid. See also *Irish Times*, 8 May 1945.
13. A. Danchev and D. Todman (eds), *Field Marshal Alanbrooke, War Diaries 1939–1945* (London: Phoenix Press, 2002), p. 220.
14. Doyle, *Soldier and Officer*, pp. 165–83.
15. Lee, *Ireland 1912–1985*, pp. 268–9.

16. *Irish News*, 31 March 1935.
17. T. P. Coogan, *The IRA* (London: HarperCollins, 1995), pp. 208–12.
18. D. O'Donoghue, *Hitler's Irish Voices: the Story of German Radio's Wartime Irish Service* (Belfast: Beyond the Pale Publications, 1998), pp. 4–18. See also 'State Within a State: the Nazis in Neutral Ireland', *History Ireland*, Vol. 14, No. 6 November/December 2006, pp. 36–9.
19. Duggan, *Neutral Ireland and the Third Reich*, pp. 59–63.
20. Hinsley and Simkins, *British Intelligence in the Second World War*, Vol. 4, pp. 16–17.
21. O'Halpin, *Defending Ireland*, p. 129.
22. *Irish Times*, 3 January 2004.
23. N. West (ed.), *The Guy Liddell Diaries 1939–1942* (Abingdon: Routledge, 2005), p. 97.
24. Duggan, *Neutral Ireland and the Third Reich*, pp. 91–100.
25. West (ed.) *The Guy Liddell Diaries*, p. 184.
26. T. P. Coogan, *De Valera: Long Fellow, Long Shadow* (London: Hutchinson, 1993), pp. 748–50.
27. Carroll, *Ireland in the War Years 1939–1945*, p. 30.
28. Kenny, *Sir John Maffey and Anglo-Irish Relationship during the Second World War*, pp. 43–50.
29. W. A. Carson, *Ulster and the Irish Republic* (Belfast: William Cleland Ltd, 1956), p. ii.
30. Ibid.
31. C. Hull, *Memories*, Volume Two (London: Hodder and Stoughton, 1948), p. 1352.
32. Ibid., pp. 1353–4.
33. Coogan, *De Valera: Long Fellow, Long Shadow*, p. 589.
34. Fisk, *In Time of War*, p. 323.
35. Longford and O'Neill, *Eamon de Valera*, p. 393. See also Coogan, *De Valera: Long Fellow, Long Shadow*, p. 594.
36. Coogan, *De Valera: Long Fellow, Long Shadow*, p. 594.
37. Longford and O'Neill, *Eamon de Valera*, pp. 397–8.
38. Hull, *Memories*, Vol. Two, p. 1355.
39. J. Bowman, *de Valera and the Ulster Question 1917–1973*, p. 250.
40. Ibid., p. 251.
41. E. O'Halpin, *Defending Ireland*, pp. 229–31.
42. Hinsley and Simkins, *British Intelligence in the Second World War*, Vol. 4, p. 195.
43. O'Halpin (ed.), *MI5 In Ireland*, pp. 82–3.
44. Carrol, *Ireland in the War Years 1939–1945*, pp. 141–2. See also Coogan, *De Valera: Long Fellow, Long Shadow*, p. 601.
45. T. Ryle Dwyer, *Irish Neutrality and the USA 1939–45* (Dublin: Gill and Macmillan, 1977), p. 185.
46. Carrol, *Ireland in the War Years 1939–1945*, p. 149.
47. E. Cunningham, 'Ireland, Canada and the American Note', in D. Keogh and M. O'Driscoll (eds), *Ireland in World War Two: Neutrality and Survival* (Cork: Mercier Press, 2004), pp. 144–58.
48. Ibid.
49. Carroll, *Ireland in the War Years 1939–1945*, p. 150.
50. W. S. Churchill, *History of the Second World War*, Vol. V, *Closing the Ring* (London: Cassell, 1952), pp. 614–15.
51. Ibid.
52. Ibid.

4

Security, Censorship and Propaganda

The Commonwealth war cemetery at Dieppe is not vast compared to many others across northern France, yet it remains a stark reminder of the disastrous 'reconnaissance in force' attempted on the nearby beaches in August 1942. Operating under the overall command of Lord Louis Mountbatten, Britain's Chief of Combined Operations, British and Canadian troops were annihilated as they attempted, with inadequate support fire, to storm the heavily prepared German positions. Nonetheless, the operation was later justified, not least by Churchill who wanted to protect the reputation of his protégé Mountbatten, as an attempt to test Germany's Atlantic Wall and for lessons learned that were applied two years later on D-Day.[1]

General, later Field Marshal, Montgomery who held a home command at the time of the operation, had questioned how good the security for it was, and one Irish military historian, J. P. Duggan, agreed with him. He later claimed that Hempel, the German minister in Dublin had, in time to alert Berlin, acquired intelligence about the Dieppe raid from Irish sources in Britain.[2] No reference to this appears in the most authoritative account of the attack which attributes its failure to haste and bad planning.[3]

Duggan also suggests that Hempel may have had access to intelligence which was instrumental in aborting British airborne operations in the Netherlands two years later. Hempel, in his account, was on close terms with Dr John Gogan, a republican who had fought in Dublin in 1916 and who was viscerally anti-British. Gogan, he claims, found out about the planned air drop of British forces from a cousin who had returned home after a spell of work in an aircraft factory. On the basis of a 1976 interview with Gogan, Duggan claims that he rushed his cousin to the German legation to brief Hempel, contributing to the heroic and costly failure of British forces to secure the vital Rhine bridge at Arnhem.[4]

Again, accounts of the Arnhem battle have not substantiated these claims though there has long been controversy over whether the landing force was sent into a trap ready made for it. It is now clear that, thanks in part to the Dutch resistance, British intelligence knew of the presence of German panzer units close to the landing area. These were understrength after their part in the Normandy fighting but still capable, as events proved, of doing severe damage to lightly armed parachute units.[5]

Even so, fears remained acute among Britain's security services that disaffected or pro-German elements within an Irish workforce recruited to sustain the war effort could pose a security risk. MI5 admitted as much at the end of the war in a report which accepted that, despite all its warnings, Britain's service and supply departments had found it essential to use Irish labour on high-risk projects like the construction of the 'Mulberry' harbour for the 1944 Normandy landings. Éire workers, with whatever information they might have gleaned, had the right to sign off at any time from such work and go home, except for the two months of intensive security controls prior to D-Day.[6]

Within Ireland itself, cross-border movement was always a potential danger. 'In spite of partition,' MI5 noted, 'Ireland has remained to all intents and purposes one country.'[7] Consideration, it agreed, had been given on occasions to closing the border except for controlled crossing points but this would have required large numbers of troops and may have led to civil disorder in nationalist localities in Northern Ireland. MI5 went on:

> This meant that throughout the war, as far as the security service was concerned, the actual crossing of the Border into or out of Northern Ireland with its Naval, Military and Air establishments, dockyards and war factories by persons resident in neutral Éire, could not be prevented or even controlled.[8]

The best hope of the security services had to be that information which might travel as a result of this movement of labour would be either low level or inaccurate and that most Irish people, while supportive of their state's neutrality, had no more wish than their Taoiseach to do active harm to the cause of Britain and its allies.

This, of course, was not true of many militant republicans. Dan Breen, an IRA hero of the War of independence and a Fianna Fáil member of the Dáil, was always a likely conduit for any information that might help the cause of the Axis powers, and may well have given whatever aid and comfort he could to German agents in Éire. He was also on good terms with Henning Thomsen, Hempel's deputy in the German legation in Dublin and a committed Nazi.[9]

Prior to the war, Breen had helped the legation draw up an Irish mailing list of recipients of its *Weekly Review of the German News Agency* which was simply a digest of Nazi propaganda, and Goertz, before his arrest, had plans to meet him, though this may not in the end have happened. In late May 1947, Breen was among the mourners at Goertz's funeral in Dublin. Other IRA members were present as he was interred in a coffin draped in a swastika flag and, among what may have been a gathering of 800, many raised their arms in the Nazi salute.[10]

Fear of security failures, and the lives they could cost, had to be a constant preoccupation of Britain's security services, and of those of the United States after it joined the war. These fears, predictably, as has been shown in the previous chapter, reached their height prior to the invasion of Normandy but Britain and its allies, as well as, it must be repeated, neutral Éire, conducted intelligence operations at a far superior level of competence to anything Nazi Germany ever attained.

A recent study of German intelligence and espionage operations in wartime Ireland has, indeed, written of them in terms of 'absolute failure',[11] using poorly selected agents, working to vague and sometimes conflicting objectives, and yielding up barely one report of any significant military use to the *Abwehr*.[12] After the early capture of an IRA transmitter by the Irish security forces, agents who did land had no reliable means of contact with their handlers in Berlin apart from the Reich's Dublin legation. Its radio contact with Berlin was, as has already been pointed out,[13] well monitored by British and Irish intelligence by late 1942, and no enemy agents had the training to use complex codes or ciphers.

Germany's failure was not just a product of anti-regime elements being entrenched within the *Abwehr* though its head, Admiral Canaris, was an opponent of the Nazis and later paid for this with his life. He was also a poor supervisor of intelligence work though, after 1935, the *Abwehr's* manpower and resources were never developed at a rate to match the rapid expansion of the Reich's armed forces. In fact, intelligence work was not a good career move in the *Wehrmacht*, and was accorded an equal and integral status to operational planning only in 1943.[14]

For the Irish state, on the other hand, given the acute numerical weakness of its own forces, intelligence and counter-intelligence work was of self-evident urgency. Officers such as Colonel Liam Archer, Éire's Director of Army Intelligence until mid-1941, and his successor Colonel Dan Bryan, both knew the value of a co-ordinated, multi-agency approach to intelligence work and of the importance of full co-operation with MI5, and later, United States intelligence services. Both, it has been pointed out,

> had the benefit, while young men, of working on the other side of the clandestine fence against the British and Bryan had then become a consummate agent runner against the republican movement until the army was pulled out of domestic intelligence gathering in 1926.[15]

Bryan and Archer went on to make an intensive study of intelligence and counter-intelligence techniques as well as a detailed analysis of the Irish state's strategic position if Britain went to war again with Germany. Perhaps the best tribute to their operational success came from John Winant, American ambassador to London. At the height of the 1944 'American note' crisis, he cabled Washington about his contacts with the Director General of MI5 and the deputy head of the United States Office of Strategic Services in Europe. Their advice was against pressing Dublin too hard on security 'since all their information suggested that the Irish already ran as tight a ship as was possible'.[16]

The necessity of effective intelligence work by Éire's forces and of co-operation with Britain and its allies was in large measure rooted in the degree to which a body of Irish opinion, not just within the IRA, was deeply hostile to Britain's cause. Activating this hostility on the side of the Axis powers had to be central to the priorities of German undercover operations in Ireland, and political developments in the Irish state prior to the onset of the Emergency had given them some reason to be hopeful of success.

When Oskar Pfaus made his clandestine visit to Éire in February 1939 to organise support there for Germany if and when war came, he made a point of meeting General Eoin O'Duffy, by then in declining health and a marginal figure whose influence was only a shadow of what it had once been. In 1922 his credentials, earned in the War of independence and as a pro-treaty commander in the civil

war, secured his appointment as commissioner of the Garda Síochána or police. He held this key position until 1933, a period in which
renewed IRA activity, that he identified with Communism, as well as
a moral decline in Irish society hardened his already authoritarian
views.

Dismissed from office after de Valera's second election victory, he
became leader of the Army Comrades Association, or Blueshirts,
ostensibly to protect Cumann na nGaedhal meetings from IRA
attacks. They were accused of starting much street violence themselves and were banned after a few months. O'Duffy then joined the
new Fine Gael Party in September 1933. It was a merger of Cumann
na nGaedhal, the National Centre Party, and the Blueshirt membership whom O'Duffy encouraged to join as the best way to fight a
Fianna Fáil government he despised and saw as a front for the IRA..

The new opposition party with O'Duffy briefly its president was
outmanoeuvred at every stage by de Valera. O'Duffy's language
became increasingly hostile to party systems and to democracy itself
which he came to equate with the cultural and moral degeneracy
brought about by alien influences at work in Ireland through film,
jazz and the ever-present danger of contraception. From there it was
a short step to espousing fascism in its Italian form and that of
Falangist Spain where O'Duffy took an Irish volunteer battalion to
fight for Franco in the civil war.

It did little fighting, and may even have returned with more men
than it went out with, but by then O'Duffy's star was waning. His
utterances became more overtly fascist and supportive, too, of Hitler's
regime in Germany. There has been much debate whether he ever had
the will to attempt a coup against the state. In August 1933 he declined
to challenge a government ban on a Blueshirt march into central
Dublin. Their membership may not have been the raw material of
fascism on the continental European model though they resurfaced
under other names after being proscribed, and their preoccupations
ran with the grain of a continuing belief in an Irish Ireland where
Catholic corporatism could define the values of a still young state.[17]

W. B. Yeats, for all that he was the product of a Protestant
tradition, for a time admired what he saw as the dynamism of
O'Duffy and the Blueshirts. One reviewer of the second volume of
Professor Roy Foster's life of Yeats has described this as being part
of the poet's drift 'further and further towards the Fascism which
had always been a wary fascination'.[18] A corporatist or even a fascist
Ireland would have been a cold house for Yeats with his belief in an
educated elite having a real role in the state. Perhaps, as Dr Conor

Cruise O'Brien pointed out, Yeats simply admired power and its determined exercise, and lost interest in O'Duffy when it was clear that power lay securely with de Valera.[19]

Pfaus quickly realised there was nothing to be achieved by talking to O'Duffy, certainly not about the possibility of German contacts with an IRA that the general loathed. Even so, it seems that O'Duffy saw no need to inform the Irish authorities of a German agent's approach to him. One of his former assistants, however, did provide Pfaus with IRA contacts though, by then, he was aware that he was under surveillance by the Garda, and curtailed his visit.[20]

Such surveillance was the work of a Dublin government which numbered among those who served it some who were at the very least ambivalent in their attitude towards the Axis powers. At the time of Pfaus's attempt to use O'Duffy as a contact, Éire's minister in Berlin, Charles Bewley, was a convinced anti-Semite and apologist for the Third Reich who used his position to deny Irish passports to German Jews trying to escape the regime's social policies. De Valera's government recalled him from Berlin in July 1939 [21] only for Bewley to settle in Italy and utilise his influence there to identify himself actively with both Mussolini's regime and that of Hitler.

Joseph Walshe, permanent secretary at the Irish Department of External Affairs also took what has been called a 'cold-blooded view of Germany's victims'[22] and saw advantage for the Irish state in a victory for the Axis powers which could deliver an end to partition. He was dangerously naive about what such an outcome would really mean and also in his belief that, under a fascist new order in Europe, Ireland would escape the fate of other small neutral states.[23]

Walshe was, of course, not alone in his anticipation of British defeat, and many in the diplomatic service shared it, albeit with less relish. An exception was Seán Murphy who represented Irish interests in France and later succeeded Walshe at the Department of External Affairs. He believed that resistance to German rule in Europe would build up over time and that Britain itself would survive. So, too, did Maurice Moynihan, the most senior official in the Department of the Taoiseach.[24]

Supporting Éire's right to non-belligerency did not have to be rooted in crude and negative anti-Britishness. For many Irish people it was a necessary act of self-assertion for a young state. The Anglo-Irish and strongly pro-British writer, Elizabeth Bowen, often stressed this in her wartime reports to the Foreign Office and Ministry of Information in London while making the point, too, that a majority was simply glad to be escaping the horror of war at first hand.[25]

Against this, Irish and British intelligence had to balance the threat from actively pro-Axis opinion in wartime Éire. Its existence was in some measure the product of hard work by German Nazis who had been appointed by successive Dublin governments to influential positions in industry, in universities and in cultural administration. Adolf Mahr who, in 1934, was chosen to be the Director of the National Museum in Dublin, had recruited actively for the Nazi party within Éire's German community. He resigned his position as party leader in Ireland only in July 1938 because, as the European situation worsened, he felt his work as museum director might be compromised. By then a sizeable number of Germans, many of them party members, had passed through Éire's universities or were still there as researchers or exchange students.[26]

The results of Mahr's efforts are not easily quantified but a xeno-phobic and authoritarian element within Irish nationalist opinion had put down its own roots in the interwar years. At one obvious level, O'Duffy's movement had given it a voice but there was also a variety of smaller groupings, such as the Saint Patrick's Anti-Com-munist League, the pro-Franco Irish Christian Front, Aontas Gaed-heal (Unity of the Gaels) and Clann na Saoirse (Clan of Liberty), which were small in numbers but overlapped in membership. Some of these had active links with the Irish Friends of Germany and, after the onset of the Emergency, their activities were monitored by the Irish intelligence service, G2. .

In the summer of 1940, as rumours grew of IRA collusion with a German invasion the first arrests were made and others followed but G2 was not over-alarmed. Most of those arrested were soon released, provided they signed pledges to undertake no activity harmful to the state. The largest and most vigorous product of a pro-Axis movement in Éire, however, was Craobh na hAiseirghe (Branch of the Resur-rection). By the end of 1941 it claimed more than 1,200 members and maintained a brisk output of leaflets on cultural issues as well as holding regular meetings. It made no secret of its pro-fascism and its ethos was anti-Semitic and corporatist on economic questions. It wanted English outlawed and a new Irish capital to be built at the ancient site of Tara.[27]

The Craobh formed a political wing called Ailtirí na hAiseirghe (Architects of the Resurrection) and in the 1944 Dáil elections it won a strong first-preference vote. This was not enough, however, to win it any seats though it had some success in council elections in 1945.[28] The People's National Party had very similar aims and also called for the expulsion of Éire's Jewish population. It claimed to have support from within Dublin's business community and, for a time, was able to maintain an office in the city and pay salaries to two of its organisers.

Another product of this subculture of pro-fascism and warped nationalism was the Young Ireland Association. Maud Gonne was its most prestigious recruit after its formation in 1941. It, too, was anti-Semitic and openly supportive of the cause of Germany and its allies. It was kept under observation by G2 and the Garda, especially when some of its adherents were suspected of breaking into the homes of army reservists in search of their weapons and of seeking to recruit support within the defence forces. At one of its meetings in 1941, soon after the unintended German bombing of Dublin, one member rose to excuse the loss of life caused, arguing that the Luftwaffe had the right to hit Irish targets because of the de Valera government's complicity in Britain's war effort.[29]

Government action closed down the Young Ireland Association by September 1942. It was in reality little more of a threat to the state than the plethora of other overlapping bodies whose members might have constituted some sort of 'fifth column' if a German invasion had happened. There was never much likelihood of that and the Dublin government avoided an overtly heavy handed response to pro-Axis subversion within Éire's borders. Many Dublin ministers, after all, had personal knowledge of conspiracy and insurrection: 'With the self-confidence born of efficiency, the police and military intelligence were content to restrict themselves to a policy of periodically lopping off the green shoots of subversion, leaving the roots to wither beneath the soil.'[30]

There is no reason to doubt that, if a German invasion and occupation had taken place, Éire's ultra-right, contemptuous as it was of the experiment in democracy which had been guided by Cosgrave and de Valera, and driven by hatred of Britain, would have yielded up a fair crop of quislings and collaborators. The IRA would have provided them as well. Short of this ultimate opportunity, there was the option, when war came, of at least serving the Third Reich in its propaganda offensive against Britain and its allies. A few Irish citizens readily availed themselves of that option.

Most of Éire's German community were able to return home in September 1939 though Mahr, possibly fearing internment, had already left with his family for a holiday in Austria. Many wanted to work for the Reich in whatever way they could and looked to *Irland-Redaktion*, German radio's Irish service, which became operational in December 1939. This was the work of Ludwig Muhlhausen, a linguist and Celtic scholar fluent in Irish and a well-known visitor to, and lecturer in, pre-war Ireland. He was an active Nazi who used his party connections to further his academic career and who also, in all probability, supplied the *Abwehr* in Berlin with potentially useful information and photographs taken during his travels in Ireland.[31]

At *Irland-Redaktion*, Muhlhausen's remit was to reach Irish listeners with whatever material might influence them. Initially he gave a series of Sunday-night talks in Irish, timed to follow on from broadcasts by William Joyce, Lord Haw-Haw to British audiences, who also had a following in Éire and in nationalist areas of Northern Ireland. Early in 1940, however, the decision was made to increase propaganda broadcasts to Ireland, and it was at this point that Muhlhausen was able to enlist the services of Francis Stuart.

Born in Australia of an Ulster Protestant family, and educated at Rugby school and Trinity College Dublin, Stuart went to prison for his support for the anti-treaty IRA in the civil war. He married Iseult, daughter of Maud Gonne, and became a prolific author whose work met with critical acclaim rather than commercial success. In 1939, with his marriage breaking up, he went to Berlin to take up a university teaching post. He still had IRA contacts and was considered by the *Abwehr* for a mission to Ireland with Frank Ryan and Seán Russell (see Chapter 5). He also took with him to Berlin a letter of introduction from Hempel, the German minister in Dublin, to the Foreign Ministry. On the basis of this he was asked, and agreed, to write some additional radio scripts for William Joyce.

Joyce found Stuart's material insufficiently anti-Semitic and, although the two met regularly in Berlin, they never got on well together.[32] Stuart remained wary of Joyce's earlier history of service to the Crown forces in Ireland and of his antagonism to Irish republicanism. His opportunity to draft and deliver his own broadcasts came as a result of a review of the Reich's radio service to Ireland, carried out by none other than Adolf Mahr. After having to turn his back on his very successful career in Ireland, Mahr had used his credentials as a loyal Nazi to find work at the Foreign Office's Irish desk and, in March 1941, he delivered a fifteen-page report on radio propaganda to Ireland.

It estimated that there were 250,000 radio sets in Éire and a potentially much larger audience in North America of those who were either Irish or Irish by descent. An Irish language in decline, Mahr argued, was of little use in reaching this audience and he carried the case against Muhlhausen for English-language broadcasts. Only a minority in Ireland, he stated, had any grasp of, or sympathy with, the ideology of National Socialism: programme content should stress instead that Éire's neutrality was neither pro-British nor pro-German but simply conceived of in terms of Irish interests. Germany must therefore respect it. This remained the Reich's public stance even as it secretly sent a succession of agents to Éire in flagrant breach of its neutrality.[33]

Francis Stuart made his debut at a microphone on St Patrick's Day 1942 with G2 in Dublin listening in as they did to most of *Irland-Redaktion*'s output. Predictably he began by denying that he was involved in the business of propaganda. He spoke, he told listeners, as an Irishman and an Ulsterman pained by the continued occupation of part of Ireland by 'foreign troops'. His concern was, he went on, to set out his view of Ireland's proper place in the world, a place best protected by its neutrality which, alone, could safeguard its ancient cultural links with the nations of Europe. 'Ireland belongs to Europe and England does not,'[34] was his concluding message.

In other broadcasts he extolled the bravery of the IRA and poured scorn on what he claimed were the double standards of Britain and its allies both in their conduct of the war and the way in which they tried to justify it. In February 1943 he praised the courage of the doomed German Sixth Army at Stalingrad: 'If I was a German I should be filled with the deepest pride; as it is, I am glad to be living among such people – glad to be here in a country that can produce such men.'[35] Yet Stuart was also an admirer of the Soviet Union which came to compromise his role as a broadcaster for the Reich.

In fact, Stuart was a rootless spirit, attracted on his own later admission to totalitarian ideologies and leaders as dynamic alternatives to a decadent bourgeois order. 'I did see Hitler [perhaps he could have added Stalin] and in hindsight I was obviously wrong, as a kind of contemporary Samson, a superman who would tear down the whole political and social system in England and Ireland,'[36] he told a newspaper interviewer nearly sixty years later. Nonetheless, he kept returning in his talks to the injustice of Irish partition and, in May 1943, he told listeners in Northern Ireland that, if conscription was brought in, they should desert to German or Italian forces. This might have landed him in serious trouble had he fallen into British hands in 1945.

Stuart was the best known of a small group of broadcasters, not all of them Irish, who worked for *Irland-Redaktion* during the war. The Dublin government, which was represented in Berlin by its legation head and Chargé d'Affaires, William Warnock, took no action against their work and indeed, on St Patrick's Day 1942, invited many of them to a party, and Warnock actually arranged for Francis Stuart to receive up-to-date copies of Irish newspapers.[37] The only representations the legation made to the German government were in response to just two of Stuart's broadcasts: one in which, in December 1942, he expressed overt support for IRA men on trial in Northern Ireland,[38] and another the following year in which he urged voters in Dáil elections to boycott Fine Gael, the opposition party. This was seen in Dublin as unacceptable interference in internal Irish politcs.[39]

Ultimately Stuart broke his links with *Irland-Redaktion*, unwilling to take the anti-Soviet line they demanded because he argued that the Soviet state's war was an honourable one which he refused to condemn though not, he insisted, being an apologist for the Communist regime in Russia. In his final broadcast on 5 February 1944, he returned to the theme of the wrong done to Ireland by partition. Earlier though, he had seemed to move away from more simplistic views of Irish unification, declaring:

> It is of no importance that the Tricolour should fly from the City Hall in Belfast instead of the Union Jack if Belfast workers find it as hard to live and support their families as before. Such freedom is mere illusion and such nationalism a farce and a danger.[40]

At the war's end there was a reckoning to be faced by non-Germans who had worked for the Nazi state's radio service. William Joyce was executed in January 1946 for treason against Britain, and some lesser figures faced prison for what they had done and the company they had kept. Francis Stuart spent a period of captivity in French hands prior to returning quietly to Ireland where he relaunched his literary career. Over the years, he sought to minimise his complicity in the evil of Hitler's Reich, reaffirming that he had broadcast no overtly anti-Semitic material that had justified the Holocaust. One of his scripts, however, found by the Allies after 1945, which may either have not been broadcast at all or simply not picked up by G2's monitoring service, had praised the *Volklischer Beobachter*, a Nazi paper notorious for its diatribes against Jews, and had also alluded to the power of Jewish-controlled finance capital.[41]

Irland-Redaktion had also, during the course of 1943, broadcast to Éire a series of talks purporting to be delivered by one Patrick Cadogan, an Irish expatriate living in the United States. These were unquestionably anti-Semitic in content and, though Cadogan's true identity has remained in dispute, some have claimed that the series was Stuart's work. This now seems unlikely, and the more plausible view is that 'Patrick Cadogan' may have been none other than the versatile William Joyce, whom German radio saw as one of its prime assets.[42]

Taking any part, however small, in the Third Reich's propaganda offensive was a contribution to its war effort and involved guilt by direct association with it and with what it did. Francis Stuart was never able to shake off this guilt. Partly, it has been said, this was because he chose to overload Éire's neutrality, an essentially pragmatic option, with more than it could carry, extolling it as he did as part of a special Celtic destiny that gave it the right not to judge Nazi Germany and that gave him the right to serve it.[43]

Part of his defence was that relatively few people in Ireland ever heard his broadcasts because radio ownership, especially in rural areas, was limited and because one of the many shortages caused by the Emergency was of batteries.[44] He may well have been right about this but it was hardly a response that helped him to retrieve any moral high ground. This remained difficult for him even as his writing won real recognition in Ireland and beyond, notably his autobiographical novel Black List Section H, which came out in 1971.

This and other work earned him, in 1991, membership of Aosdana, a state-funded academy of Ireland's outstanding artists and writers. Three years before his death, however, a Channel Four television documentary, entitled A Great Hatred, which focused on anti-Semitism in Ireland, brought public attention to his wartime role, and an ultimately unsuccessful move was launched to expel him from Aosdana. He described the programme as scurrilous but later sought reconciliation with his critics and with Jews, saying that he was 'intensely sorry for the hurt I gave to any people by appearing to support the Nazi regime'.[45]

Irland-Redaktion's efforts were, in reality, only a small part of the Nazi propaganda machine's attempt to use the Irish question against Britain and its allies. This pre-dated the coming of war. Addressing the Reichstag on 28 April 1939, Hitler drew its attention to a recent speech by de Valera in which 'strange to say, he does not accuse Germany of oppressing Ireland, but accuses England of continuing its aggression against his state'.[46] With the onset of war, Germany issued a huge volume of pamphlets and books on Irish history and Britain's malign role in it. This was a campaign, it has been said, 'to stoke the fires of righteous wrath in both Ireland and Germany but particularly Germany'.[47] Ample use, too, was made of cinema, with the full backing of Goebbels. April 1940, for example, saw the first showing in Berlin of *The Fox of Glenarvon*, a melodrama set during Ireland's war of independence. It portrayed British rule and resistance to it, in terms very similar to *Ohm Kruger*, made a year later and based on the Boer War.[48]

Despite Churchill's hostile comments on Irish neutrality in 1939 and 1940, which were echoed by much of the British press in articles, cartoons and personal attacks on de Valera,[49] there were voices in government raised in support of the case for maintaining good relations with Éire. They won an initial victory at the height of the Battle of Britain in 1940 when D notices were issued calling upon the press to tone down its criticism of the Dublin government.[50]

Cinema's newsreel coverage of the war was, in contrast, more benign in its view of Irish policy, at least in the opening months of the war. Its output had never been under the jurisdiction of the Board of Film Censorship though pressure from government could be, and was, applied to them in the pre-war period. On Ireland their tone began to change as the war on the Atlantic worsened and the issue of the Irish ports could be presented as crucial to its outcome.[51]

When war came, Britain's Ministry of Information, it has been said, 'had no policy regarding Éire and in fact questioned whether Éire should be targeted with official propaganda at all'.[52] Some of its staff simply took for granted Irish goodwill to Britain and argued that, while German radio propaganda might reach Irish audiences those same audiences could also receive BBC transmissions and buy British newspapers. In fact, on the eve of Germany's invasion of Scandinavia and the west in April 1940, British papers could claim good circulation figures in Éire: 17,000 a day for the *Daily Mail* and *Daily Telegraph* and many more at weekends for the *Sunday Times* and the *People*.[53]

If anything, it was the Dominions Office which, in the early months of the war, showed a greater sense of urgency over the matter of maintaining good relations with Éire. This was partly because the Information Ministry lacked decisive direction from the top until Brendan Bracken, a protégé of Churchill's, with Fenianism in his family history, was appointed to run it in July 1941. He was never a great well-wisher to Irish neutrality though he was an energetic minister. The Information Ministry began to address the question of how best to influence opinion in Éire, as did the BBC and, in April 1940, its Controller of Programmes issued a document to all senior staff members who might be involved in Irish broadcasts.

The directive was careful to warn broadcasters of the tense

relations that neutrality had created between the Irish state and Northern Ireland. Partition in particular was an issue to be handled with care, it stressed, in any programmes the BBC's Overseas Service might prepare for Éire. In addition, any staff working on such programmes had constantly to look over their shoulders to Belfast, where George Marshall, a Scot recruited to the BBC by his compatriot Reith, was given what amounted to veto powers over all programme content on Ireland. As one account of the BBC in Northern Ireland in these years put it: 'This became his prime occupation during the war as Belfast had ceased to be an important programme production centre with the end of regional broadcasting in 1939.'[54]

Marshall used his position to block any programmes with a cross-border content which could seem to Ulster Unionists to be failing to stress Éire's neutrality compared with Northern Ireland's participation in the war. In 1941 he opposed a BBC/Radio Éireann proposal for a joint St Patrick's Day programme as an act of appeasement. One Belfast newspaper claimed the programme was based on the pretence that Ireland was united, and a senior BBC staff member in Northern Ireland accused the corporation in London of 'shaking hands with murder'.[55]

Issues such as these dogged the efforts of broadcasters who wanted to develop talks and other programmes by the BBC which could tap into the degree of goodwill towards Britain's cause which they believed existed in Éire, even among those who supported neutrality. As a Ministry of Information minute put it in February 1941: 'The development of programmes for Irish listeners from London would be considerably simplified if it could be divorced from considerations of Northern Ireland policy.'[56]

This proved to be an understatement. Even when an innocuous series called 'Irish Half Hour' was mooted in order to reach serving members of the British forces from both sides of the border, Marshall went on the attack, condemning the programme's use of a greeting in Irish as well as its use of 'The Minstrel Boy' as its signature tune. He enlisted the support of John Andrews, Northern Ireland's new prime minister but failed to stop the series being broadcast although he took to insisting that it should be called 'Éire's Half Hour'.[57]

Sir Basil Brooke who, in 1943, ousted Andrews as premier, pressed successfully for the introduction of an 'Ulster Half Hour' which ran until the end of the war. The series had its critics, not least Sir Basil himself, who passed on to a newspaper his reactions to one particular programme: 'a Southern song spoiled for me an otherwise splendid programme. I fail to see why such a song should have been included when the producer had so many good Ulster songs from which to choose.'[58]

In the midst of a global conflict consuming thousands of lives, these exchanges vividly capture all of Northern Ireland's unresolved cultural and sectarian divisions. Nationalist opinion within the province reacted strongly to Unionist broadcasters' concern to maintain a one-dimensional image of the province, airbrushing away the heritage it shared with the rest of the island. Newspapers took up the issue,[59] and one Dublin-born recruit to the BBC, John Irwin, left an angry reaction on the record:

> I know from personal experience that the Northern Ireland Direc-
> tor's touchstone as to a programme's suitability is the opinion of
> his fellow members of the Ulster Club. This hot-bed of Orange
> fascism considers any programme which does not vilify the people
> of Éire as unsuitable for the BBC.[60]

The marvel was that out of these cross currents the BBC still managed to reach Irish audiences with material which helped Britain's cause. Those representing Britain on the ground in wartime Éire gave it all the support they could: for example, John Betjeman, who became its Cultural and Press Attaché in January 1941. Once advised of the pressure from Belfast over the 'Irish Half Hour', he threw his support behind the programme-makers, defending the series as one which 'would keep alive among soldiers serving away from home the sense of Irish nationalism in the broadest meaning of the term'.[61]

Betjeman's appointment, it has been argued, marked the real beginning of Britain's official propaganda effort in wartime Éire.[62] Sir John Maffey, Britain's man in Dublin, was an astute representative of his country's interests but was sensitive to the protocol of its relations with Éire. He also realised the potential of a propaganda front and was happy to work with Betjeman once the Information Ministry's Empire Division had assigned him to Dublin.

Betjeman saw his remit as being to convince as many Irish people as possible that Britain could still win the war while respecting their state's non-belligerent status. He believed, too, in the urgency of befriending Irish diplomats, journalists, broadcasters and writers so that he could press home the message that the war was a fight against a barbarism that was not only antidemocratic but anti-Christian. Himself a high Anglican, he had no difficulty in persuading senior Catholic clergy, as well as influential lay people from Britain, to speak in Éire in support of the war. He built up good contacts with *The Standard*, Éire's biggest Roman Catholic news-paper and also *The Universe*, a Catholic weekly printed in England but with a good circulation in Ireland. At most, Betjeman argued, it should be implied only that Britain was the upholder of Christian values, rather than hammer home the message too overtly or stri-dently to Irish audiences.[63]

He worked hard, too, to increase the output of leaflets and booklets putting Britain's case, and urged a rise in Ministry of Information funding which the BBC could draw on to increase its transmissions to Éire, even if the quality of reception there was sometimes poor, as German broadcasters in Berlin also began to realise. In all this work, Betjeman brought to bear his own distinctive and often eccentric style. A Ministry of Information civil servant, writing to him in late March 1941, observed: 'I hear you are immensely popular; but that some folk doubt your sanity. I cannot imagine a better foundation for success.'[64]

Sir John Maffey's daughter, Penelope, had met Betjeman and his wife before their arrival in Dublin. 'The couple have a big reputation here,' she wrote to her father, 'both rather eccentric and intellectual. He should be the sort of whimsical person the Irish will like and he likes them.'[65] Once arrived in Dublin, Betjeman lost no time in learning the Irish language, in which he made good progress. Before long he was starting his letters with the greeting 'A Chara' and introducing himself as Seán O'Betjeman at parties.

Some of the parties Betjeman hosted or simply attended could be uproarious events. At one, given by Erskine Childers, a Fianna Fáil politician who, in 1973, became President of the Irish Republic, Francis Macnamara, father-in-law of the poet Dylan Thomas, arrived drunk and insulted a Nigerian guest. He was ejected by Childers and an American journalist, only to take his revenge by cutting a huge swastika into the lawn, hurling the turf he had removed into the next-door garden. Betjeman stayed the night, and the following morning was able to avert a possible diplomatic crisis when he and Childers climbed a wall to retrieve the turf and replace it.[66]

The Betjemans also made friends with Seán MacEntee, a hero of the 1916 rising and minister for industry and commerce in de Valera's government. He was a powerful spokesman of the Fianna Fáil party's conservative wing and was often thought of as being anti-British. Much later his daughter Maire recalled that both her parents 'absolutely loved the Betjemans. I think the Betjemans loved them too.'[67] In June 1943 it was her parents who hosted a memorable farewell party for Betjeman and his wife on their return to London.[68]

Betjeman's close working relationship with Maffey also gave him access to the Taoiseach. Usually their meetings were in the company of Maffey but, on occasions he was invited on his own. Betjeman came to be impressed by de Valera and admired his negotiating skills. 'De Valera's position could not really be presented as heroic,' Betjeman noted after one meeting but he understood the reasons for it, adding the thought that 'he stuck to his lack of guns. He also knew that the majority of his people wanted Britain to win.'[69]

This latter thought of Betjeman's certainly described the outcome he wanted to bring about by his work in Dublin. He was also a realist, however, and knew the limits of what British propaganda could achieve given the wide-ranging power of the Irish state's censorship of the media. A striking reminder of this was the death in action of Dublin-born Brendan Finucane in July 1942. Finucane, a hero of RAF Fighter Command, had shot down thirty German aircraft and been promoted to the rank of wing commander.[70] The American press had given enormous coverage of his RAF service, leading on occasions with the story of how he flew with a shamrock painted on his Spitfire. When he was killed, the Irish press obeyed the censors and printed only the bare facts of his death with no reference to his Irish connections.[71]

Betjeman had little choice but to accept this. It was the same with film censorship, though he had worked in the Information Ministry's film division earlier in the war and valued cinema's propaganda potential. In 1941 he noted that 'only' sixty-five films had been banned outright in Éire. This number increased in the following year and, among the casualties, were now acknowledged classics of Britain's wartime cinema. They included Michael Powell's 1941 production *Forty-ninth Parallel* about a fanatical German U-boat crew who, after the sinking of their vessel, try to reach the still neutral United States from Canada.[72] The film is a compelling drama as well as a ringing affirmation of democratic and anti-fascist values. This, along with the fact that some of its funding came from the British Information Ministry, ensured that it did not get past the Irish censorship though the Irish Film Society screened it privately.[73]

While Betjeman was still in post, work started on what later became a British wartime cult classic, *The Life and Death of Colonel Blimp*, also directed by Michael Powell and Emeric Pressburger. It was based on David Low's cartoon character in the *London Evening Standard* and was both a gentle, even affectionate, satire of some outdated army attitudes as well as a call to all-out war to destroy Nazism.[74] Initially, Churchill, on the basis of little real knowledge of the film, tried to stop it going into production but then changed his mind.[75] The Irish censorship ultimately approved it but only after demanding so many cuts as to make it meaningless to audiences and not worth screening at all.[76]

Betjeman did, however, persuade Laurence Olivier that his hugely patriotic version of *Henry V*, with its obvious symbolism of an England defiant though outnumbered by its enemies, and dedicated to Britain's airborne forces, could be filmed in Ireland. The sturdy yeomen and archers who confronted the French in the film's Agincourt battle sequences were all Irish farmers who were paid extra if they brought their own horses to the locations of the film in County Wicklow. Filming began only after Betjeman's departure but it is estimated to have put more than £80,000 into the Irish economy and thus generated significant goodwill for Britain's cause. Because of the censorship, it was destined not to be seen by Irish audiences until after the war.[77]

Always a realist in his assessment of what he could achieve in his role as Cultural and Press Attache, Betjeman's single-minded energy impressed the Dominions Office and the Information Ministry in London. In January 1943 the latter's Empire Division drafted its first full propaganda plan for Éire. This really differed little from what Betjeman was trying to do. It stressed the need to spread the word as widely as possible in support of Britain's cause while allowing for the strong support which Éire's neutrality commanded as a policy. It also stressed that British newspaper distribution should be increased along with that of Ministry of Information material but the plan accepted the rigour of Éire censorship and the impossibility of getting films or broadcasts past it that were deemed to be unacceptable. It was in fact, 'more an admission of what could not be done than what could be'.[78]

What this document really changed in the conduct of British propaganda in and to Éire must remain debatable. Betjeman was recalled to London later in 1943, and his departure made front-page news in the *Irish Times*. The farewell party was an emotional occasion. Betjeman sang, in fluent Irish, the song *Dark Rosaleen* with tears rolling down his cheeks as Maire MacEntee accompanied him on the piano. To Frank Gallagher, Éire's Director of Government Information, he wrote that 'Living in Ireland has been a wonderful experience, because it is a wholly Christian country. I am sure it is my duty to go back and to help remake England one so far as I can.'[79]

Whether Betjeman's role in Dublin extended to actual intelligence gathering or even to espionage has for long been a matter of conjecture. Those who think it did have argued that the true nature of his work remained hidden because of the length of time over which records covering Britain's wartime intelligence operations in Ireland remained closed, and also that significant material was removed from them.[80] It does, however, seem to be the case that intelligence from Éire intended for the Foreign and Dominions Offices crossed Betjeman's desk, including the numerous reports by the novelist Elizabeth Bowen on Irish attitudes to the war and to neutrality.[81] She divided her time between ARP work in London during the Blitz and regular trips to Ireland to observe the political and cultural scene there, and then filed her always pointed and lively comments to London. 'Always fascinated by espionage, she was now a kind of spy,' it has been claimed. 'Her reports are headed secret and she had proposed herself for the task. Nobody in Ireland, apparently, knew of this commission.'[82]

On social occasions in Dublin Betjeman was known sometimes to refer to himself cheerfully as a spy and was later quoted as thinking that he had been one.[83] Colonel Dan Bryan, however, when interviewed long after his retirement from army intelligence work, did not believe this[84] but others sought to perpetuate the idea that Betjeman had at least dabbled in some intelligence gathering.

> He represented the acceptable face of espionage: he was a marvellous verbaliser, a lush and a bit of an eccentric, qualities which immediately endeared him to the natives. He was condescending about what he termed 'Irish gush' but he kept that to himself until he was back in Britain. Betjeman was Ireland's favourite spy and his activities in the field could be laughed off. No-one took them seriously.[85]

At the time, however, as pointed out in the previous chapter, the IRA was not so sure. It was well placed to observe and, indeed, to chat to him since some of its members, such as Brendan Behan, drank in Dublin's Palace Bar, a favourite port of call for writers and journalists.

Flann O'Brien, the great satirist and novelist who was in notional government employment, used the Palace as if it were his office, as did Tony Gray, then editor of the Irish Times books page. He was often in Betjeman's company there and recalled: 'He was very witty and very English and people loved him. He didn't at all seem to be a spy, which I suppose is a very good cover.'[86]

Betjeman and Elizabeth Bowen worked of necessity in a grey area where putting Britain's case, as well as assessing and reporting back to London on Irish opinion and morale, could overlap with the business of intelligence gathering. Their main role, however, was to circumvent, as far as they could, the Irish state's formidable censorship powers. These, it must be stressed, threw a very necessary blanket over the reality of Éire's co-operation with Britain on security and intelligence sharing, as well as on the extent of Irish people's contribution to Britain's war effort, but they were also powers deemed by the state to be essential to maintaining its declared policy of staying out of the conflict.

From the start of the Second World War, a priority of de Valera's government was to neutralise Irish opinion by a system of censorship which has been called 'wide ranging and draconian'[87] as well as being neutrality's backbone 'to be defended as forcefully as neutrality itself'.[88] Censorship was made the responsibility of Frank Aiken, the Minister for the Co-ordination of Defence, a former IRA chief of staff and an uncompromising upholder of the policy of neutrality.

A culture of censorship already existed in the Irish state, the product of a tradition of closed and secretive government as well as of Roman Catholic church power. A film censorship law, for example, was enacted in the first year of the Free State's life in June 1923. This was a result of campaigns against the moral dangers of foreign cinema output, to which the Irish Vigilance Association and Church-based pressure groups had given their support. In the first year of the film censorship's existence more than a hundred films were banned and many more severely cut. This set a pattern and, in 1939, Irish audiences were allowed to see only a heavily cut version of *Gone With the Wind*.[89]

The government's September 1939 Emergency Powers legislation amended the 1923 act to allow films to be censored, not just on grounds of obscene or blasphemous content, but because they might pose a threat to public order or offend friendly foreign states. It also allowed for the revoking of authorisation for the screening of films which had already been shown in Éire prior to September 1939. The way these powers were used in the Emergency years has already been alluded to, and the larger purpose of the legislation was to exercise control over newspapers as well as postal and telegraph communications. There was no initial provision for formal control over Radio Éireann.

It could provide only a limited news service and it broadcast for no more than seven hours on an average day. Listening access to radio was much less than in mainland Britain and, in fact, diminished during the Emergency period. Its news-gathering resources were very limited, and much of what it relayed was 'borrowed' from elsewhere, notably the BBC and Vatican Radio. Even so, in July 1941, de Valera called for Radio Éireann to be brought into line after it had broadcast material on how the trade unions were planning to fight new, and what they saw as oppressive, industrial relations laws. The press had been forbidden to carry this story so the government required that all contentious news items should, from then on, be referred to the censors before going on air.

Coverage of the war was, in fact, kept to a minimum, to the resentment of Éire's literary and intellectual community. Seán O'Faolain wrote in 1940 of how lengthy reports of the Croagh Patrick pilgrimage had precedence over events in Europe which seemed to merit only a few sentences in news bulletins. As security tightened, a Garda presence was maintained at Radio Éireann's Dublin premises and at all outside broadcasts after an incident at a Gaelic-language céilidh when an IRA supporter seized a microphone to make a political statement. Two years later, during *Question Time*, a popular quiz programme which Radio Éireann decided to relay from Belfast with BBC co-operation, a competitor was asked to name the world's best-known teller of fairy tales. When he answered 'Winston Churchill' instead of 'Hans Andersen', a mainly nationalist audience laughed and cheered.[90]

All reports of this incident were suppressed by Radio Éireann as well as by the press. The weather was another casualty of wartime censorship. Detailed meterological reports were shared secretly with Britain and its allies by the Irish Air Corps and Marine service but giving them live air coverage was felt to be of too obvious use to belligerent states. Even Gaelic sport reports and commentaries had to be broadcast without reference to the weather.

Most censorship employment was created by the interception and checking of mail. All letters and packages to and from any destination beyond Éire's borders were liable to be opened and examined. Sensitive material would be deleted or scored out but the sheer amount of mail between Éire and Britain meant that only random checking was possible. Similar spot checks were applied to cross-border mail between Éire and Northern Ireland, and the central telegraph office in Dublin was used to intercept all inland and foreign telegrams. In October 1939, *Dublin Opinion*, which liked to call itself 'the National Humorous Journal of Ireland' did manage to get away with a cartoon portraying the controlled chaos of the postal censorship office as its mostly young female staff crowded round each other to see mail with any hint of scandal, or flirted with male colleagues.

The area of censorship which has had most examination by historians has been the daily and weekly press. Controlling its content was central to a memorandum for his ministerial colleagues prepared by Frank Aiken in late January 1940. 'As a nation,' he stated,

> we have a definite grievance against the nearest belligerent [i.e. Britain], but the Government have declared with general consent that we would be unwise, in the interest of the nation, to engage in war against this belligerent. Not all our people approve of this policy, and if a certain section were allowed to talk offensively about the morals of Germany in relation to its aggression in Poland and elsewhere, we can be quite sure that others would try to express in even more offensive terms their detestation of British morality.[92]

Neither of these contingencies, Aiken stressed, could be tolerated if neutrality was to remain a sustainable policy. He was dismissive of what he called 'self-styled democrats who would hold on to the peace time liberalistic trimmings of democracy'.[93] Nothing in Aiken's background allowed him to equate the cause of Britain and its allies with democracy, least of all when the Soviet Union joined the war. Prior to that he was widely regarded as someone who was convinced Britain would lose the war but, forty years later, when interviewed by Robert Fisk, who had published in full his January 1940 memorandum, Aiken held to the simplistic moral relativism of his view of the war. He claimed that while he and de Valera had known early on of the German death camps, 'the Russians were as bad. You only have to look back at what happened in the Katyn forest.'[94]

Working under Aiken as controller of censorship was his fellow Ulsterman Joseph Connolly. Between September 1939 and February 1942, he and his successor, Thomas Coyne, were responsible for issuing a succession of emergency orders, laying down increasingly strict rules for the operation of newspaper censorship. The earlier orders were replaced on 17 February 1942 by a consolidating regulation which extended the state's powers to the printers and publishers of unacceptable material as well as to actual newspapers and journals. Censorship in wartime Éire was, in fact, much tougher than in other neutral states. In Switzerland, though a federal law in

August 1942 made it an offence to call for the country to join the war, the press carried debate and comment on the cause of the war and the case for the Allies and the Axis powers to a degree never permitted in Éire.

In Sweden, too, the press has been described as relatively free compared to Éire[95] and, as with Switzerland, Swedish newspapers undertook their own coverage of the war, sending reporters to some of the major fronts. Censorship existed but allowing the press to carry propaganda from the belligerent states and letting readers judge it for themselves was not seen as something subversive of the state's neutrality. Even in Portugal, with a well-established censorship under an authoritarian and, indeed, pro-fascist regime, newspapers not directly controlled by the government leaned towards the cause of Britain and its allies and were allowed to make this clear in their coverage of the war.[96]

In wartime Éire the censors' ultimate power was to confiscate every copy of a specific issue of a newspaper which flagrantly defied them. This happened in January 1941, when the Garda raided the Dublin and Drogheda offices of *Penapa*, the organ of the People's National Party. This was a small but rabidly anti-Semitic and pro-Nazi grouping, and the offending issue of *Penapa*, the second one, captioned on its cover with the words 'The Uncrowned King', a cartoon of a sinister-looking Jew surrounded by money bags and sitting astride a representation of the Irish economy. No further issues of the paper came out though the party resurfaced later in the war under another name.[97]

Short of the seizure of an entire issue, the censors' most serious weapon was to use their power to order a newspaper to submit every issue for scrutiny prior to publication. For many papers, especially those seeking to maintain a circulation in rural areas, this would have been tantamount to suppression because it would have made continued publication almost impossible. Others were prepared to court the risk. A notable example was the *Irish Times*. Its rotund and ebullient editor, R. M. Smyllie, or Bertie Smyllie as he was called by friends, was no respecter of the censors and had a low opinion of Frank Aiken whom he dismissed as a crass and heavy handed Anglophobe without the intellectual and moral capacity to grasp what the war was about.

Smyllie's view was, and remained, that the censorship was biased against Britain and its allies. He had been interned in Germany during World War I, became fluent in the language and was well read in the country's literature and history. He was never culturally

anti-German and, after the *Irish Times* had gone to press around four
in the morning, he would invite colleagues back to his home to listen
to Wagner and Beethoven on his gramophone and to drink with him
until dawn.[98] He had also travelled widely for the paper before and
after he became its editor in 1934 and had come to detest fascism,
especially in its German manifestation.

Putting his thoughts on paper after the war for *Foreign Affairs*, an
American journal, Smyllie declared that

> in theory the censorship was neutral; in practice it worked against
> the Allies. No paper dared to print a word in favour of the Allied
> cause. Even when the Americans came in, and Mr de Valera no
> longer had the excuse that it was a mainly British war, this rigid
> veto was maintained. Whether the Irish Government was trying to
> humbug the people of Éire, or was merely humbugging itself,
> nobody will ever know.[99]

He himself was sure that the Third Reich at least was not deceived
and knew how minimal real support for it was outside the ranks of
the IRA and some ideological zealots on the far right of Éire's
political spectrum.

Almost from the outset of the Emergency, Smyllie embarked on
what became a series of running battles with the censors. He
particularly resented their requirement that all references to Irish
people serving with the British forces be banned from the press. A
test case arose in December 1941 when HMS *Prince of Wales* was
sunk by a Japanese air attack off Malaya. Among its crew was
Johnny Robinson who had joined the *Irish Times* in 1934 but
volunteered for the Royal Navy when war came. Smyllie's tongue-
in-cheek rendering of this event was to insert a notice in the paper for
'the many friends of Mr John A. Robinson who was involved in a
recent boating accident'.[100] The report went on to say that Robinson
had survived. 'He is a particularly good swimmer and it is possible
that he owes his life to this accomplishment.'[101]

Similarly, Irishmen wounded in action with the British Eighth
Army in North Africa appeared in the *Irish Times* as being 'in
hospital suffering from lead poisoning in the Libyan desert'.[102]
The censors appear to have let pass such entries in the paper though
whether they were deceived or simply amused by them must remain
a matter of conjecture. Their response was widely believed in the
Irish Times office to be the demand for a series of trivial changes of
wording that simply delayed the paper from going to press or made it

miss the early morning newspaper trains that distributed copies outside the capital.

Smyllie and the *Irish Times* did not fight the censorship unaided. Éire's best-selling daily, the *Irish Independent* which supported the opposition Fine Gael party, incurred a raft of warnings over its handling of copy deemed to be a threat to the state's neutrality. At the height of the London Blitz in December 1940, its special correspondent there provided a series drawn from the experiences of Irish people but the censors acted to prevent its publication. Numerous other clashes arose, with Aiken using a Dáil debate in January 1941 to resurrect the case against the paper over its failure to support the 1916 rising.[103]

Another tenacious upholder of press freedom was E. T. Keane, the elderly editor of the *Kilkenny People* which, twenty years earlier, had been closed down for a time by the British authorities during the independence struggle. Keane used his own and his paper's prestige to challenge the censors repeatedly over his support for Britain and its allies. In March 1942 he defied an order to submit all editorials for scrutiny to them, quoting Yeats and Swift against the censors. He to them only submitted leading articles on a sporadic basis and, in December 1944, went so far as to run a leader in praise of Northern Ireland's war effort. This led to him being threatened with a prosecution which never, in fact, took place. Thomas Coyne who, in September 1941, had taken over from Joseph Connolly day-to-day responsibility for the censorship, admitted at the war's end that such a prosecution might have failed.

The only alternative, he agreed, might have been an occupation of the premises of the *Kilkenny People* to ensure the censorship's requirements were carried out by directing its production. Such powers, however, fell short of what the censorship could actually do.[104] At intervals during the Emergency years, the rights and wrongs of the censorship were at least debated in the Dáil and the Seanad (or Senate). In one of these debates, in October 1940, Senator Sir John Keane accused Aiken of actually seeking to censor Dáil proceedings. The minister, he claimed was taking his remit beyond state security to exercise control over opinions he and his colleagues simply found inconvenient.[105]

Aiken's answer, or part of it, was to argue that newspaper editors disliked censorship because, until the onset of the Emergency, it was they who decided what went into the press and what did not. The state censors, Aiken declared, had now, in the national interest, taken on that role: 'We are changing the function of the editor of the

Irish Times and the other papers to myself and my staff. It is now we who have final say on what to cut out, not the editors.'[106] These remarks cause a furious reaction, with Aiken's critics making the obvious but necessary point that an individual editor had no control over what went into other papers whereas the censors could excise an item they disapproved of from the entire press.

After 1942, with the Soviet Union and the United States in the war as Britain's allies, and as the tide of battle began to turn, some editors of Irish newspapers started to lose their appetite for an ongoing battle of wits with the censors. Those in day-to-day charge of the censors' office, like Coyne and Michael Knightley, began to go home earlier, devolving more responsibility to junior civil servants whom an editor such as Bertie Smyllie deemed less worthy opponents. For him and those of like mind, it became an option simply to wait for the Allies' victory.

The Emergency years also imposed a test on relations between Éire's censorship and the British press. Some papers, such as the *Daily Mirror*, had good sales on both sides of the border and, in Northern Ireland, it was, of course, subject to the requirements of the British censors. Churchill himself rashly considered having the *Mirror* closed down altogether in March 1942 over a cartoon by Philip Zec which appeared to call into question his government's competence in controlling the rationing of fuel imported at the risk of the lives of Royal and Merchant Navy crews.[107] Two years prior to that, however, another lurid *Mirror* cartoon, portraying Éire as a base for German espionage, led to Aiken and his censors issuing an order banning its import but this was lifted after only two days.[108]

British Sunday newspapers had built up particularly good Irish sales before the war. *The People* claimed a circulation of 60,000 in Éire alone when war came but it, too, clashed with the censors in April 1940 when it ran an article about espionage under the headline 'Nazis in Éire'. Again a banning order was issued and then lifted when the paper's publishers, Odham's Press, gave Aiken assurances that it would run no further copy on this subject, as well as profuse apologies.[109]

Any copy calling in question Éire's neutrality was likely to activate the censorship in Dublin. The *Sunday Dispatch* found this out in September 1943 when it published an article highly critical of Éire's stance in the war. Predictably, Aiken at once authorised an import ban but, with invasion scares long past, he settled for an agreement with its London editor that the ban could be rescinded if a follow-up article would make the case for neutrality.[110] This war between Fleet

Street and the Irish censors was in many ways a phoney one, and Thomas Coyne had been speaking the truth when, two years earlier, he had briefed the Department of External Affairs, for Washington's benefit, to the effect that not one British newspaper was excluded from Éire.[111]

The United States was concerned to have its case for joining the war on Britain's side properly heard in Éire. Gray, its strongly pro-British minister in Dublin and William Donovan, head of its Office of Strategic Services, later to become the CIA, saw Aiken as a likely impediment to this. Donovan observed that Aiken would 'make any propaganda job here a difficult one as he is almost as friendly as a disappointed rattlesnake'.[112]

Gray, with his undiminished antipathy to de Valera and his government, was the man to press the issue of reaching an Irish readership with America's view of the war. In March 1942 he raised with the DEA in Dublin the question of a Washington-funded bulletin which would be distributed in Éire. In June a trial issue was run under the title *American Newsletter*. Prepared and edited from Washington, it had a target mailing list of 18,000 and, under its altered title, *Letter from America*, it reached an even wider readership, far surpassing anything achieved by Hempel's German legation. In Gray's view its role was to 'tell the Irish people what their censorship did not want them to know'.[113]

The censors had to live with the reality that as major a belligerent as the United States would want to make its case to an Irish audience. They also had to coexist with a vibrant artistic and literary community reinforced significantly in Dublin by refugees from war and occupation in Europe. Dublin's theatre tradition was a famous one and, in fact, the 1939 Emergency legislation contained no provision for the censorship of plays. As in peacetime however, theatres could be licensed or have their licences taken from them, and the latter was a threat that theatre managements knew they had to accept as a reality.

In 1942 the capital's Olympic theatre staged *The Strings are False* by Paul Vincent Carroll. This was set during the previous year's German Blitz on Glasgow and Clydebank, and it dramatised the terror of the attack as well as the response of Irish-born people and their parish priest. One central character overcomes his anti-British instincts to join in rescue work and then volunteer for the emergency services. The play had to be much modified before the theatre management felt it could safely be staged. Even so, it gripped audiences with a script which, at least by implication addressed the nature of neutrality as a moral stance. It played to huge audiences in Dublin and then in Cork and was much discussed in the press and on Radio Éireann.[114]

A year later, Dublin's Peacock theatre took its chances when it announced its intention to stage *The Refugee*, a play whose central character was a Jew from Austria who had escaped from the Nazis. At the German legation, Hempel was quick to make representations to the Justice Ministry about what he had been advised was the script's emphasis on anti-Semitism and concentration camps. In the end, the Peacock cravenly went ahead with a version acceptable to Hempel and with vigilant Special Branch men in the first-night audience.[115]

As to the visual arts, the most contentious act of censorship in the Emergency years was not the work of government at all. Frank Aiken and his staff probably knew little of the group of avant-garde painters who lived, drank and exhibited their work in Dublin's Baggot Street area. Some of these were people displaced by war, and they were, in due course, joined by Irish artists like Jack Yeats and Evie Hone. They were much enthused when the Friends of the National Collection decided, in 1942, to buy Georges Rouault's *Christ and the Soldier* for the city's Municipal Gallery of Modern Art, only for the gallery's trustees to refuse to show it on the grounds, among others, that it was blasphemous. The resulting furore was defused only when the priests of Maynooth College offered to take the picture on loan for their dining hall. There it stayed until the gallery finally decided that it could be displayed after all.

Only in the summer of 1940 did Éire's censors assume powers over printed material other than newspapers and magazines. These powers enabled them to make representations to retailers over material deemed by them to have the potential to compromise the state's neutrality, but they were used intermittently. Sometimes it was simply put to a bookshop's owner that books or pamphlets supportive of Britain's cause or overtly hostile to the Axis powers should be sold discreetly and not given undue prominence.

In October 1942 their power was extended to printed matter of all kinds but many printers and publishers were already submitting what they saw as doubtful items for preliminary examination before they went to press. Literary and creative Ireland was, of course, no stranger to censorship. In 1929 the Free State had enacted legislation to block the publication of any writing deemed to be immoral or a danger to faith and, under its terms, an average of more than a hundred books were banned every year. These included the work of some of the country's finest writers. Samuel Beckett, Seán O'Casey, James Joyce, Frank O'Connor, Liam O'Flaherty, Seán O'Faolain and George Bernard Shaw were among them.

One way round the operation of such bans had always been the review pages of newspapers and journals. This was one reason for Seán O'Faolain agreeing, in 1940, to take on the editorship of The Bell, a new publication which dared to be intellectually innovative and even irreverent and radical in its comments upon the social and cultural situation of wartime Éire. In some rural towns it is known that, rather than openly displayed, copies of The Bell were kept under the counter by newsagents for customers who wanted it.

O'Faolain was an optimist in the sense that he felt the Emergency, for all its restrictions, could stimulate Irish writing. The war had virtually closed publishing outlets in Britain for Irish writers as it had the American market. This to him was a shameful reminder of Irish literature's dependence on publishers beyond the state's own borders but he saw the war and the Emergency forcing a cultural self-sufficiency upon the country which had huge creative potential. With regular contributions from the likes of Elizabeth Bowen, Patrick Kavanagh, Flann O'Brien, Frank O'Connor and Peadar O'Donnell, The Bell certainly reflected this.

It had, of course, to take its chances with the censors and sometimes to accept their edicts, crass as these might be. Late in 1944, O'Faolain ran a series of articles entitled 'Credo' in which people of different denominations explained their faith. In the November issue it was the turn of a Trinity College Dublin academic, A. J. Leventhal, to write on 'What It Means to be a Jew'. On viewing the proofs the censors destroyed his piece by deleting so much that it would have been barely intelligible. As the Irish Times put it forty years later in a special issue on the Emergency years: 'What was left of the text was obviously too much of a betrayal of the author to be printed',[119] and O'Faolain retained the original for publication after the war was over.

The next month The Bell had to withdraw another item, this time an editorial critical of the DEA's decision to ban a lecture at the Irish Institute for International Affairs by Ján Masaryk, a leading figure in Czechoslovakia's anti-fascist government-in-exile.[120] Even so, The Bell stayed in production and kept up its sales, using its review pages to comment upon books which the censors might seek to keep out of shops and libraries.

One major victory over the censorship via this medium was,

predictably, the work of Bertie Smyllie of the *Irish Times*. In 1942 the paper received for review a copy of *Worrals of the WAAF*, from the pen of Captain W. E. Johns, the prolific author of the patriotic adventure stories involving Biggles, the RAF pilot. Worrals was a wartime recruit to the Women's Auxiliary Air Force (WAAFs) and Smyllie at once ran off a short review. The item was banned as soon as the censors saw it, as Smyllie knew it would be.

His mischievous masterstroke was then to rewrite the piece, carefully renaming Worrals and her friends as Gretchen, Eva and Lilli and retitling the book as *Lotte of the Luftwaffe*. In its thus altered form the censors cleared the book for publication and Smyllie at once went on the offensive, accusing the censors of pro-German bias. Their embarrassment was acute while it lasted. Smyllie's very junior colleague, Tony Gray, pointed out much later that the episode simply proved that the Irish censors at this stage of the war were more afraid of Germany than of Britain, and that the German legation would be much more angered by a review item about a WAAF than Betjeman and Sir John Maffey would be by a press item on young women in a German equivalent of the Women's Auxiliary Air Force.[121]

When victory in Europe was finally secured by the Allied forces, Smyllie was ready with his revenge on the censors, and not just on behalf of the *Irish Times*. The early, country edition prepared late at night on 7 May 1945 passed the censors but, for the final Dublin edition, Smyllie personally redesigned the front page, with images of Churchill and the other leaders of the Allies, as well as commanders such as Montgomery and Brooke, laid out in the pattern of an enormous V for Victory. There was no time for any response to this final coup as the censorship was ended three days after the 8 May victory edition came out.[122]

Between 1939 and 1945 intelligence gathering and counter-espionage work were, along with a high degree of censorship, seen by the Irish state as necessary weapons in the maintenance of a non-belligerent status which carried real risks especially in the earlier years of the war. In the case of intelligence gathering, de Valera's government performed with a level of competence now well documented and which was more than satisfactory to Britain and its allies. With counter-espionage there was frustration for those such as Betjeman and Sir John Maffey whose role was to represent, as well as they could, Britain's interests in Éire. They and their colleagues simply learned to live with the censorship and work round it as and when they could.

The censorship was often driven by ignorance and prejudice, and its concern was to keep Irish people as unaware as possible of events in Europe and beyond. In any event the level of support for the Allied forces was not affected by it although equally support for Éire's neutrality remained intact as de Valera's two Dáil election victories, in 1943 and 1944; seem to suggest.

That said, it remains inescapable that the enervating effects of the censorship left an Irish public ill-prepared to confront the truth of Nazi genocide once the censorship was lifted on 11 May 1945. A significant amount of public and press comment at the time still reads as quite shamefully ambivalent in its response to scenes and images which had deeply shocked British newsreel cinema audiences and traumatised soldiers who had liberated death camps such as Belsen.[123]

That ambivalence, while it lasted, has to be seen as the dark side to the censors' work. They have been blamed for much else besides, such as reinforcing a self-absorbed and complacent Irish insularity. This charge sits uneasily with the vibrant and outward-looking artistic and literary scene which survived in Dublin in the Emergency years and attracted gifted exiles from a war-torn Europe. The authoritarian philistinism with which it sometimes had to contend both pre-dated the wartime censorship and outlasted it. Yet it is now widely disputed whether an entire people, in Plato's famous image later used by F. S. L. Lyons had been for six years condemned to live in a metaphorical cave, 'backs to the fire of life and deriving their only knowledge of what went on outside from the flickering shadows thrown on the wall before their eyes by the men and women who passed to and fro behind them'.[124]

Notes

1. W. S. Churchill, *The Second World War: Volume IV, the Hinge of Fate*, p. 459.
2. J. P. Duggan, *Neutral Ireland and the Third Reich*, pp. 177–8.
3. B. Loring Villa, *Unauthorized Action: Mountbatten and the Dieppe Raid 1942* (Don Mills, ON and Oxford University Press, 1989), pp. 204–6.
4. J. P. Duggan, *Neutral Ireland and the Third Reich*, p. 237; also J. P. Duggan, *Herr Hempel at the German Legation in Dublin, 1937–1945* (Dublin and Portland, OR: Irish Academic Press, 2003), p. 215.
5. M. Hastings, *Armageddon: the Battle for Germany 1944–45* (Basingstoke and Oxford: Macmillan, 2004), pp. 39–40.
6. E. O'Halpin (ed.) *MI5 in Ireland 1939–1945*, pp. 26–7.
7. Ibid.
8. Ibid., p. 27. See also C. Wills, *That Neutral Ireland*, pp. 150–2.

9. Duggan, *Neutral Ireland and the Third Reich*, p. 251.
10. M. M. Hull, *Irish Secrets: German Espionage in Wartime Ireland*, pp. 35, 258 and 339.
11. Ibid., p. 278.
12. Ibid..
13. Ibid.
14. Ibid., pp. 272–3.
15. E. O'Halpin, 'Aspects of Intelligence', *The Irish Sword*, 1993–34, Vol. XIX, pp. 57–66.
16. Ibid.
17. See M. Manning, *The Blueshirts* (Dublin: Gill and Macmillan, 1974); M. Cronin, *The Blueshirts and Irish Politics* (Dublin: Four Courts Press, 1977); F. McGarry, *Eoin O'Duffy: a self-made hero* (Oxford: Oxford University Press, 2005).
18. *Observer*, 12 October 2003.
19. C. C. O'Brien, 'Yeats and Fascism: What Rough Beast?' *New Statesman*, 26 February 1965, Vol. LXIX, No. 1772, pp. 319–22.
20. O'Halpin, *Defending Ireland*, p. 147.
21. A. Roth, *Mr Bewley in Berlin: Aspects of the Career of an Irish Diplomat 1933– 1939* (Dublin: Four Courts Press, 2000), pp. 55–6.
22. B. Barrington (ed.), *The Wartime Broadcasts of Francis Stuart 1942–44*, p. 48.
23. J. J. Lee, *Ireland 1912–1985: Politics and Society*, pp. 247–8.
24. Keogh, *Twentieth-Century Ireland: Nation and State*, p. 115.
25. V. Glendinning, *Elizabeth Bowen: Portrait of a Writer* (London: Phoenix Books, 1977), p. 162.
26. G. Mullins, *Dublin Nazi No 1*, pp. 47–67; also D. O'Donoghue, 'The Nazis in Irish Universities', *History Ireland*, September/October 2007, Vol. 15, No. 5, pp. 12–13.
27. R. Douglas, 'The Pro-Axis Underground in Wartime Ireland 1939–1942', *Historical Journal*, Vol. 49, 4 December 2006, pp. 1155–85.
28. A. Nc. Lochlainn, 'Altiri na hAiseirghe: a Party of its Time', in D. Keogh and M. O'Driscoll (eds), *Ireland in World War Two: Neutrality and Survival*, pp. 187– 210.
29. R. Douglas, 'The Pro-Axis Underground in Wartime Ireland, 1939–1942', *Historical Journal*, December 2006.
30. Ibid.
31. O'Donoghue, *Hitler's Irish Voices*, p. XVII; also pp. 12–16.
32. Ibid., pp. 42–3.
33. Mullins, *Dublin Nazi No. 1*, pp. 113–16; also O'Donoghue, *Hitler's Irish Voices*, pp. 57–62.
34. O'Donoghue, *Hitler's Irish Voices*, pp. 20–2.
35. Barrington, *The Wartime Broadcasts of Francis Stuart*, p. 113.
36. *Guardian*, 29 April 1999.
37. Mullins, *Dublin's Nazi No. 1*, p. 129.
38. Barrington, *The Wartime Broadcasts of Francis Stuart*, pp. 97–8.
39. Ibid., pp. 123–5.
40. Ibid., p. 192.
41. Ibid., pp. 201–4.
42. O'Donoghue, *Hitler's Irish Voices*, pp. 123–8.
43. Wills, *That Neutral Island*, pp. 380–2.
44. Ibid., pp. 203–6.
45. *Guardian*, 29 April 1999; see also his obituary by K. O'Connor, *Guardian*, 4 February 2000.
46. R. Herzstein, *The War that Hitler Won: the Most Infamous Propaganda Campaign in German History* (London: Hamish Hamilton, 1979), p. 342.

47. Ibid.
48. Ibid., pp. 343–4.
49. R. Cole, *Propaganda, Censorship and Irish Neutrality in the Second World War* (Edinburgh: Edinburgh University Press, 2006), p. 20.
50. Ibid.
51. Fisk, *In Time of War*, pp. 390-96.
52. Cole, *Propaganda, Censorship and Irish Neutrality in the Second World War*, p. 20.
53. Ibid., p. 36.
54. R. Cathcart and M. Muldoon, 'The Mass Media in twentieth century Ireland', in J. R. Hill (ed.), *A New History of Ireland*, VII: *Ireland 1921–1984*.
55. R. Cathcart, *The Most Contrary Region: the BBC in Northern Ireland 1924–1984* (Belfast: Blackstaff, 1984), pp. 114–5.
56. Ibid., p. 116.
57. Ibid., pp. 119–21; see also Cole, *Propaganda, Censorship and Irish Neutrality in the Second World War* (Edinburgh: Edinburgh University Press, 2006), pp. 94–5.
58. *Northern Whig*, 2 August 1943.
59. *Irish News*, 19 October 1943, also 23 November 1944.
60. Cathcart, *The Most Contrary Region*, pp. 133–4.
61. Ibid., p. 119.
62. Cole, *Propaganda, Censorship and Irish Neutrality in the Second World War*, p. 69.
63. Ibid., p. 70.
64. R. Cole, "Good Relations': Irish Neutrality and the Propaganda of John Betjeman 1941–43', *Éire-Ireland*, Vol. XXX, 1996, pp. 33–46.
65. B. Hillier, *John Betjeman: New Fame, New Love* (London: John Murray, 2002), p. 197.
66. Ibid., pp. 206–7.
67. Ibid., p. 203.
68. Ibid., p. 238.
69. Ibid., pp. 201–3.
70. R. Doherty, *Irish Men and Women in the Second World War* (Dublin: Four Courts Press, 1999), pp. 176–89.
71. Cole, *Propaganda, Censorship and Irish Neutrality in the Second World War*, pp. 131–2.
72. J. Richards, *Visions of Yesterday* (London: Routledge and Kegan Paul, 1973), p. 163.
73. D. O'Driscoll, *Censorship in Ireland 1939–1945: Neutrality, Politics and Society* (Cork University Press, 1996), p. 45.
74. Richards, *Visions of Yesterday*, pp. 163–6.
75. P. Addison, *The Road to 1945: British Politics in the Second World War* (London: Jonathan Cape, 1975), p. 132.
76. Cole, *Propaganda, Censorship and Irish Neutrality in the Second World War*, p. 155.
77. A. Slide, *The Cinema and Ireland* (Jefferson, NC and London: McFarland and Company, 1988), p. 28.
78. Cole, *Propaganda, Censorship and Irish Neutrality in the Second World War*, p. 152.
79. Hillier, *John Betjeman: New Fame, New Love*, p. 238.
80. Fisk, *In Time of War*, p. ix.
81. R. Foster, *Paddy and Mr Punch: Connections in Irish and English History* (London: Penguin, 1993), pp. 112–17.

82. Ibid., p. 117.
83. F. Delaney, *Betjeman Country* (London: Paladin, 1983), p. 81.
84. Fisk, *In Time of War*, p. 441.
85. Duggan, *Neutral Ireland and the Third Reich*, pp. 88–9.
86. *Guardian*, 22 April 2000.
87. D. O'Driscoll, 'Censorship as Propaganda: the Neutralisation of Irish Public Opinion during the Second World War', in B. Girvin and G. Roberts (eds), *Ireland and the Second World War: Politics, Society and Remembrance* (Dublin: Four Courts Press, 2000), p. 151.
88. Fisk, *In Time of War*, p. 162.
89. Slide, *The Cinema and Ireland*, pp. 15–16.
90. O'Driscoll, *Censorship in Ireland 1939–1945*, pp. 100–1.
91. Ibid., p. 64.
92. Ibid., p. 309.
93. Ibid., p. 310.
94. Fisk, *In Time of War*, p. 419.
95. O'Driscoll, *Censorship in Ireland 1939–1945*, p. 290.
96. Ibid., pp. 289–90.
97. Ibid., p. 186.
98. T. Gray, *The Lost Years: the Emergency in Ireland 1939–45* (London: Little, Brown and Co., 1997), p. 92.
99. Coogan, *De Valera: Long Fellow, Long Shadow*, p. 574.
100. T. Gray, *Mr Smyllie, Sir* (Dublin: Gill and Macmillan, 1991), pp. 153–4.
101. Ibid.
102. Gray, *The Lost Years*, p. 158.
103. O'Driscoll, *Censorship in Ireland 1939–1945*, pp. 171–4.
104. Ibid., pp. 181–3.
105. Gray, *The Lost Years*, p. 163.
106. Ibid., pp. 163–4.
107. P. Addison, *Churchill on the Home Front 1900-1955* (London: Jonathan Cape, 1992), p. 350.
108. O'Driscoll, *Censorship in Ireland 1939–1945*, pp. 191–2.
109. Ibid., p. 192.
110. Ibid., pp. 196–8.
111. Ibid.
112. T. Ryle Dwyer, *Strained Relations: Ireland at Peace and the USA at War 1941–45* (Dublin: Gill and Macmillan, 1988), pp. 48–9.
113. Ibid., p. 57.
114. Wills, *That Neutral Island*, pp. 217–19.
115. O'Driscoll, *Censorship in Ireland 1939–1945*, p. 53.
116. Gray, *The Lost Years*, pp. 201–12; also Keogh, *Twentieth–Century Ireland: Nation and State*, pp. 143–6.
117. M. Adams, *Censorship: the Irish Experience* (Tuscaloosa: University of Alabama Press, 1968), pp. 24–68.
118. Wills, *That Neutral Island*, p. 293.
119. *Irish Times*, 8 May 1945.
120. O'Driscoll, *Censorship in Ireland 1939–1945*, pp. 148–9.
121. Gray, *Mr Smyllie, Sir*, p. 156.
122. Gray, *The Lost Years*, pp. 234–5.
123. Wills, *That Neutral Island*, pp. 398–403.
124. F. S. L. Lyons, *Ireland Since the Famine* (London: Weidenfeld and Nicolson, 1971), pp. 557–8

5

Fanatic Hearts: The IRA, 1939–45

Soldiers of liberty! Legion of the Rearguard. The Republic can no longer be defended successfully by your force of arms. Further sacrifice of life would now be in vain, and continuation of the struggle in arms unwise in the National Interest. Military victory must be allowed to rest for the moment with those who have destroyed the Republic. Other means must be sought to safeguard the nation's right.[1]

When Éamon de Valera issued this message to the anti-treaty IRA, the Irish civil war, bloodier and more brutal than the struggle against the Crown forces, was already over and, almost a year earlier Frank Aiken, the IRA's Chief of Staff, had called upon the organisation to 'dump arms'.

This was not an act of surrender but one of defiance. It carried with it no acceptance of defeat and certainly no recognition of the Free State, whose leaders saw little reason for magnanimity to a defeated but still dangerous enemy. Kevin O'Higgins, Minister of Home Affairs, declared that there was no reason 'to settle for a draw with a replay in the autumn',[2] and raids and arrests of suspected anti-treaty activists, who often used their weapons against state forces, continued through 1923 and into the following year. There was no disarming or, in the language of the 1990s, 'de-commissioning' of weapons.

Anti-treaty sentiment and support for the IRA remained strong and registered itself in the August 1923 Dáil elections. Sinn Féin, still reeling from arrests and internment and with only a skeletal campaign organisation, managed to poll 286,000 votes against the 409,000 mobilised by Cumann na nGaedhal, the governing party. The IRA regrouped late in 1925 and restated its goal of a thirty-two county republic as well as its right to use armed struggle to attain it. It continued intermittent attacks on the new Garda Síochána, or police, and on 10 July 1927 three of its gunmen took an unforeseen chance to kill Kevin O'Higgins in what has been described as an act of 'hate filled rage'[3] for the executions he had sanctioned as a Free State minister.

De Valera was quick to condemn this killing and had already begun the process of creating a politically safe distance between himself and the IRA. In May 1926 he took a key role in the formation of Fianna Fáil (Soldiers of Destiny) as a non-violent republican alternative to Sinn Féin whom it eclipsed in the June 1927 Dáil elections, winning 26.1 per cent of the vote and forty-four seats. Sinn Féin could take only 3.6 per cent and five seats. Both parties remained abstentionist in their attitude to the Free State's legislature, viewing it as a body contaminated by its continued constitutional relationship to the Crown, but de Valera dramatically widened the gulf between himself and Sinn Féin and the IRA by leading his new party into the Dáil shortly after the O'Higgins murder.

The new party remained deeply suspect in the minds of opponents who blamed its leader for precipitating civil war only five years before. The IRA had not surrendered any weapons, and de Valera was blamed for seeming to endorse this. Some of his close allies made provocative remarks on this issue. Seán Lemass, later to be a Taoiseach, made a speech, not long after the O'Higgins assassination, in which he seemed to equate the IRA's weapons with those of the state's own forces.[4]

The Free State remained a cold house for militant republicans. Coercive legislation against them impeded ordinary political activity, and Sinn Féin was pushed to the margins of electoral support by the success of Fianna Fáil. The IRA, too, lost ground with its active membership falling rapidly, though it may still have numbered around 5,000 by the end of 1926.[5] When de Valera formed a Fianna Fáil government in March 1932, one of his first acts was to announce the release of IRA prisoners. This was a necessary act of defiance by him after a vicious election campaign in which the government party had made the most of what it claimed were his continued links to the IRA.

By 1932 these links had loosened sufficiently to give de Valera in office the freedom of action he needed but, on the issue of IRA prisoners, he did act consistently with his own condemnation of the previous government's security legislation. For its part, the IRA took a guarded view of de Valera in power, suspecting that he and his ministers would favour republican rhetoric over real action to advance the cause. As a vocal element within its ranks pressed for action on class issues, the leadership sanctioned headline grab- bing actions such as the 1932 boycott of British-made Bass ale. Pubs which sold it were raided and threatened, delivery lorries hijacked at gunpoint, and *An Phoblacht*, the Sinn Féin newspaper, put the campaign in a larger context: 'No British ales. No British sweets or chocolates. Shoulder to shoulder for a nationwide boycott of British goods. Fling back the challenge of the Robber Empire.'[6]

The IRA's continuing capacity for violence was also shown in street battles with O'Duffy's Blueshirt movement and in 1935 during a bitter public transport strike in Dublin, IRA men opened fire on police as well as on troops whom the IRA accused of protecting vehicles driven by strike-breakers. De Valera still held back from acting although, in May 1934, he had authorised the arrest and trial on arms charges of Tom Barry, a legendary hero of the West Cork IRA during the War of Independence.[7] The IRA leadership reacted angrily to this and to de Valera's reiterated warnings to it of tougher measures.

Their cause, they insisted, had a higher legitimacy than that of the new Irish state.

> The Cosgrave government ignored this issue and came into conflict with republican Ireland. The present Free State government had embarked on the same policy and it too would have to wade through the blood of republicans if it persisted in its efforts to impose Free State institutions on republicans.[8]

A week later the freedom the IRA still had was apparent when a memorial tower, 60 feet (18m) high on a hillside near Clonmel in County Cork, was raised in honour of Liam Lynch, an anti-treaty militant killed by Free State forces in April 1923.

Thousands of supporters were addressed by Maurice Twomey, an IRA Army Council member who was on the run from the police. According to one press report,

> when he came forward to speak there was not a policeman to be seen. Indeed the most remarkable feature of the day was the entire absence of police uniform in Clonmel. The IRA directed long

streams of traffic and all along the routes to the memorial, members of the IRA were on point duty.[9]

De Valera's unease at this and other exercises in IRA defiance of the state was offset by his concern at events north of the border. In 1935, a tense summer in Belfast culminated in large-scale communal violence after shots were fired at Orangemen and Loyalist bandsmen on the north side of the city. Eleven people, mostly Protestants, were killed and almost six hundred injured. More than three hundred residents had to flee from their homes and, although the British army re-appeared on the streets, so too did IRA units, using the Thompson sub-machine gun for the first time in Belfast. One account claims they 'played a vital part in the defence of vulnerable Catholic areas'.[10]

The IRA had maintained more of a military structure north of the border than in the Irish state, and de Valera and his ministers were certainly more sympathetic to its presence there than on their own doorstep, even at one point drawing on a secret service fund to pay for the legal defence of a northern republican who went on trial during this period.[11]

Ulster Unionists were quick to blame the violence of 1935 on the IRA and showed no more inclination to support an inquiry into its deeper-seated causes than did the government in London. This was despite calls for such an inquiry by the National Council for Civil Liberties and by Labour and Liberal members at Westminster.[12] The Stormont government's response was to toughen up its surveillance of all republican activity. This is apparent from a set of meticulously compiled RUC notes on hundreds of activists which only came to light by chance in the year 2005.[13] Stormont also used its powers to ban any Easter 1916 commemoration at Belfast's Milltown cemetery in April 1936, and a week later police raided premises in the city's Crown Entry, arresting thirteen leading members of the northern IRA who were attending a court martial there.[14]

This coup by the Unionist authorities came at a moment when de Valera's hand was about to be forced by the murder, in late March 1936, of Vice Admiral Somerville (see Chapter 2). The IRA unit involved may have exceeded their orders in killing the victim but their act unleashed shock waves which the state could not ignore. The killers were never caught though their identities were finally revealed in a compelling piece of investigative family history by Joseph O'Neill.[15]

This event, and the subsequent killing of an alleged IRA informer near Waterford, led the Dublin government to authorise a series of arrests and trials of IRA suspects before the state's Military Tribunal and, in June, the new Minister of Justice served notice in the Dáil on the IRA that it would soon be declared an illegal organisation because of its claims 'to have the power of life and death over its members or ex-members and other citizen' as well as its belief 'that it is entitled to use force upon the community to compel obedience to its will'.[16] In June the IRA was proscribed and its chief of staff, Maurice, or Moss, Twomey, sentenced by a military tribunal to three years' imprisonment for membership of it.

For de Valera this was truly the parting of the ways, and an act that secured him his place in the demonology of paramilitary Irish republicanism. It was also a decision made by him at a time of significant ideological division within the republican movement. One clear manifestation of this was the formation in 1931 of Saor Éire, an offshoot of the IRA, which called in its literature for a revolutionary republican leadership to unite workers and small farmers in a fight to destroy British imperialism and its Irish capitalist ally. Peadar O'Donnell, an influential radical republican activist and writer, was the driving force behind the new body, and the 1931 IRA Army Convention gave it guarded support on the ground that an alternative to Fianna Fáil was needed. Saor Éire was denounced by the Cosgrave government and declared by it to be an illegal body within only a few months of its formation.

Irish communists supported Saor Éire but with the avowed purpose of undermining it as a perceived threat to the Communist Party of Ireland which was affiliated to the Soviet-controlled Third International.[17] For its part, the IRA was alarmed by reports of its members being attracted to communism, and its army council reaffirmed a standing order preventing members from joining the party and condemned communism for its 'denial of God and active hostility to religion'.[18] This was in mid-1933, by which time Saor Éire had lost any impact that it had had but, a year later, a left-leaning element still within the IRA joined former Saor Éire supporters in calling for a new republican congress to pursue a broadly similar agenda. At its 1934 army convention, the IRA narrowly defeated a resolution commending this new initiative, prompting a substantial number of delegates to leave the convention in order to support the congress.

The army council had already condemned factionalism, branding likely congress supporters as 'deserters who will enter Leinster House',[19] where the Dáil met, and ordered the court martial of O'Donnell and George Gilmore, another articulate supporter of republicans following a socialist road. They ignored this disciplinary threat, O'Donnell later writing defiantly in the organisation's paper *An Phoblacht* that 'we were sentenced in our absence and hoped to be executed in our absence as well'.[20]

The congress met in Athlone and delivered a call to action which it hoped would unite republicans with all who were involved in class struggle on both sides of the border. One historian of Irish communism has called it 'the most representative gathering of the working class and militants seen in Ireland'.[21] It may well have been but it had little more real success than Saor Éire. Divisions developed rapidly over whether the priority of the national question might be compromised by the pursuit of class issues, while communists would think of the congress only as a united front rather than a new party.[22]

While it lasted, the congress attracted many restless spirits, such as Frank Ryan from County Limerick, 'a schoolboy Spartacus',[23] who had fought in the independence struggle and then with the anti-treaty IRA against the new Free State. As the brave cause of republican Spain began to beckon, he came to see the congress as a political cul-de-sac, and his biographer has put it that, by 1936, 'it seemed that 'all that was left to do was to put the Republican Congress out of its misery',[24] adding that the lack of real leadership left nobody to administer the *coup de grâce*.

Even as the congress foundered, the tensions it had created remained. In Easter 1936 the IRA's Dublin commemoration of the 1916 rising was marred by violent clashes between Communist Party of Ireland and congress contingents and those who disputed their right to be present at all. Divisions like these played worst of all in Irish America where Clann na Gael, a vital source of funds and political support for the IRA, opposed any leftward drift within the movement and felt that the breach with de Valera should be healed. The collapse of the congress restored the clann's political faith in the IRA but its leader, Joseph McGarrity, remained wary of rebuilding its financial support base to where it had been prior to the split.

McGarrity was a militarist with little capacity to look beyond republicanism's physical force tradition, and he had support from within the IRA's membership in Ireland. Tom Barry and Seán Russell were true keepers of the republican flame but, for Barry, the militarist tradition could best be honoured by attacks across the border, especially after the communal violence of 1935 and the complacent response to it by the Stormont and London governments. For their part the Northern IRA were desperate for a show of support from across the border but Barry's plans for providing this did not match the organisation's resources. In May 1937, however, to coincide with the coronation of King George VI, he did co-ordinate operations to destroy twenty British customs posts along the border.

Barry and Frank Ryan also led an anti-coronation rally in Dublin which was broken up after bloody clashes with the police. Barry's position as chief of staff was compromised by the IRA's failure to launch major cross-border operations, and he resigned at a time when de Valera and Fianna Fáil were pressing ahead with an agenda which they claimed was in keeping with many republican aspirations, short of actual unification. Barry's departure simply left the issue of IRA strategy on hold as often acrimonious debate over it continued. In April 1938, the same month in which de Valera was able to present the people of Éire with what he claimed was victory on the issue of the Treaty Ports, as well as the economic war with Britain, the IRA held another full army convention at which a new army council appointed Seán Russell as chief of staff.

Russell had come round to the case for a bombing campaign in Britain but, according to Irish army intelligence sources, there was only a small majority for it in the army convention. These sources also believed that Barry's doubts were shared by his German contacts who wanted an IRA offensive in Britain only when war between it and Germany had started. Barry, the intelligence people believed, saw attacks across the border as a way of triggering a rising there 'after the style of Easter Week 1916 in Dublin' which would focus world attention on the issue of partition but the 'Belfast men' were not convinced and wanted England to be hit first.[25] Russell won the argument and was admired by many in the IRA for the consistency of his militarism as well as for having no personal vices.

In a gesture heavy with symbolism, Russell then put it to the army council that they seek the backing of surviving members of the 1921 Second Dáil, a body whose republican legitimacy was, in his eyes, unsullied by any compromises. Their imprimatur was secured in December 1938 and, by then, the IRA was on a war footing. Jim O'Donovan, an experienced bomb-maker, and Dominic Adams, uncle of a more famous successor in the IRA, drew up what they called the S-Plan. This called for attacks calculated to disrupt British economic life and to hit prestige targets. There were also to be limited operations in Northern Ireland. Civilians, the plan stated, were not targets but were, of course, the inevitable victims, just as they would be in vastly greater numbers thirty years later when another IRA bombing campaign started in Belfast. O'Donovan is said to have conceived his plan while a prisoner during the Irish civil war as a way to reunite a divided movement.

The S-Plan was a dramatic departure from republican thinking, dating back to Wolfe Tone and the United Irishmen, which was rooted in the belief that any bid for Irish freedom had to be based on a reading of the international situation and the commitments it might require of Britain. Two years later Russell did form serious contacts with Nazi Germany but, in 1938, he was influenced by the siren voice of the Irish diaspora, or at least a politically myopic element within it. As J. Bowyer Bell has put it,

> Russell had come back from America determined to strike out and no-one high or low had produced a decent alternative. Whether or not the campaign was technically feasible, it was emotionally desirable. Russell and the Army Council were far from mad but they were angry. Despair, drift and delay had at last been put aside. If the odds were steep, so they had always been.[26]

On 12 January 1939, the IRA's army council wrote to the British Foreign Office demanding a final military withdrawal from Ireland and, three days later, copies of a proclamation were distributed across Éire invoking the memory of the unfinished business embarked upon by the men and women of Easter 1916. It may have been drafted by McGarrity in the United States but it bore the signatures of Russell and members of the army council. The next day, bomb attacks on electricity power stations were carried out across England, and the day after that, 17 January, the first civilian victim was killed in Manchester.

The IRA had its arms dumps, couriers, intelligence officers and safe houses in places throughout Ireland and Britain. Bomb teams had been trained, and Maurice Twomey, released from prison after his sentencing in Belfast in 1936, had undertaken a tour of inspection in England and Scotland in late 1938 to make sure that the 'army' was on a war footing. What support they really had within the Irish community in Britain is another matter. Volunteers who had gone across to implement the bombing campaign were told to keep clear of the organisation and to live on their own in rented property for security's sake. Activists within the immigrant community who had been in sympathy with Saor Éire and the Republican Congress deplored the bombings: for example, Frank Ryan who, in January 1939, was a prisoner of General Franco in Burgos with an uncertain future as the new regime's firing squads went to work around him.

A fellow prisoner later recalled Ryan's view that those who had ordered the bombings were 'irresponsible political lunatics who were doing the maximum damage to the Irish republic and the future unity of the whole of Ireland' and that they would 'alienate British public opinion against all Irish people'.[27] This was also Tom Barry's view, and the campaign certainly set back attempts to organise the Irish community politically, something admitted by Desmond Greaves, who had been working to create in embryonic form what later became the Connolly Association.[28]

The IRA's 'declaration of war' on Britain led to over two hundred bomb attacks which caused a total of seven civilian deaths. Ninety IRA members were arrested and sentenced to a total of six hundred years' imprisonment. Three of them died in prison and two were executed. They were Peter Barnes and James MacCormick who were hanged in February 1940 for their part in an attack in Coventry on 25 August 1939. A bomb left in a busy shopping centre killed five people and seventy more were injured, some severely, from flying glass and metal. The city would experience infinitely worse carnage just over a year later but, in a country not yet at war, this atrocity caused a wave of anger and revulsion.

The bomb had been intended for use against a power station on the edge of the city and may have been abandoned in panic. A third suspect was never caught and, within Irish republican circles, it is still claimed that Barnes and MacCormick were wrongly convicted. On the day of their execution, Brendan Behan, a Dublin-born teenage IRA volunteer, was about to stand trial for his part in the bombing campaign. The hangings were scheduled for 9 a.m. and Behan, handcuffed to a prison officer, was driven to court in Liverpool in a prison van.

He could glimpse newspaper boards on the pavement proclaiming 'Irish murderers to die'. The moment drew closer as his journey continued:

A church bell rang out a little later. They are beginning to die now, I said to myself. As it chimed the hour, I bent my forehead to my handcuffed right hand and made the sign of the Cross by moving my head and chest along my outstretched fingers. It was the best I could do. The screw who was handcuffed to me on my right looked at me and I looked back at him. If he was going to say anything, he changed his mind and we both looked ahead of us again, towards the windscreen.[29]

Because of his age, Behan was sentenced to only three years, to be served in a young offenders' institution, or borstal as it was then called. He refused to recognise the court and delivered a barnstorming oration before he was taken down. He later wrote:

> The world would know that my two comrades now lying in the clay this few hours past were not so soon forgotten. Thousands had marched in mourning all over Ireland and in the United States, but I was the only one privileged to stand up for these humble men openly and defiantly in the midst of our enemies – great as they were with their money, their Army, Navy and Air Force, their lions, unicorns and ermine robes to hide their hangman's overalls.[30]

De Valera and his old opponent Cosgrave in fact worked hard to impress upon London the case for leniency after the verdicts in the Coventry case. They used their access to Sir John Maffey in Dublin to put their view, stretching his patience in the process. He passed on their case for clemency to the Cabinet in London which was mindful of the likely reaction of Irish Americans if the hangings went ahead. The evidence in the trial had, however, shown that Barnes and MacCormick had smuggled into England the explosives used in Coventry and had assembled the device itself even if they had not intended to detonate it where it went off.

Much of Ireland had indeed gone into mourning for Barnes and MacCormick. Flags flew at half mast in Éire, many shops and businesses closed; special Masses were held in most churches and many sports events were cancelled.[31] This high emotion masked the failure of a bombing campaign in which many operatives were inexperienced and poorly trained. Brendan Behan was arrested soon after he arrived in Liverpool with what he called his 'Sinn Féin conjuror's outfit'[32] of gelignite and detonators in his suitcase:

> Friday in the evening, the landlady shouted up the stairs 'Oh God, oh Jesus, oh Sacred heart. Boy, there's two gentlemen to see you.' I knew by the screeches of her that these two gentlemen were not calling to inquire after my health, or to know if I had had a good trip.[33]

Many operations carried out by IRA units in Britain were improvised and, because of communication problems, carried out with little reference to the original S-Plan. A degree of disruption of ordinary life was achieved as police had to search letter boxes, railway stations and telephone kiosks but the result for the Irish community was a heavy burden of intensified police raids on their homes. Severe sentences on convicted IRA suspects became the norm and, in July 1939, special legislation provided for the screening of all arrivals from Ireland, registration of Irish residents, deportation of suspects and extended powers of detention. Volunteers' morale suffered badly as the Irish state began to use its special powers, on 9 September arresting most of the IRA's general headquarters staff in Dublin. This crippled the campaign which was effectively over by the time Brendan Behan made his court speech.

Behan rejoined the IRA on returning to Dublin after the completion of his sentence. His time in borstal was a formative period for him because he made warm relationships with many working-class English boys serving their sentences for strictly non-political crimes. He later wrote with affection about them but with ridicule of a puritanical Belfast IRA man who visited Behan to warn him against the moral laxity and foul language of fellow prisoners who had become his friends.[34] By the time his borstal memoirs were published in 1958, he had radically re-examined the beliefs that had taken him to England as a teenage bomber twenty years earlier.

In Éire itself, the IRA's offensive capacity was initially blunted by arrests, coercive legislation and heavy police surveillance but, in October 1939, one of its Dublin units managed to infiltrate explosives into Mountjoy prison. A large bomb was then detonated against the prison's outer wall in an unsuccessful attempt to enable the arrested GHQ staff members to escape. Plans for a second bid to free these prisoners were abandoned in favour of other operations, These culminated in the huge propaganda success of the Magazine Fort raid on 23 December 1939, although the arms and ammunition taken were quickly recaptured by state forces.

The state forces had to remain on high alert, as Patrick Campbell found out during his period of service with the Dublin Port Control unit. Not all of this was spent out in Dublin Bay and, in the course of 1940, he found himself guarding a cargo shed at the far end of the North Wall where the River Liffey joins the sea. He was told by an army sergeant to set up barbed wire and sandbags outside the shed but queried whether this would deter the German navy if it arrived. 'To hell with the German navy,' the sergeant replied. 'It's the IRA I'm worried about. I've got thirty-three rifles and three thousand rounds of ammo in there.'[35] To Campbell, this seemed ominous proof that the state's forces were 'more concerned about our ability to defend our weapons against raids by fellow Irishmen than to defend the Republic against the invader'.[36]

Such fear of the IRA was justified in the first winter of the war, and de Valera himself had reason by the end of 1939 to regret his decision to release IRA prisoners who had started a hunger strike in November. One of these was Patrick McGrath, the IRA's chief operations officer, who had played a key role in the independence struggle and still carried a British bullet in his body. He was never, as events would soon prove, going to repay the leniency of the state by giving even tacit allegiance to it, and his release and that of his fellow hunger strikers was soon followed by the Magazine Fort Raid.

More arrests followed the raid and seven prisoners began a new hunger strike in protest against the government's Offences Against the State (Amendment) Bill. Two men, Tony D'Arcy and Jack McNeela, died on this protest in Mountjoy prison before the IRA called it off. One prisoner, Michael Traynor, survived the protest but only just. 'Our beds,' he later recalled,

> were fibre mattresses with a spring upon an iron bed. After a while, we had to have all our joints bandaged because they were only skin and bone and bedsores or gangrene would have set in easily. After a bit, I remember, I couldn't even turn in the bed without help. We had to be rubbed down each day with olive oil to prevent the bedsores. I could smell death off myself, a sickly nauseating stench.[37]

The macabre theatre of prison protest would repeat itself but on the outside the IRA fought on, increasingly targeting members of the Garda. On 2 January 1940, Thomas MacCurtain, son of the Lord Mayor of Cork murdered by Crown forces in 1920, shot dead a detective while resisting arrest. His death sentence was commuted to life imprisonment but others were less fortunate. Patrick McGrath, the recently released hunger striker, and Thomas Harte were found guilty by a military court of killing another detective during a house raid in Dublin. Their appeal was rejected and they entered republican song and legend from Mountjoy's scaffold on 6 September 1940. An IRA order for cinemas to close in respect for the memory of McGrath and Harte was, however, widely ignored, a major indication that the organisation's already limited support base was starting to crumble.[38]

This process was accelerated by a sequence of disastrous events for the IRA in 1941. Unrest at the organisation's failure to achieve more militarily began to be voiced within the ranks, especially in Northern Ireland where, by September 1939, there existed a stronger unit structure than elsewhere in Ireland. Unrest developed into suspicion which focused on Stephen Hayes, Russell's successor as chief of staff. Hayes, who had been promoted within the IRA by Russell himself, lacked his austere authority. He came from Wexford, where he had excelled in Gaelic football, but was also thought of as a heavy drinker.

On 30 June 1941, Hayes's enemies moved against him, abducting him at a routine IRA meeting he was due to attend in Dublin. He was held by his captors for a two-month period during which they beat out of him a confession to having informed the Éire government of IRA operations. His chief prosecutor was Seán McCaughey, from Ardoyne in North Belfast, and predictably Hayes was found guilty and sentenced to death. He was able to buy time, however, by persuading the court martial to let him embellish the already lengthy and improbable confession he had signed. This, it has been rightly said, 'would not have disgraced a Stalinist show trial'.[39]

When Hayes escaped, his first move was to seek the protection of the despised Garda and make known to them and to the press his treatment. The IRA's credibility, even among those sympathetic to it, never fully recovered. Hayes had not been a traitor and was later convicted for IRA offences but the whole bizarre and brutal episode consumed IRA energies for many months. His more likely offence, as he later told Tim Pat Coogan, was to have tried to spell out to activists the clear limits to what armed action against the state could achieve, given the build-up of its forces and its formidable armoury of emergency powers.[40]

After 1941, IRA activity was no more than intermittent but it could still be lethal, as in September 1942 when they carried out the well-planned killing of a Garda Special Branch sergeant, Denis O'Brien, in Dublin. Their victim had an uncompromising track record against the IRA but there were no political gains for republicanism in a cold-blooded execution in the presence of the victim's wife. Another Special Branch officer was shot dead during the intensive search operations which followed the O'Brien killing.

Charlie Kerins, who succeeded Hayes as chief of staff, was eventually convicted of O'Brien's murder and executed in 1944. For some of his time on the run he stayed, under the assumed name of Pat Carney, in the Waterford home of the writer Dervla Murphy who was then twelve years old. Her parents were not IRA supporters though her father's sister was, and she was staying with them at the time. Thinking later of how her parents had handled this crisis, she wrote: 'From their point of view an awkward situation was being compounded by the need to impress on me that giving refuge to "Pat" did not mean condoning his crime.'[41] In any event, neither of them betrayed their fugitive and armed guest who was always polite and considerate to them and their daughter. Kerins was later arrested in Dublin and, prior to his execution, he sent Dervla a note of gratitude for her company while he was in hiding with her family, with a silver ring as a parting present.

'With him died the last fragile symbol of IRA continuity,' one history of the organisation has claimed of the execution of Charlie Kerins:

> For the first time in generations the line had been broken. There was no longer a Chief of Staff or a GHQ or an Army Council or even an IRA. The prisons and the camps held those who would not quit but few of these men looked forward to more than their own freedom and the chance to lead quiet private lives.[42]

It was premature to write off the IRA but it had lost much of its active nucleus to arrests and internment. Brendan Behan finished the war in the Curragh, in his case as a convicted prisoner, having rejoined the organisation after completing his sentence in England. His account of the Dublin IRA in the later part of the war shows that at least it still clung to its rituals of commemoration. At a 1942 Dublin rally to honour the rebels of 1916, he recalled 2,000 people being present '. . . not all of them active members of the IRA. Some of them were indeed British soldiers on leave but in mufti.'[43] Mufti, or civilian clothes, was a requirement for all Irish members of the British forces while on home leave.

Around 2,000 republicans and IRA members were interned during the Emergency, most of them in the Curragh camp, a dismal complex of identical wooden huts behind quadruple lines of barbed wire. One new arrival remembered long afterwards as he arrived and took in 'the dead, drab look of the place'.[44] The huts were heated with turf stoves but could still be damp and cold in winter while sometimes suffocatingly hot in summer. Surveillance by guards was intense and the food was poor, though perhaps much the same as that of the Irish defence forces, and tension could easily build up, as it did in December 1940 over a reduction in the butter ration. Huts and bedding were set on fire and one internee was shot dead during violent clashes with the army.

Internecine IRA tensions were a reality the internees lived with, especially as a result of the fallout from the court martial of Stephen

Hayes. Eventually a majority of internees took the official IRA line on this, many influenced by Pearse Kelly who became and remained officer commanding in the camp for much of his five years there and proved effective at representing the interests of the men. He was able to secure an end to physical punishment of internees by military police, increased fuel allowances and facilities for education, camp concerts and Gaelic sports.

Education courses were a success in the Curragh as in the 'university of Long Kesh' thirty years later, but they became an issue with the arrival in the camp of Niall Gould, a communist who had settled in the Soviet Union in 1932 and had declared his support for the Republican Congress. A son of the Anglo-Irish gentry and educated at Cheltenham College and London University, Gould was an accomplished linguist and a gifted teacher. He went beyond giving courses on Russian to offering classes on Marxism–Leninism which rekindled some of the tension which had divided republicanism in the 1930s. Kelly used his position as camp OC to communicate in secret with Joseph Keogh, Bishop of Kildare and Leitrim, whose diocese included the Curragh.

Kelly's claims that Gould's teaching posed a threat to faith and morals in the camp met with a prompt response. The bishop informed the prison authorities and, within three days, Gould was transferred to Mountjoy in Dublin and released in 1943.[45] Prison was thought of by many internees as a preferable option to the regime of the military police at the Curragh but the concern of a state wary of offending the Church was to create a safe distance between Gould's alleged influence and the biggest single concentration of internees.

German prisoners, mostly Luftwaffe aircrew who had crashed on Irish soil, were also housed in a separate part of the Curragh complex. Their presence and its implications appear to have impinged very little on IRA internees during their time there, any more than did that of a limited number of British and Canadian aircrew. Like the Germans, they enjoyed paroles and other privileges which put them in quite a separate category from republican inmates of the Curragh.[46]

Close to the war's end Brendan Behan, who was classified as a hard-core convicted prisoner with no immediate prospect of amnesty, recalled being handcuffed and chained to other prisoners prior to being moved to a different part of the camp. Their route took them close enough to German and Canadian internees for both groups to jeer at them. One German tried to attack the IRA internees but was restrained by army guards. 'The reason they attacked us, I suppose,' Behan reflected, 'was that the Canadians believed we were neutral or in favour of the Germans and the Germans believed we were neutral or in favour of the Allies, whereas in actual fact we were in favour of one side only: that was our own.'[47]

This preoccupation with 'our side' or even 'ourselves alone', amid huge global events which dwarfed the issue of the Irish border and the six counties, was well captured in Behan's admission that 'As a rule I didn't take much interest in what British fughing convoy was going where or how the Allied armies were stretching themselves in occupied territory.'[48] Hitler's suicide on 30 April 1945 was greeted with cheers by internees and prisoners when the news reached the Curragh, not just by left-wing republicans who had fought in Spain but by the much larger number who simply hoped it would hasten their release.[49]

The moral myopia of so many Irish republicans of this era could simply take the form of apparent indifference to dramatic and historic events beyond Éire's borders. Ernie O'Malley, a writer of enormous talent, had been an IRA divisional commander in 1921 and took the anti-treaty side in the civil war but later left the organisation. When war came in 1939, he did join the Local Security Force but he concentrated his energies on managing a farm in Mayo and on expanding his art collection. He kept up his Dublin literary contacts, but a recent study suggests that events in Europe simply passed him by and that he had little or nothing to say about them.[50]

Others saw the armed struggle within a context of suffocating self-righteousness, such as the Belfast IRA man whom Brendan Behan encountered while serving his first sentence in England. In spring 1940, Josephine Plunkett protested to Cardinal MacRory that her son Joseph, whose father had been executed in 1916, might find himself as a prisoner in Mountjoy alongside 'sexual degenerates'.[51] The matter was brought to de Valera's notice, and assurances were provided that there was effective segregation of republican prisoners and no moral danger to them from Dublin's underclass.[52]

Twenty-six IRA men went to their deaths in the Emergency years on both sides of the border and as a result of the 1939–40 bombing campaign in England. One of modern Ireland's finest historians, Joseph Lee, has made the point that the Irish state itself glorified a tradition of insurrectionist violence, as did its school syllabus, and that these mostly young volunteers who died on hunger strike, on the gallows or in gun battles with state forces, 'could not unreasonably claim to be the logical products of the official political culture which now sought to suppress them'.[53]

'Forties men', as IRA volunteers of this period are sometimes called in republican circles, are invested with heroic attributes by the movement's hagiography. Offsetting such claims is the fact that, among their number, were those who refused to see any moral imperative in the need to destroy the Third Reich and its monstrous tyranny across Europe. Some, indeed, were resourceful in their apologetics for Hitler's regime and prepared to work both with it and for it.

One of them, Seán Russell, IRA chief of staff at the time of his arrival in Berlin in the summer of 1940, now has a statue in his honour in Fairview Park in North Dublin. It was installed there by the republican movement. Today's Irish state, it has been said, must be the only one in the European Union to accept the presence of a public memorial to a man who showed himself to be indifferent to Nazi Germany's brutality and to its aggression in Europe and who would have worked with it had it invaded and occupied his own country.[54] Sinn Féin luminaries, such as Mary Lou McDonald, now one of its MEPs, have addressed commemorative events beside Russell's statue but, at the start of January 2005, it was attacked and the head knocked off and removed. The unnamed group responsible later gave a statement to the press saying that their action had been in honour of all Holocaust victims and also to 'banish Seán Russell into the dustbin of history'.[55]

In the summer of 1940 Nazi Germany was planning to invade Britain and had already waged war on five neutral states. Its brutality, particularly in Poland, was becoming known to the world. None of this deterred Seán Russell from accepting the status of an honoured guest in Berlin and enjoying every privilege accorded him: a comfortable villa and a chauffeur-driven car were all part of the package. So, too, was access to a high-security German army base where he was given training to update his skills in sabotage and guerrilla warfare. He also met leading Nazis, such as Edmund Veesenmayer, who specialised in preparing armed subversion in other countries and was also a brutal anti-Semite found guilty at Nuremberg of war crimes.

Russell's whereabouts at this stage were a mystery to Irish and British intelligence services though he had wanted German support for IRA operations for some time and hoped that plans for these would be incorporated within Operation Sea Lion, the code name for the German cross-Channel invasion. His contacts with Germany went back to 1936 and left-wing and anti-fascist republicans had condemned him for them. With the failure of Saor Éire and the Republican Congress many of them had left the movement. Others, such as Frank Ryan, went to fight for the Spanish republic without seeking the IRA's authorisation. For them it was a bitter pill to swallow when, in July 1940, the IRA leadership commended Hitler and Mussolini for the part they had played in securing a Roman Catholic regime in Spain.

Increasingly pro-German and anti-Semitic IRA 'War News' bulletins appear to have left Russell untroubled, and he was eager to co-operate with Veesenmayer and others in preparations for Operation Dove. This involved landing Russell by submarine in Ireland where he would activate IRA units in support of a German invasion when it came or in defence of the Treaty Ports should Churchill seek to retake them. According to legend, which seems to be all that it is, the signal for the IRA to act was to be the placing of a flowerpot on a windowsill of the German legation in Dublin's Northumberland Road. Apologists for Russell have claimed that he simply saw himself as a military man and he did declare to Colonel Lahausen of the *Abwehr*: 'I am not a Nazi. I'm not even pro-German. I am an Irish man fighting for the independence of Ireland.'[56]

Russell, of course, was guilty of the most crass and simplistic self-deception and, like many of his compatriots, gave no thought to what would have happened if the Third Reich had won the war and whether there was the remotest likelihood of it respecting the independence of a small and unaligned Irish state. He certainly gave even less thought to what the fate of Éire's 4,000 Jews would have been, or the fact that a victorious Germany would doubtless have demanded that they be handed over to them. He and other IRA men like him could well have ended up as active collaborators in a German occupation of their own country with all its brutal implications for Jews, anti-fascists, socialists and democrats.

To suggest that Russell occupied a moral vacuum in 1940 may even be to flatter him, given the high level of his contacts with a Nazi regime which thought the future belonged to it. His myopia was shared, however, by others not in the IRA who supported de Valera and held office under him. Conor Cruise O'Brien, who had joined the Irish foreign service, later described incisively the mindset of many of his contemporaries in this period: 'The idea that Nazism differed from all previously known forms of imperialism as AIDS differs from the common cold was quite a new idea and unassimilable within our culture.'[57]

In late July, Russell was joined in Berlin by Frank Ryan. Ryan's release from Spanish captivity into German hands had been arranged by Éire's minister in Madrid, Leopold Kerney, who was known for his republican sympathies. These had compromised his position in the foreign service earlier in his career but he was reinstated in 1932 when de Valera took office. He later claimed he had intervened on Ryan's behalf to secure residence for him in the United States.[58] In the event, agents for the Nazi state, with whom Ryan was ready to co-operate, spirited him safely into Germany and, despite the rigours of captivity in Franco's prisons, he was ready to join Russell in Operation Dove.

As the time for launching this plan approached Admiral Canaris, the *Abwehr*'s head, became increasingly doubtful about what it might achieve militarily. It was, however, driven forward by von Ribbentrop's ministry and by Veesenmayer at a time when the IRA's bombing campaign in Britain had lost any real momentum and when the organisation on both sides of the Irish border was being hit hard by arrests and internment.

Soon after the U-boat that was to take Russell and Ryan to Ireland set sail, Russell was taken ill with agonising stomach pains and died soon afterwards. He was buried at sea with appropriate German naval honours. Sixty years later files released by Britain's MI5 revealed that Lahausen, the *Abwehr* officer who had worked with Russell, had told his interrogators in prison after the war that he believed Ryan had poisoned Russell. This, he claimed, was because of their bitter disagreements over what political strategy the IRA and the republican movement should follow.[59] Little has emerged to substantiate this though Lahausen's testimony did emphasise the *Abwehr*'s doubts about the whole operation. Russell's death, it has been argued, may well have saved his *Abwehr* and Foreign Office handlers from an embarrassing failure, given his imprecise remit and the weakness of the IRA.[60]

His demise also created a dilemma for Ryan. He had to consider how old comrades on the republican left would view his arrival on Irish soil under Nazi auspices and what on his own he would be able to accomplish without Russell's senior IRA rank. Given the choice by the U-boat commander, he decided to return to Germany. Once safely back, he found that Veesenmayer wanted to maintain contact with him over the prospects of cross-border IRA operations and moves to bring down de Valera. Francis Stuart, the Irish writer who had settled in Berlin at the start of the war and who later broadcast from there to Ireland, was quick to appreciate Ryan's difficulties.

'Ryan was in a very ambiguous position,' Stuart told an interviewer in 1989. 'Starting off fighting for the International Brigade
and ending up as an adviser to the SS Colonel Veesenmayer, a Jew
exterminator.'[61] The precariousness of Ryan's role in wartime Berlin
in fact worsened despite the privileges bestowed upon him by the
regime, such as a free apartment and a diplomat's rations of food and
drink. In 1941 Stuart was struck by the incongruity of spending an
evening in a Berlin nightclub drinking champagne with Ryan and a
Nazi party member who was wearing the party's swastika badge.[62]

Ryan, it emerges from letters of his seen much later by Irish army
intelligence, was desperate to justify his own position. Writing in
December 1940 to Leopold Kerney, the Irish minister in Madrid who
had facilitated his transit to Germany, Ryan impressed upon him
that he should not feel responsible for any political consequences of
his move: 'I remain my own man,' he wrote. 'Nobody can make me do
anything I don't want to do.'[63] This, he stressed, had not happened,
and added: 'I have met only gentlemen.'[64] Perhaps he included
Edmund Veesenmayer in this category.

Ryan also began to feel guilty about his own comfortable circumstances in Berlin. In a letter which he attempted to post out of the city
to his sister Eilish in Ireland in late September 1941, he told her that
he knew of the worsening fuel and food situation there.

> Every time I stick a fistful of tea in the pot I think of your half
> ounce and wish I could send you some. I have spent the summer (5
> months) living in a lovely bungalow and now I'm packing up to go
> into a flat.[65]

A few weeks later, again writing to Kerney in Madrid thanking him
once more for his work in getting him released from captivity, Ryan
said of his status in Berlin: 'I am treated – not merely officially but
genuinely – as a distinguished guest'[66] and he went on to claim that,
as far as the German Reich was concerned, he was 'a non-party
neutral.'[67]

In fact, Ryan clung to the illusion shared by Seán Russell that a
victorious Germany would give more respect to Ireland's case for
national self-determination than it had done to the rights of the
countries it had already invaded and occupied.[68] To him, it has been
said, 'the devil Ireland did not know could be no greater enemy to
Irish unification than the devil it did'.[69] Ryan claimed increasingly to
detest Hitler's regime, especially after its onslaught on the Soviet
Union, even as he continued to enjoy all the privileges it gave him. He

had to be circumspect, however, about expressing such views as his fear grew of Gestapo surveillance, yet he could still fantasise about a German victory. Even as the *Abwehr* distanced itself from any further operations in Ireland, Francis Stuart claimed he had heard Ryan declaring that 'When Germany wins the war I will be a member of the Irish government.'[70] He was not alone in such fantasies. Jim O'Donovan, the bomb-maker who had masterminded the 1939 S-Plan, was later classified by Irish Army intelligence as 'someone who fancied himself as the future Irish Quisling or Fuhrer'.[71]

Ryan continued to be seen as a potentially useful pawn for both the *Abwehr* and the German Foreign Office though, in the Reich's often poorly co-ordinated intelligence and espionage war, these two bodies were capable of working at cross purposes to each other. Veesenmayer continued to press the case for using Ryan, missing no chance to stress his republican credentials and his supposed contacts with de Valera. In 1941 he drew up a plan for an operation, code named Sea Eagle, in which Ryan and other IRA men would be landed in Éire to operate with German backing. The plan was shown to Hitler himself at a conference in early September but no action on it was taken.[72]

Against his better judgement Ryan, homesick for Ireland, fearful of the Gestapo and under pressure to help the regime with broadcasts to Irish America, does seem to have envisaged a role for himself in an Irish Vichy. There were degrees of collaboration with the Nazi state during the Second World War, and Ryan's may have been akin to that of Subhas Chandra Bose, the founder of the Japanese-backed Indian National Army.[73] In the end, however. it has been said that his own 'useless culpability was borne in upon him'.[74]

One abortive German project Ryan allowed himself to be drawn into was the attempted recruitment to Hitler's cause of Irish soldiers in the British army who had become prisoners of war. Jupp Hoven, a German officer who had studied in pre-war Éire and made IRA contacts, was assigned the task of sounding out the loyalties of a group of more than a hundred Irish prisoners selected for transfer to Friesack, a special camp near Berlin. Hardly any among them were tempted to serve the Germans, thanks in large part to the authority and strong personality of their senior officer, Lieutentant Colonel John McGrath.

Essentially, McGrath strung along the Germans while keeping officers at his original camp informed of what Hoven and his agents were trying to do. Two prisoners from Friesack, however, did accept release to undertake special training with the German army as saboteurs and radio operators. One of them was John Codd who had served as a regular soldier and been wounded and captured in 1940. He was an accomplished, though self-taught, linguist who had impressed Hoven. Along with fellow prisoner Frank Stringer, he arrived in Berlin in the autumn of 1941 where hospitality was on offer from their compatriot Frank Ryan though, to them, he used the alias Frank Richards.

Codd had become an unpopular man at Friesack because of what were thought to be his pro-German views and, for a time, his life may have been at risk because of this. He might also simply have been an opportunist who had had enough of prison-camp life. Irish army intelligence officers, who reported on his case after he returned to Ireland, were unsure about him. 'Whether he was genuinely pro-German is subject to doubt but his fellow prisoners regarded him in that light,'[75] they noted. Codd went on to undergo extensive training with the *Wehrmacht* for unspecified missions but, in the end, was never assigned to any of them. In part, this was because of his drinking and his affairs with women which made him a liability both to Ryan and to his German handlers.

His fellow prisoner, Stringer, and another Irishman, James Brady, who also accepted release from Friesack, ended up, with some reluctance, training with the Waffen SS and took part in some of its final operations late on in the war. Their story has now been told very fully, along with that of Codd.[76] After the war, both Stringer and Brady had to face trial by court martial and were given heavy sentences for treason, though these were later reduced. Codd was more fortunate and more resourceful. Passing himself off as a French prisoner of war married to a German woman, in 1945, he made his way back to Dublin via France. Once there, he made a voluntary statement to Irish army intelligence about his wartime role. This was received with some scepticism though it has been kept on file.[77]

The whole episode alarmed Ryan and heightened his concern that his whereabouts might become known beyond his immediate family in Ireland and Kerney in Madrid with whom he continued to correspond.[78] One particular visit he made to Friesack upset him when he was recognised and greeted by name by some of the Irish prisoners. The last thing he wanted was attention to be drawn to his presence in Berlin or for it to be used by British propaganda to smear the republican cause.

Ryan's health had deteriorated rapidly during his time in Germany, and he died alone in a Dresden hospital in June 1944, though Francis Stuart and a few German friends were there for his burial.

Many more attended his reinterment in Dublin's Glasnevin cemetery in 1979, a ceremony carried out with full republican honours as a new IRA waged implacable sectarian war north of the Irish border.[79] Songs in his honour can still be heard in republican clubs though they tend not to refer to his years as a guest of the Third Reich.

Frank Ryan was a brave but politically confused man. He had shown himself willing to fight the insurgent generals in Spain and their Nazi and Italian fascist backers but was either unable or unwilling to make a moral connection between that struggle and Churchill's hazardous choice to fight it out with Hitler. If Seán Russell had not died at sea in the summer of 1940, Ryan would have found himself in Ireland on a mission to co-ordinate IRA operations against Britain with Hitler's support. This would have taken him back into the fold of the organisation he had joined twenty years earlier but it would have been a deeply flawed choice, given that '. . . faced with one of the twentieth century's genuinely world-threatening tyrants, the IRA had opted for alliance rather than opposition'.[80]

Some republicans came to feel bitter regret for their blinkered decision. One of them was the grandmother of Joseph O'Neill who, late in her life, agreed to talk to him of the events of half a century earlier. For O'Neill this was a cathartic moment in his troubled journey of discovery of his own family's history. 'During the Second World War,' his relative told him,

> we didn't know how bad the Germans were; we saw it only after, on the screens and heard it on the radio. What Hitler did . . . Oh my God, what he did. At the time, anyone that was beating the English, we were for them. But how wrong we were. How wrong we were.[81]

Militarily, the IRA never posed a serious threat to an Irish state which, from the outset of the Emergency, was equipped with for-midable powers to keep its activists under surveillance and have them charged or interned. The real danger would have been if Germany had ever been able to co-ordinate operations of its own on Irish territory with the IRA, and the *Abwehr* did have contacts with it which pre-dated the outbreak of war. It had its intermediaries in Éire, such as Carl Petersen, who worked for the German News Agency in Dublin, and Helmut Clissmann, an academic researcher on Celtic studies who moved between Ireland and Germany in the period after Hitler came to power.[82]

Clissmann cultivated the acquaintance of leading republicans, such as Frank Ryan and, provided useful introductions for Eduard Hempel after he became German minister in Dublin in 1937. So, too, did the ethnographer and folklorist Jupp Hoven but, by July 1939, British intelligence knew of their activities and, at the end of August, MI5 and Éire's Department of External Affairs agreed to share information about German espionage in Éire and attempts by its nationals there to make IRA contacts.[83]

Clissman and Hoven returned to Germany after war broke out and thereafter any link-up with the IRA by the German military or its intelligence services depended on infiltrating agents into Éire. One of these, Oskar Pfaus, had been there in the early part of the IRA's bombing offensive against Britain and had made contact with Jim O'Donovan, the bomb-maker and army council member who had travelled to Germany and prepared some of the ground for Seán Russell's 1940 visit.

The German agent who remained at large for longest in wartime Éire was Hermann Goertz. What he achieved remains very questionable and it is now accepted that his *Abwehr* handlers overestimated his abilities.[84] During the eighteen months that he remained free, he became increasingly sceptical of the IRA's capabilities. This scepticism dated from his initial access, in the summer of 1940, to the organisation's 'Plan Kathleen' which was based on a cross-border operation by German troops landed in Northern Ireland and backed by IRA units. Though news of the plan's capture by the Irish security forces unleashed a wave of rumours, it appears to have been rated no more seriously by Goertz than by German intelligence.

Goertz's eventual arrest in November 1941 was followed by that of O'Donovan, his most important IRA contact but, by then, the organisation was capable of little more than sporadic attacks on members of the Garda and erratic distribution of copies of its proscribed *War News*. Huge damage had been caused by the Stephen Hayes case, which may be why, in its immediate aftermath, the poet John Betjeman, a cultural attaché to Sir John Maffey's Dublin office, was actually considered as a possible target, if only to move the spotlight away from the IRA's internal tensions.

Betjeman was a popular figure in wartime Dublin though some claim his role merged with that of gathering for London whatever intelligence came his gregarious way. Indeed, he has been described as 'the acceptable face of espionage'[85] but the IRA took him more seriously. One of its Dublin-based intelligence officers, Diarmid Brennan, used to drink in the Palace Bar, next door to the *Irish*

Times office where Betjeman used to socialise with journalists and civil servants and where he would have been an easy target.

Brennan began to have doubts, however, and took action to avert any operation, though Betjeman's reports on Irish opinion on the war and levels of support for the IRA were read with care in London. His poetry also appealed to Brennan. More than twenty years later he went public with his recollections of the episode: 'I came to the conclusion that a man who could give such pleasure with his pen couldn't be much of a secret agent. I may well be wrong.'[86]

The IRA's disarray after the Hayes court martial, and its rapidly dwindling capacity for serious operations against the Irish state, meant that, after the capture of Goertz, other German agents sent to Ireland began to operate independently of it. They concentrated their efforts on reporting back to Berlin on shipping movements, army dispositions in Northern Ireland and on estimates of air-raid damage to cities in England from Irish contacts who had left for wartime work there.

The wartime diaries of Guy Liddell, who was head of MI5's counter-espionage work and whose brother Cecil ran its Irish operation, convey no real sense of a major IRA threat to Britain or of German agents having any success in working with it. In one 1941 entry, on Colonel Liam Archer of Éire's G2 intelligence unit, Liddell noted: 'He seemed to have reached the same conclusions as ourselves about the German intelligence service. His experience so far of all the agents who landed in Éire is that their plans were singularly ill-conceived and badly carried out.'[87]

As to Northern Ireland, Liddell was concerned that policing operations there were driven primarily by the deep-rooted fear of an internal enemy, the IRA, rather than by the external threat of German agents who might seek either for intelligence or to co-ordinate attacks with it. One MI5 agent, TA, or Tommy Robertson, reported back to Liddell on the RUC in November 1939. Liddell wrote: 'Robertson's impression of the local police is somewhat similar to the one I gained more than a year ago. The issue between the Orangemen and the IRA is the thing that really counts and espionage matters are of secondary importance.'[88]

This early appraisal of the RUC was confirmed at the war's end in a report compiled by MI5 on the work of its Irish section. The RUC, this argued, entered the war ill-equipped to monitor German espionage partly through its lack of qualified linguists. It was also jealous of what it saw as its own rights and responsibilities and wary of the 'amateur interference of Intelligence Officers who lack local

knowledge'.[89] This attitude in fact deterred Britain's security services from sending a regional officer to the province where he 'could
have performed valuable services for both the Security Service and
the RUC'.[90]

As big a concern as IRA operations for Liddell was the need to be
circumspect about the degree of co-operation between Britain's and
Éire's intelligence services. In October 1941 a real problem over this
arose when Sir Charles Wickham, inspector general of the RUC in
Northern Ireland, came close to compromising the secrecy that was
essential to protect this relationship. The point at issue was the plan
then being run to trap Goertz and end his mission to Éire. Wickham
wanted to make available to his own officers information about
Goertz and his IRA links which had come to him from the Garda
Síochána and from British sources, too.

Wickham, Liddell noted in an irritated entry to his diary in
October 1941,

> had evidently misunderstood the whole position. He does not
> realise that Liam Archer and Dan Bryan have already been at
> great pains to conceal that they obtain any information from us
> and that our position is therefore an extremely delicate one. The
> fact is that Northern Ireland is so concerned about the IRA and
> obtaining information from the South that they are not inclined to
> give much consideration to other matters.[91]

Northern Ireland had reason to be concerned about the IRA in late
1941 because what was left of the organisation had decided to
concentrate on operations there. Prior to the bombing campaign in
Britain, the army council had accepted the case for a northern
command which would cover the six counties and also Donegal.
The organisation had, despite arrests and constant RUC surveillance, maintained a military structure, with possibly as many as five
hundred volunteers in Belfast alone in 1939.[92]

It claimed to have defended nationalist areas of the city during the
communal violence of 1935 and conducted limited border operations
in 1937. Some of its leaders, notably Dominic Adams, uncle of the
Sinn Féin president Gerry Adams, were key figures in planning the
1939 bombing offensive against targets in English cities. During the
Easter weekend in April of that year, the Belfast IRA staged a
significant show of strength with parades starting off from three
different locations to mark the anniversary of the 1916 rising. At
these parades and others in Northern Ireland, a statement was read

out which declared: 'The expeditionary forces of the IRA are waging war against the invader on her own soil – something that no other nation in the world has ever attempted – and this war will continue while British troops or institutions remain in Ireland.'[93]

The biggest of the Belfast parades was on the Falls Road where five hundred volunteers marched:

> People in the district, hearing the measured tramp of feet and seeing the columns of marching men and youths swing past, thought that another rising was taking place and women especially called words of encouragement for the 'phantom army' that had suddenly materialised in their midst.[94]

No attempts were made by the different parades to go near Milltown cemetery where the republican burial area was sealed off by a heavy police presence. This show of strength put the security forces on even fuller alert and, when war came in September, forty northern IRA members were quickly interned. Local units were still able to mount raids, however, notably on the British army camp at Ballykinlar in County Down, in February 1940, when thirty rifles were taken in what was not the last raid on this target.

As Hitler's armies advanced relentlessly through the Low Countries and into France itself the IRA's northern command in Belfast issued a call to the 'Men of Ireland' to resist conscription. They claimed recruitment in the North to be at a standstill and that Lord Craigavon was making the case to Churchill for conscription to be extended there. This was close to the truth, and the statement finished by declaring that 'Only the strength of the IRA stands between you and conscription.'[95]

A few weeks later, a further statement by the northern command acclaimed German victory in the west:

> The present crisis caused by the intervention of Germany and Italy and the success of their campaign makes our job easier. The enemies of England are, by that fact, the friends of Ireland. We are no more Nazi or Fascist than Connolly and Pearse were Imperialistic in seeking the aid of Imperialistic Germany in 1916.[96]

This latter disclaimer sat uneasily with the presence of Russell and Ryan in Berlin as honoured guests of the Third Reich and with the northern IRA's commitment to disrupting Britain's war against Hitler.

The IRA, in fact, had started 1940 in Northern Ireland with a series of bomb attacks on buildings in Belfast and in Londonderry. Cinemas in both cities were treated as targets, in the latter's case for showing what the IRA claimed were pro-British films, and the city's opera house was destroyed by fire on 9 March. The internment of seventy-six more IRA members in early May did not halt the northern offensive. A wave of fund-raising bank robberies followed and, in Armagh on 25 July, the RUC foiled one of them, though they came under heavy fire from the IRA's favoured weapon, the Thompson sub-machine gun.

The six-man IRA unit fled south by car towards the border but were trapped by police at Cullyhana. After what the RUC called a 'grim gun battle' the IRA men were disarmed and arrested but on one day, 20 September, there were further raids on seven banks and post offices in west Belfast.

The RUC's response was to remain on high alert and, when the diarist Moya Woodside left her own middle-class neighbourhood to do voluntary work in a nationalist area, it came as a shock to her to see how heavily fortified police stations were. She wrote descriptions in her diary of ugly brick structures built out on to the pavements for machine guns to fire from and graffiti on nearby walls proclaiming opposition to both conscription and to the ARP, that is, the Air Raid Precaution Service.

Neither a Catholic nor a nationalist, she hated the Unionist regime and saw semi-fascist tendencies in the way it was using its Special Powers legislation as well as what, in her view, was its excessive recourse to media censorship.[98] Moya Woodside joined the Northern Ireland Labour Party but was pessimistic about its capacity to tackle the province's sectarian tensions or to drain what she called its 'wells of hatred'.[99]

She was right about this, of course, though Northern Ireland, contrary to republican flights of rhetorical fancy, was neither a one-party state nor an apartheid one. Yet it had been devised in 1920 to perpetuate the rule of Unionists who were the majority within its borders, and the state's major institutions were a reflection of this. Its fault lines as a society, however, were defined by social class as well as by sectarianism. Many Protestants suffered acute deprivation and poverty but so, too, did Catholics whose prospects of either low-paid labour or unemployment were even greater, and they could blame this on a political settlement which embodied what they saw as the injustice of partition.

All this was soil from which the IRA could feed, and they followed their attacks of 1940 with more of the same the following year. Banks and businesses, however, became harder to raid as police protection for them increased, so their targets shifted to smaller shops and to individuals thought to have money in their homes. For those arrested by the RUC, retribution was severe. Courts applied a tariff of heavy sentences, ten to twelve years for firing on the police; five years for illegal possession of firearms and often fifteen strokes of the cat (a whip formed by knotted lashes) for convicted young offenders.

The IRA in Northern Ireland saw itself as the cutting edge of opposition to the Stormont state and to the British presence it seemed to them to represent. Paddy Devlin, the Belfast-born socialist and trade unionist, as a boy before the war joined the Fianna Éireann, the IRA's youth wing, attracted to it, he was to say later, by its green berets and tunics as well as by the white lanyards. He kept this a secret from his parents, keeping his uniform in a friend's house in order to attend drills and parades.[100] In early 1940, aged fifteen, he was accepted into full membership of D Company of the organisation's west Belfast battalion on the Falls Road. Much of its northern Command leadership was recruited there though arrests both before and since the start of the war had taken experienced activists off the streets.

Despite being in some disarray because of this, the Belfast IRA could still carry out fund-raising robberies and collect what was, in effect, protection money from local shops, pubs and bookmakers. It also beat up those it identified as being 'antisocial' elements within the community. In his memoirs, Devlin wrote of how unpopular these disciplinary exercises were and that the unit that carried out most of them, once its members were interned by the government, was ostracised by other internees.[101]

Apart from attending basic weapons training, Paddy Devlin was ordered to take part in the monitoring of all troop movements in the Belfast area as well as the locations of all war-production factories. These data were meant to be recorded on maps and in note form for the use of the IRA's pro-German leadership but the limited education of many rank-and-file volunteers meant that this work was often poorly done, if it was done at all.[102] One of Devlin's assignments was to commandeer a car from a street close to Clonard monastery. When he arrived to tell the owner, a factory worker with a special ration of petrol, that the IRA needed his vehicle his reward was to be told: 'Fuck off, you wee bastard, or I'll give you a toe up the arse.'[103]

Police surveillance, arrests, internment and a strong British army presence severely limited the IRA's operational capacity in Northern

Ireland, and its attacks there became fewer as 1941 wore on. Another major factor in this was the devastating impact of the German Blitz on Belfast in April and May of that year which did not discriminate between Loyalist and Nationalist areas of the city. Even so, there were those in authority south of the border who thought they might be able to use the IRA. Early in March 1941, General Hugo MacNeill, who held a divisional command on Éire's side of the border, met Maurice Twomey of the IRA's army council, at a Dublin restaurant.

MacNeill's purpose was to ask Twomey what the northern IRA might know about British deployments and whether it was still planning any cross-border operations. Twomey arranged for two members of the Belfast IRA, Seán McCaughey and Charlie McGlade, to talk to a Garda Special Branch officer at Dublin Castle. He in turn sent them in to meet the private secretary to Frank Aiken, the Defence Minister. What came of these contacts is not known and Aiken later denied that he had ever met the IRA's Belfast emissaries.[104]

What the Irish state forces, given the high quality of their own intelligence work, could really have learned from the northern IRA has to be problematic. Men like McGlade and McCaughey saw the IRA's struggle as an all-Ireland one but, at this point in the war, their immediate priority was a renewal of operations against the Stormont state and its security forces.

When the IRA leadership sanctioned an intensification of offensive operations in Northern Ireland, the IRA's northern command was only too ready to respond. At an army convention in late March 1942, delegates voted unanimously for renewed and all-out attacks on the RUC. They voted, too, and again unanimously, for a resolution from the northern command that 'if the Germans enter Ireland with the consent of a Provisional Government of the Irish Republic, Óglaigh na hÉirean (the IRA) should assist the German forces.' Further resolutions, also carried, stated that if there were renewed German air attacks on Belfast, 'picked men' would be deployed in attacks on the RUC and the fire service, also on emergency water tanks and on the city's electricity supply. Perversely, gas supply installations were not to be hit 'in an effort to avoid undue strain and distress to the civilian population'.[105]

The response of local IRA units to this authorisation of new attacks was swift and brutal. On 4 April 1942, one of them shot dead Thomas Forbes in Dungannon. He was a married RUC constable with ten children, and his killing was intended to serve notice that the IRA was back on the offensive. The RUC certainly saw it that way. In a retrospective report near the war's end they declared that 'Generally speaking the year 1942 shows perhaps the greatest amount of IRA activity that there has been in this country for a long time.'[106]

The very next day, Easter Sunday, the IRA's army council had a statement ready for distribution to all its units and for reading at a commemoration of the 1916 rising in west Belfast's Milltown cemetery. 'England is still the one and only enemy of Irish freedom,' it read.

> She and she alone holds us in bondage. Her imperialism is the root cause of all our National and social evils. To break the connection with England, to get rid of her invading forces, to prevent her dragging Ireland into a war in defence of her Empire, these are our immediate objects.[107]

The commemorative ceremony at which this document was to be read was banned by the Stormont authorities, who used the Special Powers Act to ban all political gatherings for seven days over the Easter period. For its part, the IRA prepared diversionary actions to enable the commemoration to go ahead. 'Belfast was split into five areas,' as described by Joe Cahill who became a leading member of the Provisional IRA in the 1970s and 1980s. 'In three of the areas shots were to be fired over a patrol – over a patrol – I want to emphasise that. And in the other two areas (with RUC attention diverted) marches were to be held.'[108]

Cahill was one of a six-man unit from the IRA's C Company which opened fire on a police vehicle as it approached Clonard Street. One shot smashed a window, but missed the occupants, and a sergeant and two constables got out and gave chase as the unit withdrew into the neighbouring Cawnpore Street to hide its weapons in a safe house. It was quickly sealed off by the RUC but the IRA unit opened fire killing Constable Patrick Murphy. He was a Roman Catholic from the area, popular with local children and with whose son Paddy Devlin had often played football.[109] Some accounts claim Murphy wanted to persuade Cahill and his comrades to lay down their weapons because he knew their identities, a reminder of how cohesive and close a community Nationalist Belfast was and still is.[110]

Constable Murphy, though hit by five bullets, was able to return fire before he died, hitting Tom Williams, the commander of the IRA unit, wounding him severely but not fatally. Williams then ordered

the unit to give themselves up to the RUC. A few weeks later
Williams, Cahill and the other four unit members were sentenced
to death, and Nationalist Ireland on both sides of the border at once
orchestrated a campaign for their reprieve. De Valera gave it his
support although, earlier in the year, his own government had
sanctioned the hanging of another IRA volunteer, George Plant.

This did not stop the Taoiseach using his Department of External
Affairs to send a message to Churchill urging him to use his
influence on Stormont in the interests of clemency:

> the saving, at this moment, through your personal intervention, of
> the life of young Williams who is due to be executed on Wednes-
> day morning in Belfast, would profoundly affect public feeling
> here. I know the difficulties but results would justify it, and I urge
> strongly that you do it.[111]

Similar representations by the Dublin government to Roosevelt and
American politicians achieved as little as the eleventh hour appeal to
Churchill who did not even mention the matter in his history of the
war.

In late August the Stormont Cabinet reviewed the case and, acting
on their recommendations, the governor of Northern Ireland announced that, apart from that of Tom Williams, the death sentences
would be commuted. His hanging went ahead on the morning of 2
September 1942 in Belfast's Crumlin Road prison. A large Catholic
crowd gathered close to the prison to pray and say the rosary as the
moment of execution approached; they were taunted by Loyalists
chanting and singing in side streets which linked the Crumlin Road
to the Shankill.[112]

Tom Williams was nineteen years old, a devout Roman Catholic
who had done mostly casual work since leaving school. Though he
knew little except the streets of the Falls area, he was, in Paddy
Devlin's recollection, a quiet boy who liked to read Irish history and
literature and who joined the Fianna with him.[113] It is possible that
Williams did not fire the fatal shot but confessed to it, perhaps from
a premonition of his own death from tuberculosis and also to save
the lives of a unit he had commanded and for whom he felt
responsible.

From Berlin, where he enjoyed the hospitality of a regime already
carrying out the wholesale slaughter of Jews and of all who opposed
it across occupied Europe, Francis Stuart devoted a special broadcast to this execution, the only one of an IRA member carried out in

Northern Ireland during the Second World War. Willliams, he told his listeners, 'was legally murdered by the British administration for no other crime than for being loyal to his nation'.[114] Stuart went on to heap praise on another Irish rebel, de Valera, though omitting any reference to executions of IRA men already sanctioned by his government.

Tom Williams was buried in an unmarked grave within the forbidding walls of Crumlin Road prison. Joe Cahill saw this taking place from his own cell window and vowed, like the rest of the republican movement, that the remains would one day be reinterred in the heart of west Belfast. Nearly sixty years later this was accomplished, after a sustained campaign by former IRA members in the National Graves Association. Cahill, who some republicans continued to think had fired the fatal shot which killed Constable Murphy,[115] took a leading part in it and in the macabre street theatre of the reburial of Williams on 19 January 2000.

Shops and businesses closed in west Belfast and thousands lined the streets to see Joe Cahill take his turn carrying the coffin, with an Irish tricolour over it, to Milltown where it was buried alongside other members of the Williams family. Many tributes were paid by the Sinn Féin leadership, including Gerry Adams, and in local newspapers read by the Nationalist community. One of these came from the Irish Republican Socialist Party, gunmen of whose armed wing the Irish National Liberation Army (INLA), murdered Constable Murphy's grandson, himself a former RUC constable, in 1982. The priest who officiated at the Mass prior to the reburial offered prayers for Williams, for Constable Murphy and for his grandfather.[116]

The IRA was planning to step up its operations even before the date for Tom Williams's execution. The northern command enlarged upon its March statement by calling for orchestrated attacks on ARP posts across Belfast and for senior officers in the RUC and its B-Special reserve, as well as Unionist politicians, to be 'exterminated'.[117] As well as attacks on electricity generating plants, cinemas all over the city were to be attacked on 19 August. This was rooted in the leadership's intention 'that from then until we achieve our object the population be kept in a state of picture-less tension. With less cinema-going they may have more time to think.'[118]

Cinema and its allegedly alien, by which they quite often meant Jewish, cultural influence had been a republican target before and remained one, as demonstrated in the brief career of the IRA hero Seán South who was killed fifteen years later on 1 January 1957 in a border raid. Putting Belfast's cinemas out of action could well have been politically counterproductive but it was well beyond the IRA's resources. So indeed, was much of what featured in the brutal language of northern command's statements during 1942.

As the time for the hanging of Tom Williams drew near, IRA units were ordered to be ready for reprisal attacks on the security forces. The RUC, however, was also ready and, three days before the execution, it carried out raids on the edge of west Belfast, seizing weapons caches intended for these operations, and shooting dead Gerry O'Callaghan who had been guarding one of the caches. Within hours of the hanging, police patrols came under attack and, on 5 September, two constables were killed by IRA units in Clady, County Tyrone.

On the same day, four IRA men were arrested in west Belfast after shots were fired at a police patrol. One of them was a sixteen-year-old Gerry Adams who was later charged with attempted murder of two RUC constables and with the illegal possession of a firearm. A police report prior to his trial and sentencing said that 'he has been honest, sober, industrious, and generally of good character – except for the fact he was known to associate with members of the IRA'.[119] This was apparently a personality flaw shared by two of his brothers, one of whom, Dominic, may well have ordered the 1939 Coventry bombing,[120] and certainly by his more famous son, now the Sinn Féin president.

Tension in Belfast reached a point where a curfew was imposed on Nationalist areas, and two more RUC men were killed in IRA gun attacks in October, while others were wounded. Early in the month, Hugh McAteer, the IRA's new chief of staff, was arrested in Londonderry and given a fifteen-year sentence. He was an archetypal IRA member of this era, one of a large family with a long history of allegiance to the cause, schooled by the Christian Brothers, and a teenage recruit to the Fianna.[121] His arrest was a severe blow to the IRA, not least because it was the work of a boyhood friend who had joined the RUC.[122]

McAteer, with a famous Belfast republican Jimmy Steele and two others, made a dramatic escape from Crumlin Road prison on 15 January 1943, after securing access to its roof from a lavatory and using knotted bed sheets to get over the perimeter wall. An even more dramatic escape from Londonderry prison, on 21 March, involved twenty-one IRA men tunnelling their way out, and it helped to maintain republican morale amid more arrests and internments of activists. So, too, did the commandeering of a cinema in Broadway, off the Falls Road in Belfast, by McAteer and Steele, who read out to the audience the Easter 1916 proclamation and an IRA policy statement before making their escape.[123]

These exploits served to mask the real weakness of the IRA. Paddy Devlin knew that his own internment was inevitable after the violence which had followed the Williams execution and, by the end of 1942, he found himself on D wing of Crumlin Road jail with many other republican inmates. His three years there were a formative time for him as he used them to learn Irish and to read widely but he also sensed growing disenchantment with a futile armed struggle. By late 1943, he later wrote, 'morale had hit rock bottom and the wing [the internees' D wing of the prison] was no longer run on military lines'.[124]

Initially, Devlin was upset by the low spirits of some who had been incarcerated since 1939 and 1940 with no certain prospect of any release date until the war in Europe ended. By the time of his arrival on D wing, a significant number of IRA men, especially those who were married with families, were ready to go before the government's release tribunal, even if this meant co-operating with the RUC in order to get out. Devlin got what he described as a 'biff on the gob'[125] for berating one of these men and decided he should keep his views to himself.

Sporadic IRA operations continued and, in October 1943, they killed another RUC officer during a raid on a mill in Odessa Street in Belfast, but Devlin's impression of declining morale was shared by the police. Their surveillance work and fire power continued to trap and kill wanted IRA men such as James Burns, one of the Londonderry jail escapers whom they shot dead in Belfast city centre on 10 February 1944.

His death was seen as a turning point for the RUC as a report by them at the end of the year made clear: 'From this date onwards the IRA began to show a rapid decline and it seemed as if complete demoralisation had set in. Many internees applied for release from internment which in most cases was granted'.[126] Those released, the report noted, were not returning to the organisation's active membership, and it went on to say that, while the IRA was not completely dead, 'the close of the year 1944 finds it more or less inactive, without money and with very few arms'.[127] Overall, the report recorded, IRA action had done minimal damage to Britain's war effort and left British service personnel untouched.

Paddy Devlin's own doubts began to grow with his reading and participation in political debates with fellow prisoners as well as visiting lecturers to Crumlin Road. He found himself wondering about the legitimacy of armed action by a movement which seemed to have no prospect of majority support on either side of the Irish border. The thought, too, that the war with the Axis powers might indeed be a just one also began to preoccupy him:

> It was surprising to hear words of praise for Britain's part in fighting the Fascist forces of Hitler and Mussolini. I began to understand better the reasons for the war. and to recognise that there were many admirable values in the British people.[128]

For him, prison was an invaluable breathing space within which to examine his relationship with the ingrown values of Irish republicanism. Others found that an impossible journey to make, and they still speak to us from the pages of the novel, *Odd Man Out*, published in 1945 and later to provide the script for a memorable film. Its author F. L. Green, knew Belfast well and he created a bleak and dark vision of the wartime city within which the IRA operated, though he never called the IRA by that name, only 'the organisation'.

At one key point in Green's narrative, three IRA men who are on the run after abandoning their wounded chief of staff, Johnny McQueen, during an armed robbery, hear late at night a ship's siren from Belfast Lough:

> It proclaimed oceans and wide lands, and rendered small and trivial by comparison the meagre territory and the unrelenting civil strife which were all that these three outlaws had known from earliest infancy, hatred, fanaticism and murder, within a tiny island beyond which they had never ventured and outside of which their stunted imagination could not extend.[129]

Green's novel and his characterisation of the IRA, especially the celibate and sexless McQueen, has been criticised for misrepresenting what drew young Irishmen and women to the republican cause. That cause was, after all, able to appeal to the generous spirits of Brendan Behan and Paddy Devlin but they both, over different periods of time, broke their links with it.

There still remained, however, a few ready to play out to the end their part in the 'patriot game'. One of them was Seán McCaughey, who had been a key figure in the IRA's northern command. Born in Aughnacloy in County Tyrone, but raised in Ardoyne in Belfast, he 'joined up' in 1934 when he was eighteen years old. Much of his subsequent life was a sacrifice to the cause, either in prison or on the run.

He was a keen hurler and Gaelic footballer and sufficiently accomplished in Irish to teach it to children at an Ard Scoil, or language school, in Divis Street in west Belfast. He was also a violent man who, in 1941, had taken a central role in the interrogation and sentencing of Stephen Hayes. On his arrest in Dublin in September of that year, he was sentenced to death by a special military tribunal for his part in the Hayes 'trial', an episode which did irreparable damage to the movement. His sentence was commuted to life imprisonment but, from its outset, he demanded political status and, when this was denied him, he refused to wear prison clothes and spent four and a half years in Portalaoise prison clad only in a blanket.

After the ending of the Emergency, having served most of his sentence in isolation, McCaughey finally, in April 1946, went on a hunger and thirst strike and died an agonising death after twenty-three days. One witness to his end described his tongue as being the size of a threepenny piece.[130] It was the Hayes case, and his own brutal part in it, which brought him south and to his arrest, though his unyielding commitment to the republican cause may well have meant that he was in any case living on borrowed time. There is now an imposing mural to his memory in Ardoyne in north Belfast.

The Emergency years drew the IRA into attacks on both sides of the Irish border and in Britain which proved to be beyond its resources. It was severely hit by coercive measures applied against it by both the Stormont and Dublin governments and, by 1945, there was little its leadership could claim to have achieved. Regrouping and new political thinking were needed. At the end of 1956, the IRA launched an abortive border campaign but its real rebirth came in response to events in Northern Ireland in 1969. The cause endured, especially for those, to adapt slightly the words of W. B. Yeats, who were born with or acquired 'fanatic hearts'.

Notes

1. C. Foley, *Legion of the Rearguard: the IRA and the Modern Irish State* (London: Pluto, 1992), p. 32.
2. T. de Vere White, *Kevin O'Higgins* (Kerry: Anvil Books), 1988, p. 150.
3. R. English, *Armed Struggle* (Basingstoke: Macmillan, 2003), p. 44.
4. J. Horgan, 'Fianna Fáil and Arms Decommissioning', *History Ireland*, Vol. 5, No. 4, winter 1997, pp. 49–53.
5. B. Hanley, *The IRA, 1926–1936* (Dublin: Four Courts Press, 2002), p. 11.

6. Foley, *Legion of the Rearguard*, p. 119.
7. *Irish News*, 3 May 1934.
8. Ibid., 1 April 1935.
9. Ibid., 8 April 1935.
10. Foley, Legion of the Rearguard, p. 156.
11. E. O'Halpin, *Defending Ireland*, p. 124.
12. *Irish News*, 25 and 27 May 1936.
13. Ibid., 18 June 2005.
14. Ibid., 27 April 1936.
15. J. O'Neill, *The Blood-Dark Track: a Family History* (London: Granta, 2000), pp. 292–4.
16. *Irish News*, 17 June 1936.
17. E. O'Connor, *Reds and the Green: Ireland, Russia and the Communist International 1919–1943* (Dublin: UCD Press, 2004), pp. 173–4.
18. Ibid., pp. 198–9.
19. Foley, *Legion of the Rearguard*, p. 138.
20. Ibid.
21. M. Milotte, *Communism in Modern Ireland* (Dublin: Gill and Macmillan, 1984), p. 154.
22. Foley, *Legion of the Rearguard*, p. 144.
23. *An Phoblacht/Republican News*, 9 December 2004.
24. A. Hoar, *In Green and Red: the Lives of Frank Ryan* (Dingle, Co. Kerry: Brandon Press, 2004), p. 140.
25. M. Ryan, *Tom Barry: IRA Freedom Fighter* (Cork: Mercier Press, 2003), pp. 305–6; also Irish Military Archives (henceforth IMA), G2X/0093, undated 1939 report; also G2X/0093, 23 November 1943, letter by unnamed officer.
26. Bowyer Bell, *The Secret Army: the IRA 1916–1979* (Swords: Poolbeg Books), p. 152.
27. Hoar, *In Green and Red: the lives of Frank Ryan*, pp. 234–5.
28. Foley, *Legion of the Rearguard*, p. 191.
29. B. Behan, *Borstal Boy* (London: Hutchinson, 1958), pp. 130–1.
30. Ibid., pp. 131–2.
31. Foley, *Legion of the Rearguard*, p. 196.
32. Behan, *Borstal Boy*, p. 1.
33. Ibid.
34. Ibid., pp. 173–7.
35. Campbell, *My Life and Easy Times*, p. 168.
36. Ibid.
37. Coogan, *The IRA*, p. 144.
38. Ibid., p. 149.
39. O'Halpin, *Defending Ireland*, p. 249.
40. Coogan, *The IRA*, pp. 153–4.
41. D. Murphy, *A Place Apart* (London: John Murray, 1978), p. 29.
42. J. B. Bell, *The Secret Army: the IRA 1916–1979* (Swords, Poolbeg Books, 1970), p. 234.
43. B. Behan, *Confessions of an Irish Rebel* (London: Hutchinson, 1965), p. 30.
44. Coogan, *The IRA*, p. 196.
45. U. MacEoin, *The IRA in the Twilight Years* (Dublin: Argenta Books, 1997), pp. 919–23; also O'Neill, *The Blood-Dark Track*, pp. 158–9.
46. See T. Ryle Dwyer, 'Guests of the State', in D. Keogh and M. O'Driscoll (eds), *Ireland in World War Two* (Cork: Mercier Press, 2004), pp. 107–26.
47. Behan, *Confessions of an Irish Rebel*, p. 74.

48. Ibid., p. 71.
49. Ibid., p. 69.
50. R. English, *Ernie O'Malley: IRA Intellectual* (Oxford: Clarendon Press, 1998), p. 55.
51. Lee, *Ireland 1912–1985*, p. 221.
52. Ibid.
53. Ibid., p. 224; also F. S. L. Lyons, *Ireland Since the Rising*, p. 550.
54. H. McDonald, *Colours: Ireland from Bombs to Boom* (Edinburgh: Mainstream, 2004), pp. 116–17.
55. *Sunday World*, 2 January 2005.
56. Hoar, *In Green and Red: the Lives of Frank Ryan*, p. 243.
57. O'Brien, *My Life and Themes*, p. 91.
58. O'Halpin, *Defending Ireland*, p. 194.
59. *Irish News*, 20 April 2000.
60. M. M. Hull, *Irish Secrets: German Espionage in Wartime Ireland, 1939–1945* (Dublin and Portland, OR: Irish Academic Press, 2003), p. 273.
61. D. O'Donoghue, *Hitler's Irish Voices: the Story of German Radio's Wartime Irish Service* (Belfast: Beyond the Pale Publications, 1998), p. 51.
62. Ibid., pp. 57–8.
63. IMA, G2X/0093, Ryan to Kerney, 11 December 1940.
64. Ibid.
65. Ibid., 27 September 1941, F. Ryan to E. Ryan.
66. Ibid., 6 November 1941, Ryan to Kerney.
67. Ibid.
68. Ibid., G2X/0093, 27 September 1941, F. Ryan to E. Ryan.
69. Hoar, *In Green and Red: the Lives of Frank Ryan*, p. 260.
70. G. Gelborn, *Francis Stuart: a Life* (Dublin, Raven Arts, 1990), p. 157.
71. IMA, G2X/0093, 21 December 1945, Colonel D. Bryan to J. Walshe at the DEA.
72. Hull, *Irish Secrets: German Espionage in Wartime Ireland 1939–1945*, pp. 186–90.
73. E Staunton, 'Frank Ryan and Collaboration: a Reassessment', *History Ireland*, autumn 1997, Vol. 5, No. 3, pp. 49–51.
74. Hoar, *In Green and Red: the Lives of Frank Ryan*, p. 261.
75. IMA, G2/4949, 18 June 1945.
76. T O'Reilly, *Hitler's Irishmen* (Blackrock, Co. Dublin: Mercier Press, 2008).
77. IMA, G2/4949, 18 June 1945.
78. Hull, *Irish Secrets: German Espionage in Wartime Ireland 1939–1945*, pp. 218–27.
79. *An Phoblacht/Republican News*, 9 December 2004 (a review of A. Hoar's book, *In Green and Red: the Lives of Frank Ryan*).
80. English, *Armed Struggle: the History of the IRA*, p. 65.
81. O'Neill, *The Blood-Dark Track*, p. 160.
82. F. H. Hinsley and C. A. G. Simkins, *British Intelligence and the Second World War*, Vol. 4, pp. 16–17.
83. Ibid.; also J. P. Duggan, *Neutral Ireland and the Third Reich*, pp. 60–5.
84. Hull, *Irish Secrets: German Espionage in Wartime Ireland 1939–1945*, pp. 75–96.
85. Duggan, *Neutral Ireland and the Third Reich*, pp. 88–9; see also B. Hillier, *John Betjeman: New Fame, New Love* (London: John Murray, 2002), pp. 230–2.
86. *Guardian*, 22 April 2000.
87. N. West (ed.), *The Guy Liddell Diaries*: Vol. 1, *1939–1942, MI5's Director of Counter-Espionage in World War II* (Abingdon: Routledge, 2005), 21 May 1941, p. 149.
88. Ibid., 14 November 1939, p. 44.
89. O'Halpin (ed.) *MI5 and Ireland 1939–1945: the Official History* (Dublin and Portland, OR: Irish Academic Press, 2003), p. 25.

90. Ibid.
91. Ibid., 17 October 1941, p. 184.
92. Foley, *Legion of the Rearguard*, p. 193.
93. *Irish News*, 10 April 1939.
94. Ibid.
95. PRONI, HA/20A/1/24.
96. Ibid.
97. M Woodside, Diary, 16 August 1940.
98. Ibid., 4 August 1940.
99. Ibid., 21 February 1941.
100. P. Devlin, *Straight Left: an Autobiography* (Belfast: Blackstaff, 1993), pp. 22–3.
101. Ibid., p. 28.
102. Ibid., p. 30.
103. Ibid., p. 29.
104. MacEoin, *The IRA in the Twilight Years*, p. 847; also C. Foley, *Legion of the Rearguard*, p. 202.
105. PRONI, HA/20/A/1/24.
106. PRONI, CAB 3A/78B.
107. PRONI, HA/20/A/1/24.
108. *Irish News*, 22 January 2000.
109. Devlin, *Straight Left*, p. 33.
110. Jordan, *Milestones in Murder*, p. 65.
111. Coogan, *De Valera: Long Fellow, Long Shadow*, p. 622.
112. *Irish News*, 3 September 1942.
113. Devlin, *Straight Left*, p. 33.
114. B. Barrington (ed.), *The Wartime Broadcasts of Francis Stuart* (Dublin: Lilliput Press, 2000), pp. 91–2; also D. O'Donoghue, *Hitler's Irish Voices*, p. 102.
115. *Guardian*, 28 August 1999.
116. *Irish News*, 20 January 2000; also *An Phoblacht/Republican News*, 27 January 2000.
117. PRONI, HA/20/A/1/24.
118. Ibid.
119. PRONI, HA/9/2/650; see also D. Sharrock and M. Devenport, *Man of War, Man of Peace, the Unauthorised Biography of Gerry Adams* (London and Basingstoke: Macmillan, 1977), pp. 5–9.
120. Jordan, *Milestones in Murder*, p. 62.
121. Coogan, *The IRA*, pp. 162–4.
122. Ibid., pp. 183–4.
123. Ibid., pp. 184–6.
124. Devlin, *Straight Left*, p. 46.
125. Ibid., p. 41.
126. PRONI, CAB 3A/78B.
127. Ibid.
128. Devlin, *Straight Left*, p. 49.
129. F. L. Green, *Odd Man Out* (first published London: Michael Joseph, 1945; London: Sphere Books, 1991), pp. 45–6.
130. Coogan, *The IRA*, p. 199; see also *Belfast Graves* (Dublin: National Graves Association, 1985), p. 53.

6

Éire in the Emergency and the Irish in Britain

It was in September of thirty-nine.
And the sky was full of lead.
Hitler was heading for Warsaw.
And the Irish for Holyhead.

These humorous lines by The Dubliners open one of their great songs, *McAlpine's Fusiliers*, which is dedicated to Ireland's migrant workers in Britain. They do less than justice, however, to the thousands of Irish people who would, before long, make the opposite journey to join Britain's armed forces or its wartime labour force. But Chamberlain's declaration of war on Germany on 3 September 1939 was followed by a sizeable movement of Irish men and women whose initial preference was to return to neutral Éire as soon as they could.

For several days they packed the mail boats from English and Scottish ports, as well as from Holyhead in Anglesey. By 5 September the numbers landing at Rosslare and Dun Laoghaire were such that John Dulanty, Éire's high commissioner in London, made representations to the Dominions Office about whether the influx could be controlled.[1] Basil Brooke, a Stormont Unionist MP who, in 1943, became Prime Minister of Northern Ireland, had been in Scotland when war broke out, and observed in his diary of his return journey to Belfast: 'Masses of Irish on Glasgow boat. Running away.'[2]

Apart from the widely shared anticipation of air attack, conscription was what many among these homeward travellers feared and, in some cases, resented. It had been introduced to Britain but not to Northern Ireland under legislation of June 1939. It applied to those aged twenty-one, and those a year older became liable under further legislation in December. Relatively few young Irishmen in Britain were, in fact, liable for call-up because they were protected by the Free State's 1935 Citizenship and Nationality Act. This made Irish citizenship available to those born out of Ireland but with just one Irish parent.

Four months into the war, de Valera set out his view of the position in a speech to the Dáil.

> Every person who acquired Irish citizenship by virtue of the constitution of 1922 or who has acquired or acquires citizenship under the 1935 act, possesses Irish nationality only and should not be liable to military service in the event of war, whether permanently or temporarily resident in Britain.[3]

He also argued that permanent residents in Britain born of Irish parents were not liable either and that conscripting them would be in breach of the 1930 Hague convention on citizenship, signed by both states.

His words were gladly reported in the *Glasgow Observer and Scottish Catholic Herald*, a newspaper read by many Irish people who were resident in Scotland at the outbreak of the war. Their legal position was no different from that of their compatriots living in England, or so they hoped, but in fact de Valera had not been able to secure overall exemption from the call-up for Irishmen in Britain. Its national service legislation of 1939 and 1940 decreed that anyone who had lived there for two years was liable but that they could be exempted if they wished to return permanently to Éire. They then needed an exit permit and documentary proof from Éire's high commissioner in London that they had homes in Ireland.

The permit was valid for the journey home only and, if anyone granted it returned to Britain, he or she would at once be liable for military service. Some who sought exit permits complained of their treatment by the authorities who, in some places, clearly categorised them as defaulting nationals. 'This is not our position at all,' one group of young Irish workers told the press. 'We are quite willing to return to Éire and renounce all claims to England's hospitality.'[4] Another group was quoted by their parish priest: 'Our sympathies are neither English nor German: we dislike the Nazi mentality, but for us the British Army has associations of a more personal and much more bitter sort.'[5]

Many young Irishmen remained anxious about the operation of the exit permit system and wrote to the Department of External Affairs in Dublin stressing their intention of joining the Irish state's defence forces once they returned. A Glasgow-based body, the Irish Citizens League and Advisory Bureau, was set up in 1940 to help them and to make sure that exit permits were fairly granted.[6]

A letter survives from May of 1940 which is a reminder of how some of the Irish in Britain felt about the call-up. Leo Casey was from Belfast but living in Scotland where he seemed to think he was safer than he would be south of the border. A letter home to his brother made clear his sympathies: 'I scan the paper carefully every day for Republican news . . . For God's sake don't go to England until their war is over. Believe me, they'll conscript you if you can walk.'[7]

Life had always been hard for the Irish who had crossed to England and Scotland in search of work. In April 1940 one group of labourers brought over to a heavy construction job near Inverary in Argyll decided to go home for reasons unrelated to the war. Their major grievance was that the nearest church where they could hear Mass was 30 miles away in Dunoon. Ten of them walked further than that, to Oban, to seek transfers from their employer back to Ireland. Their complaints included overcrowded accommodation, sometimes fifteen to a hut, verminous bedding, bad food and sanitation and arbitrary pay stoppages. 'All over the country Irishmen are up against the same thing,'[8] a sympathetic newspaper reported.

In their case, unless they could find work right away on their return home they might wait up to six weeks for any benefit payments from the Irish state. For many others who made the same journey in the opening months of the war, the future was an uncertain one. Concern was acute in government circles in Dublin about the war's economic implications. Éire needed the British market for most of its exports, and it imported almost all its coal as well as essential machinery and machine tools for its manufacturing industry, limited though that was.

In May 1940 de Valera had talks with the state's leading bankers to seek their advice about funding increased emergency expenditure. He was also concerned to alert them to the politically dangerous potential of increased unemployment. This seemed an inevitable result of the war to Seán Lemass, an energetic minister who, in July, took over the new Ministry of Supplies. He did his best to convince his Cabinet colleagues of the need for interventionist economic policies to combat the disastrous job losses which would arise from a possibly total economic isolation of Éire.

Such isolation seemed a real possibility in 1940. Churchill's utterances about the Treaty Ports and the war at sea, and his anger at de Valera's rejection of his June unification offer, fuelled Irish fears that economic sanctions by Britain were imminent. The first clear call for these came from the head of the Northern Ireland civil service, Sir Wilfrid Spender. Early in November, he wrote two letters to Lord Hankey, Chancellor of the Duchy of Lancaster in Churchill's government, arguing that de Valera's policy ought to result in a degree of hardship for Éire's people.[9] Hankey circulated the letter to colleagues and replied to Spender that his comments had met with agreement 'in the most important quarter to which I sent it',[10] meaning Churchill himself. Churchill was quick to seek advice on how best to apply pressure on Éire, and singled out the extent to which, under existing trade agreements, Éire's exports to Britain were, in fact, subsidised. 'Pray let me know how these subsidies could be terminated,' he wrote to his chancellor, Sir Kingsley Wood, in a memorandum on 1 December 1940. He went on to ask 'what retaliatory measures could be taken in the financial sphere by the Irish', observing that 'we are not afraid of their cutting off our food, as it would save us the enormous mass of fertilisers and feeding stuffs we have to carry into Ireland through the de Valera-aided German blockade'.[11]

These last words were unjust as de Valera had agreed that RAF aircraft operating from bases at Lough Erne in Northern Ireland could fly over Irish state territory to shorten flying times during vital convoy protection duties in the battle of the Atlantic. Churchill did recognise this gesture in a later letter to Lord Cranborne, his dominions secretary though, in it, he confused Lough Erne with Lough Swilly, but his language was still uncompromising and even vengeful:

> No attempt should be made to conceal from Mr de Valera the depth and intensity of feeling against the policy of Irish neutrality. We have tolerated and acquiesced in it, but judicially we have never recognised that Southern Ireland is an independent sovereign state.'[12]

His chancellor of the Exchequer had already provided Churchill with a plan of action to make Éire feel the consequences of its neutrality. On 16 December 1940 he advised the prime minister how Éire's shipping space for crucial imports could be drastically cut. Éire had been able to charter ships, acting through Britain, but Wood proposed that pressure could be put on other countries not to make shipping available 'except to Allies or co-operators'. He offered other proposals for shutting off most of Éire's imports of fuel, food, fertiliser and machine tools from Britain as well as the freezing of its sterling balances which would seriously disrupt the country's ability to pay for other imports.

Such measures were were potentially punitive but, in December 1940, Churchill, writing to Roosevelt about the war at sea, was careful to justify the imminent change in policy towards Éire in terms of national necessity. He told the President:

> We are so hard-pressed at sea, that we cannot undertake to carry any longer the 400,000 tons of feeding-stuffs and fertilisers which we have hitherto convoyed to Éire through all the attacks of the enemy. We need this tonnage for our own supply and we do not need the food which Éire has been sending us.[13]

With all of Britain 'digging for victory' as shortages worsened, this last assertion was debatable but Churchill did express regret to Roosevelt for the hardships Irish people might suffer, while going on to justify the phasing out of subsidies to Irish food exporters.

Sir Kingsley Wood, provider of the economic strategy to be deployed against Éire, justified it to the Cabinet in very similar terms and, in January 1941, the plan to block Éire's chartering of ships was implemented. The results were almost immediate. Petrol rationing had to be introduced, private motorists' allowances were cut by 75 per cent and the amount of already rationed tea available in shops was halved.

The full apparatus of sanctions against Éire which had been laid before Churchill was not implemented. He and his ministers, after all, had to balance their desire to make the Irish state and its people pay some part of the price of their neutrality against the hope that de Valera would make further covert moves to help Britain's fight or even to join the war, as Churchill seemed to hope he might after the Japanese attack on Pearl Harbor.

For Irish people as a whole, the war meant adaptation to worsening shortages but there was no general rationing until June 1942. Because of the loss of shipping capacity, coal, which came entirely from Britain, had to be rationed in January of 1941 and, in September of that year, Dublin's supply of domestic coal went down at one point to just enough for one week. Supplies of meat and potatoes remained adequate but staples such as butter, margarine and above all tea became scarce. At the worst point in the Emergency years, the weekly allowance of tea went down to under an ounce (28g) per person while sugar was cut to 8 ounces (225g) and butter to 6 (170g).

Bread was rationed in 1942, and restrictions in the supply of other commodities inevitably drove up prices both on the open market and in the less official networks of sale and distribution which developed. As the coal-supply crisis grew acute, trains began to run on timber and straw as substitutes. The rail system as a result slowed down to the point where, in the winter of 1942, the 200-mile journey from Killarney to Dublin took twenty-three hours. One Dublin train travelling to Athlone along a line parallel for some distance to the Royal Canal was passed twice by a barge.[14] The crisis, in fact, reached a point where the city of Limerick opened up a stagecoach service to Adare, complete with horse teams and a post horn player.[15]

By 1943 private motoring had almost ceased as petrol supplies threatened to dry up entirely and, to ease the crisis in coal supplies, a propaganda campaign was launched to encourage the use of turf and peat. In towns and cities traditional skills in drying peats and turfs had to be relearned. Long strips of both hanging over suburban washing lines became a familiar sight, while Dublin's vice-regal Phoenix Park became a storage area for emergency supplies which were sometimes stacked there to a height of 30 feet (9m).

Cutting and loading turf were back-breaking jobs and, when de Valera announced in 1941 that an extra 3 million tons would be needed that summer, desperate measures were set in motion to find the necessary labour. Schools were encouraged to release older pupils to help; as many private firms as could be found were brought in; and, at one point, local councils were employing 16,000 men on this work. Conditions and accommodation were often atrocious, especially on the great Bog of Allen in County Kildare, and some councils brought severe pressure to bear on unemployed men to take work 'on the turf' or to have their benefits suspended if they left it 'without cause'.[16]

Wages never compared with those known to be available in wartime industry in England and Scotland, but so urgent was the need for fuel that, in July 1941, the Dublin government was considering acquiring powers to control the movement of labour out of the state, especially that of workers who were needed for fuel or food production.[17]

Even with these shortages there was, apart from coal and petrol, plenty to buy for those with money. People from Northern Ireland were free to travel to Dublin and were often astonished at the food which still seemed to be available. Moya Woodside, the Mass Observation diarist, visited Dublin in September 1940 and recorded her reaction to what she saw: 'Britain must have some good political reasons for allowing two thirds of Ireland (thanks to the British Fleet) to be a land thriving with milk and honey.'[18]

Others reacted similarly, such as the English journalist J. L. Hodson, who arrived in Dublin fresh from covering London life under the Blitz, to find his hotel still serving a seven course dinner at ten o'clock at night.[19] A week later he returned on the ferry to Holyhead and the reality of a dismal meal: 'I began to understand the irascibility of the Irishmen who come over from a land of plenty to this – unreasonable as that irascibility may be.'[20]

Real hardship was not always immediately apparent to those who made only brief visits and stayed in good Dublin hotels. Two decades earlier, war had meant record prices for Irish exports to Britain, particularly farm produce, but, from 1940 onwards, rationing and strict price controls as part of a wartime planned economy meant that Éire's export earnings were minimal. This, along with the drastic reduction in the flow of crucial raw materials from Britain, brought a serious fall both in industrial output and in employment in Éire.

A sharp decline in working-class spending power resulted, worsened by the freeze on wages imposed under an emergency powers order in 1942 which was not lifted until 1946, while living costs soared in a wartime economy defined by shortages. One survey of Cork city carried out by its local University College and completed in 1944, though not published, used Seebohm Rowntree's basic 'human needs standard' and found that 45 per cent of households there were living in poverty.[21]

Éire's child and infant mortality rose sharply during the Emergency years as did the incidence of tuberculosis. Two years after the end of the Emergency, deaths from it were still higher than they had been in 1939 while, in Northern Ireland they had already been brought below pre-war levels by 1945. Dublin, with one-fifth of the state's population, suffered one-third of its deaths from TB between 1936 and 1941. Noel Browne, a young Irish doctor, who had himself been treated for the illness and who had completed his medical studies in wartime Britain where he had seen a national health care system in embryonic form, returned to Éire in 1944 and was affronted by the shortcomings of the hospital service there and its attitude to low-income patients, especially tuberculosis victims to whom he had a special commitment.[22]

That same year, Dr John Dignan, Bishop of Clonfert, wrote a pamphlet in which he described Éire's Medical Assistance Service, on which the poorest of the population depended, as tainted by 'destitution, pauperism and degradation'.[23] Dealing with such issues, however, simply did not take centre stage in political debates in wartime Éire. As early as July 1940, Seán Lemass, when appointed Minister of Supplies, made the case in the Cabinet for actively inter-ventionist policies to tackle the unemployment and poverty which he judged would worsen because of the war. Lemass has been seen as a moderniser in Irish politics after the Emergency period but, during it, he was thwarted by 'the inertia and conservatism of his own party and colleagues',[24] notably Seán MacEntee, the finance minister.

The Catholic Church made some attempt to increase its involvement in social questions and, in April 1941, some of its bishops formed the Catholic Social Service Conference to formulate alternatives to any statist approach to tackling poverty and inequality. When the 1942 Beveridge Report, with its commitment to full employment and a welfare state, became a best-seller in Britain, the de Valera govern-ment's reaction has been called one of 'vulgar political fear'.[25] The Taoiseach himself saw a structure of church-based and privately funded charity as the practical alternative to Beveridge, and Arch-bishop McQuaid of Dublin led the ideological counterattack with zealous support from MacEntee in the Cabinet, who constantly invoked the 1937 constitution's articles on the primacy of the family in responsibility for matters of education and welfare.

De Valera had real problems in confronting the realities of poverty and palpably inadequate welfare services. In one speech during the 1943 Dáil election campaign, he insisted that 'there is nobody in this country who is not getting proper food' and that 'every section of the community has had the careful regard of the government.'[26] The year 1943 was also the one in which, as part of a Saint Patrick's Day broadcast, he famously set out his essentially pastoral vision of his ideal Ireland:

> . . . the home of a people who were satisfied with frugal comfort and devoted their leisure to things of the spirit – a land whose countryside would be bright with cosy homesteads, whose fields and villages would be joyous with the sounds of industry, with the romping of sturdy children, the contests of athletic youths and the laughter of comely maidens, whose firesides would be the forums for serene old age. It would in a word, be the home of a people living the life that God desires that man should live.[27]

The actual attainability of this demi-paradise was doubted by some of those close to de Valera, not least Seán Lemass. With the support of the Ministry of Finance, he challenged the case for the further settlement of families in smallholdings unlikely to provide them with adequate income. Many farmers hard hit by the Emergency agreed and, in the 1943 Dáil elections, a party representing them, Clann na Talmhan (party of the land) won fourteen seats and 11 per cent of the total vote, much of it in areas previously strong in support of de Valera's own Fianna Fáil party.

The Labour Party, which had been gaining rapidly in branches and membership and had the support of Irish Communists after they dissolved their own small party in 1941, won seventeen seats and over 15 per cent of the vote. This was proof at last that it could run Fianna Fáil close for the urban working-class vote. It was, however, a false dawn for Labour. The legendary Jim Larkin, hero of the 1913 Dublin transport workers' strike, who had espoused Marxism and been a delegate at the founding Congress of the American Communist Party, had joined Labour and won a Dáil seat with its backing in 1943. A group of Dáil Labour TDs (Teachta Dála or deputies) feared Larkin's influence so much that they resigned from the Dáil the following year to form a new National Labour Party. Labour's advance was halted in the snap Dáil election called by de Valera in 1944. Its vote was almost halved and it lost nine seats.

Fianna Fáil, and particularly Seán MacEntee, seized the chance to attack Labour in the most lurid terms, using the red-scare tactics of which they themselves had been victims at the hands of their opponents before de Valera took office in 1932. The new party's emergence in fact split the political labour movement at the very point when it might have developed a radical alternative to the infirmity of purpose on social issues shown by the state's two main parties.

Leading members of the Catholic hierarchy and lay organisations too eagerly supported this offensive against Labour. The Cold War began early in Ireland and trade unionism was also a victim. The Irish Congress of Trade Unions was led by the reformist, William O'Brien, who had prior to 1914 worked with James Larkin. His aversion to what he thought Labour had become led him to disaffiliate his own Irish Transport and General Workers Union from the party, then to take it out of the congress itself because of what he saw in the latter as the excessive role of left-leaning British-based unions. He formed a breakaway Congress of Unions and the resulting split within organised labour was a further impediment to change though, even before this, campaigns against the de Valera government's 1941 wage freeze and its legislation to restrict union rights had achieved no real success.

A society as conservative and Church dominated as Éire was in 1945, needed a strong Labour movement, just as Britain did to make a reality of its people's wartime aspirations to social justice. Once back in Ireland, the young Noel Browne, committed as he was to a state-backed campaign against the tuberculosis which had ravaged his own family, and to welfare reforms, was clear that the Labour party did not want his membership. He threw his support behind the new party formed by Seán McBride, Clann na Poblachta. This was the measure of Irish Labour's failure in the Emergency years.

For the Irish state and its people, the social memory of the period 1939 to 1945 was defined by the relative deprivations brought about by the Emergency. Without the movement of labour to Britain these would have been much worse but hardship became acute for the urban and rural poor who remained. Despite the words of the 1916 Easter proclamation, a self-governing Irish state had signally failed to 'cherish all its children equally', and the Emergency had worsened the plight of many of them.

Even so, the reality of the war that confronted the people of Warsaw, London, Leningrad and latterly Germany itself, never really came home to Éire. 'At the time I suppose we thought we were going through hard times,' one middle-class Dubliner wrote forty years afterwards. 'It was only later when we realised what was happening in other parts of Europe – the saturation bombings, the concentration camps, the sheer horror and misery – that we recognised what a comfortable war we had had.'[28]

There were the bodies washed ashore on the west coast, mostly those of British sailors as the U-boat war took its toll, and there were the German air attacks of 1941, the products of navigational errors by the Luftwaffe. The worst of them was on the night of 31 May when a well-lubricated Bertie Smyllie left the *Irish Times* office wearing a steel helmet and with a broom on his shoulder as if it were a rifle. He had borrowed both items from the paper's Air Raid Precaution Post but his services were not required.[29]

The Dublin government registered a protest with Berlin, and Hempel at the German legation was greatly shocked by the raid. Some IRA sympathisers were prompt, of course, in blaming Britain, even claiming that the RAF had used reconstructed German aircraft for an attack which might help bring Éire into the war on the side of the Allies.[30] It remains possible that the RAF's ability to jam German radio signals had thrown off course some aircraft tasked to hit targets in Wales[31] but, in any event, the post-war West German government paid compensation to the Irish state. The 31 May bombing destroyed or damaged three hundred houses, mostly in Dublin's North Strand area. Thirty-four people were killed and ninety injured, only a fraction of Belfast's death toll a few weeks earlier.

The real war for Irish people was that experienced by those who made their decision to enlist in Britain's forces, and their story has begun to be told and belatedly to be recognised by the Irish state itself. No official figures were published on the numbers from both Éire and Northern Ireland who served in the British armed forces during the war, and some wildly differing estimates have been made, with the Irish Consul General in New York in 1945 claiming 300,000 for Éire alone.[32] No final figure has emerged though some patient recent work has arrived at just under 100,000 volunteers from both sides of the Irish border who served in the British army. Slightly more of these, 50,644, came from Éire.[33]

In the Free State, or Éire, as it later became, there were many who continued to serve in the British forces. With the army, particularly, this could be because of family tradition. It was also a result of the fact that the new state's defence forces were, from the conclusion of the civil war in 1923, kept small for for financial and for political reasons.[34] With service in the British forces continuing to offer substantially better pay and opportunities, the outbreak of war in 1939 accentuated a pattern which had already been set.

One sergeant in the Irish Guards put it well when, at the height of the battle for the Anzio beachhead in 1944, he was asked by an English-speaking German prisoner why, as a citizen of a neutral state, he was fighting for Britain. His reply was simply: 'They've fed me for seven years. Now I'm earning my keep.'[35] A few weeks earlier, his battalion had been piped on to their landing craft at Naples to tunes such as The Minstrel Boy and The Wearing of the Green. They were en route to a battle of attrition which destroyed them as a unit and which their chaplain described as being worse than that which he had experienced on the Western Front a generation earlier.[36]

Though the Irish Guards had always taken pride in recruiting from both sides of the border, they had also to rely on non-Irish conscripts to bring their units up to full combat strength. This was true of other Irish regiments but it was never allowed to dilute their distinctive ethos, certainly not those who were part of the 38th Irish infantry brigade to whose formation Churchill gave his strong support in 1942 even though John Andrews, the Northern Ireland prime minister, took strong exception to this move. For him there was a sinister all-Ireland agenda involved, as he wrote to Clement Attlee, Churchill's deputy, objecting to what he claimed was a policy 'calculated to obliterate or blur the distinction between the belligerency of Northern Ireland and the neutrality of Éire'.[37] His objections were overruled, and an existing brigade was simply renumbered and its English battalions replaced with Irish ones. One of these was the Sixth Royal Inniskilling Fusiliers. This formation took part in severe fighting in Tunisia, Sicily and Italy. During a respite in the brutal battle for Monte Cassino, the Inniskillings held a St Patrick's Day party and ceilidh which seems, according to its unit diary, to have taken on a life of its own. During it, as the revelry grew, greetings were sent out by telegram to King George VI, to the Duke of Gloucester, the regiment's colonel-in-chief, as well as to the Roman Catholic Church and Church of Ireland archbishops of Armagh and also to de Valera. Most of these greetings were acknowledged and reciprocated but the latter's reply is not on record.[38]

Less than a year later, the Eighth Army, with which the Irish brigade was serving, had reached the northern plains of Lombardy and was given its place in the assault crossing of the River Po. A Church of Ireland rector's son was there as a young infantry lieutenant and later recalled the preparations:

> The Irish turned up in force. Not only were there battalions of the Royal Inniskilling Fusiliers, and the London Irish Rifles carrying the fighting tradition of the historic Irish brigade, but there were the North Irish Horse and thousands of Irishmen from the 'neutral' South who had infiltrated every unit in the country – all keen to get into the fight while applauding de Valera's astuteness in keeping them out of the war.[39]

The Irish had 'turned up' on many other fronts, too, and they were also serving with the Royal Navy and the RAF. Brian Inglis, a writer and journalist, volunteered for aircrew duty while remaining a believer in the Irish state's right to go its own way.[40] Another RAF volunteer, Fergus Duffy from Bantry, later declared in a newspaper interview that he had 'no problems with Irish neutrality'[41] and that he met many in the RAF who were well able to see the reasons for it.

The British armed forces could not, of course, accept all the young Irishmen who offered themselves for service. At the Inniskilling Fusiliers depot at Omagh in County Tyrone, or in Armagh where the Royal Ulster Rifles were based, recruiting sergeants could take pity on some of those who arrived in the hope of joining up.

Each day there were four, five, six boys from the South of Ireland came over the border, some of them literally in their bare feet, because at that time there was very little work in the South and they came and joined up for two shillings a day,

recalled one Armagh-based soldier who also described the aspiring riflemen as 'small, under-nourished, with a hint of desperation'.[42]

The British military authorities also had to establish, so far as they were able, whether Irishmen seeking to enlist had, in fact, deserted from their own country's defence forces. Their rates of pay had never compared favourably with those on offer in Britain, and compulsory deductions also applied for haircuts, laundry and 'welfare'. Even when a private soldier's basic wage was raised to fourteen shillings a week (70 pence in today's money) in 1942, payment of half of the one shilling increase was deferred until the end of the Emergency.

All of this, along with the prospect of overseas service and real action, tempted serving soldiers to offer their experience and basic knowledge of drill and weapons to the British forces. Similarly with the Air Corps, whose relationship with the RAF had been close anyway through the purchase of aircraft and the provision of instructors, pay and conditions in British service were a temptation, especially once any real threat of a German invasion of Éire had clearly passed. Moreover, as one Air Corps man who crossed into Northern Ireland to join the RAF put it: 'most of the Army Air Corps men would have been fairly sympathetic to the British'.[43]

How concerned the British services were to identify whether Irish recruits had unofficially left Éire's defence forces remains questionable. General McKenna, the Éire army chief of staff accepted in 1943 that desertion to the British forces had become a real problem, given that 'those who have a natural taste for military life are more inclined to join the British services, where a more exciting career is expected'.[44] A high incidence of desertion occurred in units serving close to the border,[45] and G2, the Irish army intelligence service, reported in 1945 that over 5,000 non-commissioned officers and privates were on 'absence without leave', some for as long as three or four years and 4,000 for more than twelve months.[46]

All who made this decision were, of course, liable to court martial if they returned home. Two who did, in 1945, Patrick Kehoe who had left the defence forces to volunteer for aircrew duty with RAF Bomber Command, and Patrick Shannon who had joined the British Army in 1941 and fought in North Africa and Italy, were both arrested. Kehoe told his prosecutors that the suffering of his relatives under the Blitz in England had made him decide that he wanted to 'get a crack' at Hitler. Shannon's defence was that he joined the British army 'so that he could support his mother'. The officer assigned to their defence argued that desertion meant leaving one's post to escape danger but that this could not apply in cases where men had opted to leave safety to face danger and death. Kehoe and Shannon were found guilty and were each sentenced to 156 days' detention, sentences which were at once commuted and both were discharged from the defence forces.[47]

The issue of how the Irish state should treat those who had left its defence forces to enter British service became a contentious one after the Emergency. Some Dáil members demanded the enforcement of an order under emergency powers legislation which could have applied seven years of 'civil disability' to deserters who returned to Éire, no matter how distinguished their war service might have been. There were some rancid contributions to this debate: for example, from one Fianna Fáil TD who crudely and gracelessly told the chamber that:

> We hear this song and dance about Belsen camps and so forth and about the glorious place the Irishmen who were in the British army won for themselves . . . Freeing deserters to a possible enemy is simply putting a premium on desertion and a premium on treason.[48]

Sanctions which would have penalised those who had enlisted in Britain's cause were not applied and, after all, the Irish government had never attempted to place any impediment in their way. As Dr F. H. Boland, assistant secretary at the DEA during the Emergency, put it later in a memoir dictated to his daughter:

> There was a suggestion after the war that these ex-members of the National Army who had deserted to join the British Forces, should lose their eligibility for unemployment benefit. Dev was opposed to this, and when it was put to him, he said 'No'.[49]

Even so, for far too long the Irish state and Irish society remained ambivalent and ungenerous to those of its citizens who had played their part in a victory over Hitler which most Irish people welcomed. These men and women, when they took home leave during the war, had to discard their uniforms and wear civilian clothes provided by the British government in agreement with Éire. Facilities for this were made available at Holyhead and other ferry ports but, in a real sense, this need to conceal their choice outlasted the war in a way that many in today's very different and far more inclusive Ireland take no pride in.

Their fate was also to be pressed into service by those who wanted to argue that neutral Éire had, in fact, provided more volunteers in Britain's cause than super-loyal Northern Ireland. Even before the war in Europe ended, the government of Northern Ireland was becoming fearful of such claims. Often they were much exaggerated, and they continued to be, especially after the outbreak of the Troubles in 1969. Robert Fisk showed that, actually, the figures for Éire and Northern Ireland were not dramatically different, allowing for the former's larger population. He also performed a service by stressing the overall absurdity of an argument which, in its petty point scoring, was unworthy of those who joined up from both sides of the border.[50]

Richard Doherty, in his work, made a reasoned contribution to the debate, drawing upon sources such as the British army's honour roll and the records of the Commonwealth War Graves Commission. His findings brought him close to Fisk's conclusions. He made the questionable assertion, however, that Irishmen who had been resident in Britain long enough before the war to become liable for conscription can be regarded as volunteers because they had the option of departing to Éire once their call-up papers arrived.[51] In reality, Irish people long settled in England or Scotland, with homes and jobs, who were of military age could not necessarily return to an Éire hard hit economically by the war and where employment would not have been guaranteed.

Like their Scottish and English counterparts, many of them were ready to 'do their bit' in the war but they remain a problematic group to quantify for those who want to be exact in their assessment of an overall Irish contribution. Significant numbers of Irish and Ulster people, wherever they found themselves living in 1939 and after, acquiesced in, or volunteered for, war service in Britain's cause. Their choices and the reasons for them have begun to receive the recognition, and also the examination, that they deserve.[52]

The variety of reasons behind their choices should take nothing from that recognition. Who would want it to in the case of the fictional RAF volunteer in Brian Moore's novel *The Emperor of Ice-Cream*? A product of Belfast's middle-class Nationalist community, he asks the novel's narrator: 'So you think anyone ever joins up for purely patriotic reasons, even the English? Fellows join up because they want to leave home, have some excitement, stuff girls, and so on. All of them.' Becoming more eloquent at the bar during a former pupils' dance, he goes on: 'At least I won't die wrestling to get my man in between the thighs of some cold Irish virgin. This uniform is going to liberate me.'[53]

At the war's end, Seán O'Casey, who had lived in England since 1926 and adhered to the British Communist Party's view of the war, reserved most of his praise for the part played by the Soviet Union and the Red Army. As to the Irish contribution to victory he simply wrote of it as the continuation of a long history of 'England's wars' always drawing in the Irish. He cited a roll call of names of Irish soldiers who had earned their keep in foreign wars and offered the thought that: 'there'll always be blossoms of blood on our sprigs of green. Are we proud of these men? Not a bit.' and he added: 'their names are never mentioned at home'.[54]

He was wrong there but it took time for justice to be done to their memory. A writer such as Robert Fisk, who was not Irish, helped the process along with his ground-breaking 1983 study of Éire's neutrality and how Northern Ireland and Britain responded to it. Six years later an eminent Irish military historian, J. P. Duggan, who had fully supported de Valera's stance during the war, wrote of the utter evil of Nazi Germany and the role of his compatriots in fighting it: 'Thousands of Irishmen died at the tip of the spear – that's where they generally were – on the battlefields,'[55] he declared and the history of the war clearly bears him out.

Duggan added to his tribute the thought that 'Thousands more worked in Britain's munition factories, farms and hospitals. It was an extraordinary, unsung contribution.'[56] If it was unsung at the time, it was so in the sense that Éire could make no official acknowledgement of the extent of it any more than could the British authorities, if doing so would embarrass de Valera or in any way serve to compromise his policy of neutrality.[57] Like enlistment in Britain's armed forces, the role of the Irish on its 'factory front' and in other industries and services desperate for labour was something for Éire's state censors to exclude, so far as they could, from press and radio coverage of the Emergency.[58]

Some accounts suggest that as many as 180,000 Éire citizens moved to Britain to obtain work during the Emergency years.[59] The figure is probably not quite as high as this because not all those who received travel permits to work in Britain necessarily used them in the end. Éire's Department of External Affairs figures point to more than 172,000 permits being granted from 1941 until 1945.[60] In any event, the process was still a huge one which altered the spatial pattern of Irish movement to Britain away from Scotland and

Lancashire to the English Midlands where there was a vast concentration of war-production plants. This shift continued to mark the post-1945 years though London retained its importance as a destination for the Irish-born to work and often to settle in.[61]

Prior to 1939, Irish citizens had the right of free movement to Britain. This right was unaffected by the Free State's introduction of Irish passports and it, like Éire under the 1937 constitution, remained part of a Common Travel Area within the British Commonwealth of which it was still a member.[62] By then migration had passed its peak though this had not prevented some rancid campaigns against the immigrant Irish.

A writer as popular as J. B. Priestley succumbed very easily to such prejudice. Writing of Liverpool in 1933 he declared that.

> a great many speeches have been made and books written on the subject of what England has done to Ireland. I should be interested to hear a speech or read a book or two on the subject of what Ireland has done to England. If we do have an Irish Republic as our neighbour, and it is found possible to return her exiled citizens, what a grand clearance there will be in all the Western ports, from the Clyde to Cardiff, what a fine exit of ignorance and dirt and drunkenness and disease.[63]

At the same time, and over much of the interwar period in Scotland, the Church of Scotland's General Assembly and its Church and Nation Committee issued regular calls for action to curb Irish immigration as a threat to the country's religious and cultural identity. One secretary of state for Scotland, Sir Godfrey Collins, raised the issue without success in the Cabinet in 1933 and, in both Edinburgh and Glasgow, locally based and viciously sectarian and anti-Irish political movements gained significant, though only temporary, support.[64]

When war came in 1939, control over Irish movement to Britain was already in operation as a security measure made necessary by the IRA's bombing campaign. Under legislation enacted in July of that year, all newly arrived Irish people had to register with the police and also to report to them if they changed their addresses or places of employment. Fear and uncertainty created by the war had an initial impact on travel to Britain but seasonal and temporary migration by Irish farm workers continued, although they needed to have temporary residence visas.

As it became clear that the war was going to be a long one, Britain's requirements for labour became paramount and, starting in the winter of 1940, it had contact through the Ministry of Labour with the Dublin government over the practicalities of recruiting workers in Éire. Some British firms, such as ICI and Ford, which were handling large war contracts, already had offices and agents in Éire to carry out recruitment. By early 1941, applications for work in Britain were putting severe pressure on Éire's labour exchanges and, in July of that year, agreement was reached by the two governments on ways to facilitate the movement of Irish workers to Britain.

Under the July terms, the Ministry of Labour could not set up its own agencies in Éire to co-ordinate recruitment there, and the Irish government in turn would have the right to block recommendations for the issue of travel permits by the ministry's liaison officers. Their criteria for doing this were that only people without work and for whom none seemed available should get permits. Whether Irish labour exchanges which issued the permits enforced these rules fully is another matter though, in October 1941, they had to do so when the age limit for applying was raised to twenty-two.

From this point onwards direct recruitment by British firms was halted. They had to work through liaison officers assigned to Éire by the Ministry of Labour, the Ministry of Supply and later by the Royal Ordnance factories and the Ministry of Aircraft Production. Even so, some in Éire continued to see the hand of British employers seeking to denude Éire of its youth. Dr Michael Browne, the Bishop of Clonfert, told a newspaper in late August 1941 that Ireland had

> been invaded by agents of foreign firms who are trying to get strong young Irishmen to leave the country for work abroad. I am surprised that these are allowed to operate so freely, for they are a danger to their victims and to the nation.[65]

The danger he feared was to young Catholics going to live in Britain but the Dublin government's attitude had to be a more pragmatic one. This was to let British employment liaison officers and agents do their work, interviewing applicants for work and travel permits without actively encouraging them to leave Éire, as well as using the censorship to prevent the press from advertising job vacancies outside Éire. The agents' work was time-consuming and slow because of the fuel crisis and its impact on public transport links. Hotels were often used discreetly for interviews, with generous tips for staff to maintain at least a degree of secrecy. Results could be slow, and some agents reported back to the Ministries of Labour and

Supply that as many as half those they had interviewed either failed the necessary medical tests or changed their minds, sometimes under the influence of parents or clergy.[66]

Not all Catholic clergy tried to talk their parishioners out of migrating to Britain for wartime work. In February 1943, Nancy Lyons was in her early twenties and was the oldest of three brothers and four sisters, working long hours on a farm owned by ageing parents. A local priest who was also her cousin told her to break away. 'The only thing I can see for you at the end of your days is having a lot of cats around you. You're going to stay until you are so old nobody else is going to want you. They're all going to go away.'[67] She made her decision and got her travel permit to start nursing training in a London hospital.

The uptake of travel and work permits by Éire citizens increased year on year in response to Britain's ceaseless demand for labour. It began to slow down only in 1944 as a result of intensive security measures and travel restrictions prior to the Normandy invasion. Inevitably, the implications for Éire's economy and for urban and rural society were discussed at government level. In September 1941, the Department of Industry and Commerce set out in a memorandum a case for controlling the level of migration, partly to protect the country's agricultural output.

Dr Enda Delaney has charted the debate which followed, with the Department of Finance making the first response. Its officials made the case that it was better for the moral fibre of workers to take employment in Britain or in Northern Ireland than to live on state benefits at home. The Department of External Affairs was also drawn into the debate. Its assistant secretary, F. H. Boland, focused on the possible social turmoil within the state if migration was curbed. For him the priority was to find the right balance in policy which would avoid a labour shortage at home and also minimise threats to social order. He looked further ahead to the war's end and argued that there would need to be negotiations with Britain to avoid the abrupt repatriation of a workforce 'who will, no doubt, have imbibed a good deal of leftism in Britain'.[68]

In May 1942, when a crisis in agricultural output seemed imminent, the Dublin government did act to control the migration of those with experience in farm work and turf cutting. The debate among ministers and civil servants, it has rightly been said, revealed real double standards, with pious talk about emigration's moral and cultural dangers neatly balanced against fear of class unrest if it was held back by state action. As to concerns about Irish war workers returning home when hostilities ceased, events would show that civil servants and ministers were happy enough for them to extend their stay in Britain indefinitely.[69]

Yet the whole process had huge effects upon Irish society. Women had been conspicuous and often predominant among the numbers leaving for Britain. This had a marked effect on the population's gender balance given that, in Éire's twenty-six counties, males had outnumbered females in every census since 1911. 'Whole communities withered, their roots torn away, whole villages became totally deserted and rural Ireland in particular went into a dramatic decline. As the social and economic opportunities diminished even further for those left behind, another cycle of emigration was ensured.'[70] The scene was set for some of the bleakest imagery in the post-war fiction of William Trevor, Edna O'Brien and others.

For those who secured clearance to take work in Britain, there could be ordeals ahead before actual embarkation. The Irish authorities came under pressure from Britain to ensure that migrant workers carried no infections, and this took on more urgency after an outbreak of typhus in Western Ireland in 1943. Leaving delousing procedures to the British port authorities evoked Famine memories of the degrading treatment of Irish people arriving in Britain during those years, so the Dublin Department of Local Government and Public Health instituted a health embarkation scheme which processed 55,000 people between 1943 and 1947.

On arrival in Dublin, prospective migrants, as well as those enlisting in the British armed forces, were referred to two hotels, one for men and one for women, for medical inspection. Then they were assigned to public baths from which the water had been drained. Dr James Deeny, an adviser to the department and later chief medical officer in Dublin, and a man of humane instincts, later described the scene at the baths.

> There I saw something I will not forget. The baths had been emptied. On a floor of a pool were large sherry half-casks. Men with rubber aprons and Wellington boots were hosing people down and bathing them with disinfectant in the casks. All around were naked men, seemingly in hundreds. The place was full of steam and the smell of disinfectant.[71]

After all this, embarkation, too, could often be a bleak business as one observer of it at Dublin's ferry terminal later recalled in somewhat staccato sentences:

Everything swathed in seeping mist. Steerage passengers still cattle-herded in tin-roofed quayside shed. Lumpy baggage in brown paper parcels, cracked fibre suitcases. Shiny faced pippin cheeked girls and youths. One or two whey-faced middle-aged men. All, or nearly all, hatless. All with coat-collars upturned – like umbrellas blown out by the wind. Wretched looking. The song knocked out of them. As they stumbled on board noticed why: each wore a label like stock cattle. 'British factories' it said simply. As if on their way to be spam-canned.[72]

Arrival at their destinations in a drab and austere wartime Britain could often be a traumatic experience, especially for younger migrants. Noreen Hill from Cork had a rough crossing on the upper deck of a cattle boat. Once arrived in Leicester, she fell ill, not just with the asthma which had not got in the way of her medical clearance to travel. 'I couldn't believe that homesickness would kill you, because that's how I felt – that I was dying.'[73] She hated the food offered her, 'gravy over everything and powdered eggs' but she recovered and adapted to twelve-hour shifts in an aircraft factory, with alternating weeks on night shifts, and posted half of each week's wages home to her mother.

The average age of women recruited from Éire was lower than that of men, and one ICI plant reported in 1942 that, of its 560 workers recruited through the Ministry of Labour's agents, many women were fitter and better workers than men.[74] They could adapt, too, to what was required of them, as was noted by the historian of wartime labour in munitions production: 'Among those who settled down in the heat and racket of the drop forging shops in the mirk of the Black Country there were some who had rarely if ever seen a motor car until their journey to Dublin en route for England.'[75]

Most war work taken on by the Irish was punishingly hard and the hours long. For those laying out runways for RAF airfields in the flat expanses of East Anglia, there was basic accommodation in Nissen huts and monotonous food. Often they were joined by others who had roamed Britain for work long before the war, men such as Seán Killeen, into his sixties, gentle and quietly spoken and well liked by all his workmates:

All his life a pick and shovel man, he pulled more than his weight with a gang – until three months ago. He was crushed by a sand-lorry against a hangar-wall and had three ribs broken. Then came pneumonia. On release from hospital they put him on light work,

an ablution orderly. Two days ago he got fierce pains in his chest
and died before the doctor could be called. Union stewards take
a whip-round in the canteen. Thirty-five quid is collected to pay
the expenses of sending his body home to Tipperary – money to
send the emigrant's remains to the old country. It's a poignant
but not uncommon story. Old, poor and without friends – a brief
obituary.[76]

The welfare officer on the site where Seán Killeen died was an
Irish priest who worked hard on behalf of the men employed there.
He was also a hot-tempered disciplinarian ready to use his fists on
late-night revellers who disturbed the peace of the huts and those
sleeping in them.[77] In fact, the well-being, especially the moral well-
being, of Irish war workers in Britain became an issue from the time
that the July 1941 agreement was negotiated between the Ministry of
Labour and the Dublin government.

> The clergy should warn those who seek employment in Great
> Britain of the danger to faith and morals which they will encounter
> – dangers, alas, to which not a few have already succumbed, and
> should impress upon them the desireability of insisting before they
> emigrate that adequate provision is made for the exercise of their
> religion.[78]

This was part of a statement issued by the Irish Catholic bishops in
October 1941. The Church of Ireland's Young Men's Association,
however, took the view that an unjust slur was being cast on the
British people, and one speaker at its October 1941 meeting pointed
out that 'the morals of Éire which they [the emigrant workers] have
left, are not what they should be'.[79]

The Scottish Catholic newspaper which carried the bishops'
warning about the dangers faced by emigrants felt concerned to
stress that there were already good contacts between clergy on both
sides of the Irish sea and that, as part of the July 1941 work and
travel agreement, the personal details, employment destinations and
addresses of emigrant workers were being sent to the relevant
dioceses and parishes 'across the water'.[80]

As part of his many sided role in representing British interests in
Éire, John Betjeman was drawn into the issue. This was after a
meeting in Dublin of the Mercier Society, a body set up with the
support of Archbishop McQuaid to promote Catholic and Protestant
dialogue. A speaker raised the issue of the threat to faith and morals

that lay ahead of young Irish migrants to Britain. Betjeman was prompt to respond, and minutes of the meeting record him declaring that 'he had to rise to defend his country from aspersions. Irish immigrants were well taken care of in religious matters: the Ministry of Labour saw to it that chaplains were provided and facilities given for attendance at Mass.'[81]

It was often young women workers who were more aware of Church surveillance, though the lengthy hours they worked and the fact that they almost all lived in works hostels or lodgings set limits to any opportunities for sexual liaisons. Noreen Hill, whose experiences have been mentioned earlier in this chapter, recalled arriving in Leicester with a character reference from her priest which she showed to her first employer. The Legion of Mary also called on her landlady once a month to check that she was going to Mass, though she didn't think this necessarily happened to all women workers.[82]

By the time of her arrival, memories of the IRA's bombing campaign in Britain were beginning to recede but, while it was at its height, it had created real fear in the minds of Irish people. In Coventry after the August 1939 bomb attack there, some left their homes for fear of what the reaction against them might be, and there were reports of people refusing to work with the Irish in some factories. Some 2,000 aircraft-production workers marched into the city centre to hear their shop stewards condemn the IRA. A resolution was carried calling for tougher security measures but without overtly racial overtones. Such measures, the resolution stressed, would be in the best interests of innocent Irish people living in Britain.[83]

Mass Observation surveys show intermittent evidence of workplace prejudice against the Irish.

> The Irish girls stick together and they've only got to open their mouths to get any money they want. They've got all the best jobs in the factory – you never hear of an Irish girl being put off a job to make room for a Birmingham girl.[84]

These remarks were recorded in an aircraft production plant midway through the war. At another factory in Aston, which made steel tubes for the Admiralty and where Irish women were a sizeable element of the workforce, there was also some resentment towards them. A Mass Observation diarist reported that.

I'm afraid very few of them are here to do 'war work'. It's the money that brings them over – they're eager to earn as much as they can. That's why most of the Irish girls work pretty well on the whole. There's very little evidence of them having the right spirit towards their work.[85]

Given the mounting level of workplace unrest in wartime Britain, not having the 'right spirit' towards work was an accusation that could have been directed at non-Irish workers, too. Irish workers, moreover, were hardly alone in seeking the best wages they could get on Britain's 'factory front'. For many of them in the engineering industry, talk of high earnings when they were recruited in Éire made the reality of piece-rate payments for many of them a disappointment, especially since most of them were of an age to be sending a part of their wage home every week to families in Éire.[86]

Irish workers, women and men, showed themselves resistant to the more draconian manifestations of factory discipline. At Ford and Briggs Bodies plants at Dagenham in Essex, which both employed a high proportion of Irish workers, pre-war immigrants and wartime recruits played a major part in maintaining and expanding trade union organisation,[87] something agreed upon both by the *Catholic Worker* newspaper and the Marxist Connolly Association. This latter body recruited actively among politically aware and militant Irish workers in Britain and at its 1943 conference, Desmond Greaves, later to become well known as the biographer of James Connolly, declared confidently that 'British workers are finding not only good workmen among the Irish, but staunch Trade Unionists and good comrades who, never averse to a fight, are prepared to fight with them against their mutual exploiters'.[88]

A succession of delegates reported to the conference on their work to unionise the Irish and to build solidarity between them and English and Scottish workers. One Ford's shop steward told the audience that the Dagenham plant where he worked had 'almost as many Irish to the square yard as Dublin'.[89] Others spoke of a vigorous billeting campaign to improve the standard of accommodation for Irish war workers, and condemnation was expressed of those elements within the British press which still sought to fan anti-Irish prejudice. Flann Campbell, who had worked tenaciously among the Irish on East Anglia's airfield construction sites, assured the conference that such attitudes were absent from the workforce within which he was active.

'There is no race hatred here,' he stated.

The border too is forgotten here. Belfastman and Dubliner work side by side and neither have any time for any Fascist propaganda. Unscrupulous employers who think they can split our ranks by dividing British from Irish workers will get short shrift from Irishmen united in defence of their class rights.[90]

Other speakers rallied the conference with calls for an end to partition and in support of Éire's right to neutrality. This latter was upheld unanimously in a resolution but several speakers made it clear that support for de Valera on this issue implied no sympathy whatever for fascism, and a booklet on the conference took care to enumerate the Victoria Crosses and other awards for gallantry given to Irish members of the British forces.

One conference guest, Captain Henry Harrison, writer and former friend and secretary to Charles Parnell, was well received when he declared:

I am a defender of Ireland's neutrality under existing circumstances, but if it were not for my age I would be fighting against the Germans at the present moment. But that does not mean in any way that I condemn Ireland for her neutrality and I am sure that you are up against almost daily reproaches because the country from which we come is neutral.[91]

It is hard to know how far the issue of neutrality was ever a divisive one in the workplace or in day-to-day relations between Irish war workers and the host community. One Dublin woman with a republican background who arrived to work in London in 1943 later recalled some arguments over the neutrality issue: 'People couldn't understand why Ireland couldn't see the cause of Britain being their cause. They couldn't see in any way that Ireland had any right to separate itself in its policy from Britain.'[92]

A potentially much more divisive workplace issue was, in fact, anti-communism and the extent to which Catholic organisations sought to promote it there. A Catholic Workers Guild movement had begun to make its presence felt early in the war and, in some workplaces, proved capable of mounting a real challenge to communist shop stewards. Guided by Vatican social encyclicals and one of the few Catholic movements where lay people made the real decisions and carried them out, it was active in its support of workplace trade unionism and in campaigns for post-war social justice.

George Orwell wrote dismissively of Catholic Irish workers in wartime Britain: 'They vote Labour and act as a sort of silent drag on Labour Party policy but are not sufficiently under the thumb of their priests to be Fascist in sympathy.'[93] This was unjust to the activists in the Connolly Association, as it was also to those Irish workers who were drawn to the guild movement, even if shop-floor divisions resulted.

They were inevitable where communists were as well entrenched as they were in much of the war-production plants of west and central Scotland in 1940 and 1941. The Catholic Archdiocese of Glasgow and the local Catholic Union which it controlled were calling for anti-communist vigilance late in 1940 and contributing frequent copy to the local Catholic press on the party's allegedly malign influence within bodies such as the Home Guard, as well as within the trade unions and the armed forces.[94] One of the most forceful exponents of the Church's fears was Anthony G. Hepburn.

Until his enlistment in the RAF in 1942, Hepburn showed himself to be a committed and talented polemicist, best known for a thirty-two page booklet he wrote and had published in 1941 entitled *Communism in Scotland*. On its opening page, he declared that the party's goal was to achieve power in Scotland 'by an armed civil war. It contains many men who went specifically to Spain for military experience likely to be useful in the future.'[95] Its rising membership, he went on, 'presents a problem for every worker who is a Catholic. Above all the Communist knows us as his greatest enemy.'[96]

The venom of his attack on the party was driven in part by what he saw as its support for the August 1939 Nazi–Soviet pact and its apparent indifference to the fate of Catholic Poland as well as its stated opposition to an imperialist war. All this would soon change but Hepburn and his close friend and supporter, James Darragh, kept up their attacks on both the party and the Soviet Union after it joined the war in late June 1941. By August 1941, Hepburn and Darragh were claiming a membership from thirty trade unions[97] and any Catholic Irish workers assigned to work in the Glasgow area had a choice to make when they arrived at this workplace battleground of value systems and beliefs.

The Catholic guild movement was active elsewhere but it has been claimed that, in Glasgow and on the Clyde, its shop-floor influence acted as a brake on the growth of communist support.[98] It may have done but Catholic and Irish workers were ready for strike action especially when Catholic Workers Guild activists openly challenged communist shop stewards over the way they had followed the new party line after the Soviet Union came into the war. This involved them in calling for support for joint production committees and avoiding strike action when possible.

A vivid example of this was provided by events in 1943 at Glasgow's huge Hillington engineering plant. This made aero-engines for Rolls Royce and employed nearly 20,000 workers, over 40 per cent of whom were women. Communist shop stewards there found themselves dangerously outflanked in a strike of national significance in which the Catholic Workers Guild threw its full support behind demands to end blatant gender inequality in the grading and payment of work.[99]

Signs saying 'No Irish need apply' became less common in wartime Britain as its labour crisis intensified but there were public figures who assumed that the new arrivals off the Dublin ferries must constitute a problem. The Duke of Kent quite early on in the war was taken on a tour of Glasgow's production factories by its Lord Provost, Patrick Dollan, himself the son of Irish immigrants. The duke at one point remarked to him that 'he must have a difficult time because of the number of Irish in Govan and elsewhere'.[100]

Dollan was equal to what the situation required:

> I told him that I had represented Govan for 30 years during which I had never had trouble with any of the citizens and that he was on his way to inspect the Govan Civil Defence Force. At the end of the inspection, he had a tremendous reception from the Govan boys and when we went out into the street I said, 'you have just now been seen by the Irish and the Scots of Govan. Could you tell me which was Irish and which was Scots?'[101]

Notes

1. Fisk, In Time of War, pp. 104–5.
2. Ibid., p. 105.
3. Glasgow Observer and Scottish Catholic Herald, 5 January 1940.
4. Ibid., 19 January 1940.
5. Ibid.
6. Wills, That Neutral Island, pp. 105–8.
7. PRONI, 20/A/1/24, L. Casey, letter, 30 May 1940.
8. Glasgow Observer and Scottish Catholic Herald, 3 May 1940.
9. PRONI, D 715/15, Spender Diaries, Spender to Hankey, 9 November 1940.
10. Fisk, In Time of War, p. 293.
11. Churchill, The Second World War, Vol. II, Their Finest Hour, p. 535.

12. Churchill, *The Second World War*, Vol. III, *The Grand Alliance*, p. 645.
13. Churchill, *The Second World War*, Vol. II, *Their Finest Hour*, p. 536.
14. Share, *The Emergency: Neutral Ireland 1939–1945*, p. 53.
15. Ibid., p. 56.
16. *Glasgow Observer* and *Scottish Catholic Herald*, 22 May 1942, report from its Irish correspondent.
17. E. Delaney, *Demography, State and Society: Irish Migration to Britain 1921–1971* (Liverpool: Liverpool University Press, 2000), pp. 120–3.
18. M. Woodside Diaries, 17 September 1940.
19. J. L. Hodson, *Towards the Morning* (London: Victor Gollancz, 1941), p. 50.
20. Ibid., p. 79.
21. L. Ryan, 'Urban Poverty', in S. Kennedy (ed.), *One Million Poor* (Dublin: Turoe Press, 1981), p. 38; also Delaney, *Demography, State and Society*, p. 113.
22. N. Browne, *Against the Tide* (Dublin: Gill and Macmillan, 1986), pp. 85–8.
23. Patterson, *Ireland Since 1939: the Persistence of Conflict*, p. 75.
24. B. Girvin and G. Murphy (eds), *The Lemass Era: Politics and Society in the Ireland of Sean Lemass* (Dublin: University College Dublin Press, 2005), p. 2.
25. Patterson, *Ireland Since 1939: the Persistence of Conflict*, p. 71.
26. Ibid., p. 74.
27. T. Ryle Dwyer, *Eamon de Valera* (Dublin: Gill and Macmillan, 1980), p. 122.
28. *Irish Times*, 8 May 1945.
29. Gray, *The Lost Years*, p. 125.
30. Duggan, *Neutral Ireland and the Third Reich*, pp. 139–41.
31. Fisk, *In Time of War*, pp. 503–5.
32. Y. McEwen, 'Deaths in Irish Regiments 1939–1945 and the Extent of Irish Volunteering for the British Army', *The Irish Sword*, Vol. XXIV, No. 95, pp. 81–98.
33. Ibid., p. 86.
34. See Chapter 2.
35. P. Verney, *The Micks: the Story of the Irish Guards*, p. 23.
36. D. J. L. Fitzgerald, *A History of the Irish Guards in the Second World War* (Aldershot: Gale and Polden, 1949), p. 243.
37. PRONI CAB 9CD/85/8, Andrews to Attlee, 23 January 1942. See also Fisk, *In Time of War*, p. 525.
38. R. Doherty, *Clear the Way: A History of the 38th (Irish) Brigade 1941–47* (Dublin: Irish Academic Press, 1993), p. 158.
39. B. Harpur, *The Impossible Victory: a Personal Account of the Battle for the River Po* (London: Granada Books, 1980), p. 169.
40. B. Inglis, *West Briton* (London: Faber and Faber, 1962), p. 60.
41. *Irish Times*, 1 May 1995. This interview and the previous source are referred to by C. Kavanagh in B. Girvin and G. Roberts (eds), *Ireland in the Second World War: Politics, Society and Remembrance* (Dublin: Four Courts Press, 2000).
42. R. Doherty, *Irish Men and Women in the Second World War* (Dublin: Four Courts Press, 1999), pp. 42–3.
43. A. McElwaine, 'The Oral History of the Volunteers', in Girvin and Roberts (eds), *Ireland in the Second World War: Politics, Society and Remembrance*, p. 117.
44. O'Halpin, *Defending Ireland*, p. 167.
45. Ibid.
46. Keogh, *Twentieth-Century Ireland: Nation and State*, p. 123.
47. Doherty, *Irish Men and Women in the Second World War*, p. 42.
48. G Roberts, 'Three Narratives of Neutrality: historians and Ireland's war', in Girvin and Roberts (eds), *Ireland and the Second World War: Politics, Society and Remembrance*, p. 173.

49. *Irish Times*, 8 May 1945.
50. Fisk, *In Time of War*, pp. 522–4.
51. Doherty, *Irish Men and Women in the Second World War*, pp. 25–6.
52. Work on this by R. Doherty and by Girvin and Roberts in *Ireland and the Second World War: Politics, Society and Remembrance*, has already been cited. See also I. S. Wood, ''Twas England Bade Our Wild Geese Go: Soldiers of Ireland in the Second World War', in P. Addison and A. Calder (eds), *Time to Kill: the Soldier's Experience of War in the West* (London: Pimlico, 1997), pp. 77–92.
53. Moore, *The Emperor of Ice-Cream*, p. 169.
54. L. Daiken (ed.), *They Go, the Irish* (London: Nicolson and Wolson, 1944), p. 17.
55. Duggan, *Neutral Ireland and the Third Reich*, pp. 258–9.
56. Ibid.
57. K. Lunn, ' "Good for a few hundreds at least": Irish Labour Recruitment into Britain during the Second World War', in P. Buckland and K. Lunn (eds), *The Irish in British Labour History* (Liverpool: Liverpool University Institute of Irish Studies, 1992, p. 102.
58. O'Driscoll, *Censorship in Ireland 1939–1945*, pp. 256–7.
59. Salmon, *Unneutral Ireland*, p. 130.
60. T. Connolly, 'Irish Workers in Britain during World War Two', in Girvin and Roberts (eds), *Ireland and the Second World War: Politics, Society and Remembrance*, p. 122.
61. Delaney, *Demography, State and Society: Irish Migration to Britain, 1921–1971*, p. 151.
62. E. Meehan, *Free Movement between Ireland and the UK: from the 'common travel area' to the Common Travel Area* (Dublin: Trinity College Dublin, Policy Institute, 2000), pp. 22–4.
63. J. B. Priestley, *English Journey* (London: Heinemann and Gollancz, 1933), pp. 248–9).
64. T. Gallagher, *Glasgow, the Uneasy Peace: Religious Tension in Modern Scotland* (Manchester: Manchester University Press, 1987), pp. 133–81; also R. Findlay, 'Nationalism, Race, Religion and the Irish Question in inter-war Scotland', and S. Brown, ' "Outside the Covenant": Scottish Presbyterian Churches and Irish Immigration 1922–1938', both in *Innes Review*, Vol. XLII, spring 1991, pp. 46–67 and 19–45 respectively.
65. Delaney, *Demography, State and Society: Irish Migration to Britain 1921–1971*, p. 153.
66. P. Inman, *Labour in the Munitions Industries* (London: HMSO and Longman Green, 1957), pp. 167–75.
67. M. Lennon, M. McAdam and J. O'Brien (eds), *Across the Water: Irish Women's Lives in Britain* (London: Virago, 1988), p. 173.
68. Delaney, *Demography, State and Society: Irish Migration to Britain 1921–1971*, pp. 120–3.
69. Ibid.
70. Lennon, McAdam and O'Brien (eds), *Across the Water: Irish Women's Lives in Britain*, p. 25.
71. J. Deeny, *To Cure and to Care: memoirs of a chief medical officer* (Dublin: Glendale Press, 1989), p. 78.
72. Daikin, *They Go, the Irish*, p. 65.
73. Lennon, McAdam and O'Brien (eds), *Across the Water: Irish Women's Lives in Britain*, p. 94.
74. P. Inman, *Labour in the Munitions Industries*, p. 174.
75. Ibid.

76. Daiken, *They Go, the Irish*, pp. 52–3.
77. Ibid., p. 51.
78. *Glasgow Observer and Scottish Catholic Herald*, 24 October 1941.
79. Ibid.
80. Ibid.
81. Hillier, *John Betjeman: New Fame, New Love*, pp. 217–18.
82. Lennon, McAdam and O'Brien, *Across the Water: Irish Women's Lives in Britain*, p. 96.
83. Buckland and Lunn (eds), *The Irish in British Labour History*, pp. 105–6.
84. Sheridan (ed.), *Wartime Women: A Mass Observation Anthology – the Experience of Women at War* (London: Mandarin, 1990), p. 170.
85. R. Croucher, *Engineers at War 1939–1945* (London: Merlin Press, 1982), p. 281.
86. Ibid., p. 287.
87. Dooley, *The Irish in Britain* (Watford: Connolly Association, 1943), pp. 7–8.
88. Ibid., p. 6.
89. Ibid., p. 7.
90. Ibid., pp. 10–11.
91. Ibid., pp. 10–12.
92. Lennon, McAdam and O'Brien, *Across the Water: Irish Women's Lives in Britain*, p. 65.
93. G. Orwell and I. Angus (eds), *The Collected Essays, Journalism and Letters of George Orwell*, Vol. 2: *My Country Right or Left 1940–1943* (London: Penguin, 1968), p. 176.
94. *Glasgow Observer and Scottish Catholic Herald*, 3, 10 and 17 January 1941.
95. G. Hepburn, *Communism in Scotland* (Glasgow, John S. Burns, 1941), p. 1.
96. Ibid., p. 8.
97. Gallagher, *Glasgow, the Uneasy Peace: Religious Tension in Modern Scotland*, p. 218.
98. Ibid., p. 220.
99. Croucher, *Engineers at War*, pp. 285–92.
100. P. Dollan, *Unpublished Memoirs*, Vol. 2, pp. 134–5 (Glasgow: Mitchell Library).
101. Ibid.; see also T. Gallagher, *Glasgow the Uneasy Peace: Religious Tension in Modern Scotland*, p. 223.

7

Northern Ireland at War

In 1944 Seán O'Casey wrote with optimism about the prospects of radical political change on both sides of the Irish border. An anti-fascist war and the heroic role in it of the Soviet Union had, he believed, energised the Irish working class. They now, he argued, had new heroes besides King William of Orange and Brian Boru:

> The North is realising that William is too long dead to be able to keep the auld house together when unemployment comes, and the South is beginning to be aware that the Pope isn't near enough to bring a hot meal on a plate to a hungry child.[1]

His optimism was premature in respect to both Éire and Northern Ireland. Éire's 1944 Dáil elections saw a divided Labour movement lose ground. In Northern Ireland, while Unionism had lost much of its confidence earlier in the war, the Ulster Unionist party maintained its domination of the province's Westminster representation in the 1945 British general election. It also triumphed in the Stormont elections in June of that year. As always, opposition to it was split between the Nationalist party and parties of the left who, in fact, mobilised a strong vote though the Northern Ireland Labour Party had split over the nagging issue of what its attitude to partition should be.[2]

The praise which Churchill heaped upon Northern Ireland for its part in Britain's victory steered well clear of its continuing sectarian divisions which shocked many British and American service men and women who were stationed there during the war. These have already been alluded to in this book for the bearing which they had in debates on whether conscription should be extended to Northern Ireland and on the organisation and recruitment of the Home Guard. The IRA's intermittent violence could also drive communal tension to dangerous levels.

When war came in 1939, Northern Ireland was still scarred by some of the worst poverty and deprivation to be found anywhere in the British Isles. Industries, such as shipbuilding and textiles, had begun to lose markets after 1918, and Britain's decision in 1925 to take Britain back on to the Gold Standard pushed up the bank rate, with severely adverse effects on both investment and exports. Unemployment among insured workers in Northern Ireland averaged 15 per cent over the years prior to the Wall Street crash in 1929, and between 1931 and 1939 the figure averaged 27 per cent. The year 1935 was one of brutal sectarian violence which brought British troops back to Belfast's streets. It was also in economic terms the lowest point with over 100,000 of the insured workforce unemployed.

Three years earlier the long-term unemployed, who had been driven on to the starvation rates of outdoor relief paid by Belfast's Poor Law Board of Guardians, had marched in protests which briefly brought Roman Catholics and Protestants together. The Unionist government's approach was to fall back on the batons, guns and armoured cars of the RUC.[3] Most local councils evaded what house-building responsibilities they had, and Belfast Corporation, which was suspended for its corruption in 1942, was barely fit to discharge them anyway. Working-class housing in Belfast still shocked British troops who arrived to patrol the city's streets in 1969 and 1970.

In April 1932 the Maternity and Child Welfare Committee of Belfast Corporation was told by one of the city's medical officers that, from January to the end of July of that year 679 deaths of children under one year old had been registered in the city. 'The high infant mortality rate is largely due to poverty'[4] the committee was informed. Six years later, when the Northern Ireland parliament met after elections at its grandiose Stormont building, a Unionist back-bencher, William Grant, launched what a newspaper called a 'scathing criticism'[5] of his party's failure to tackle unemployment and housing. He was followed by an Independent Unionist, J. W. Nixon, whose first priority was to welcome all new members 'to this Protestant Parliament for a Protestant people',[6] merely echoing the words of the prime minister, Lord Craigavon.

Little had changed for the better a year later when Belfast's High Sheriff moved at the corporation's General Purposes Committee that representations be made to the British government to declare the city a distressed area. He was supported by an alderman who spoke of the 'white scourge' of tuberculosis that was ravaging working-class areas of the city. It was pitiable, he went on,

> to interview cases who had been refused dole and transitional benefit and were obliged to seek poor-law relief . . . Something very formidable will have to be done at once to protect the people from this terrible scourge and to provide them with decent living conditions and something to maintain them properly.[7]

The motion was declared by the corporation to be out of order and no action was taken.

An administration led by the ageing Lord Craigavon was unlikely to respond with much greater energy to the contribution of Northern Ireland to the war. His death in late November 1940, and his replacement by John Andrews, did little to allay concerns that not enough was being done to mobilise Northern Ireland's resources for war and to bring its full workforce into employment. A junior Board of Trade civil servant in London, Harold Wilson, reported on the need for this in January 1941,[8] and Churchill himself later in the month minuted to Ernest Bevin, his Minister of Labour, on 'the little use which is being made of the resources of Ulster in manpower and industry for the war effort,' adding: 'I am told that more than one fifth of the insured workers are now unemployed.'[9]

Bevin followed up with representations of his own to Stormont for a full statement on manpower use in the province.[10] Results could not come right away, and the Queen's University vice chancellor, Sir David Lindsay Keir, who had earlier voiced his concern at Northern Ireland's indifferent enlistment levels, drafted a reply of his own to Harold Wilson's report. This still reads as a revealing insight into the anxieties of those who were close to the Stormont government, as Keir told Sir Basil Brooke, the energetic commerce minister, of the content of his reply in advance of it being sent.

Keir had clearly reacted badly to the Stormont government's widespread use of the British Ministry of Labour's poster with the rousing message 'Go to it' borrowed from a David Lowe cartoon in the *Daily Mirror*. 'The situation is very bad indeed and seems to be getting worse,' he began.

> Those who are loyal, are, as you say, disheartened and disillusioned by there being nothing to 'go to'. Among the others

extremism of all kinds, e.g. Communism and the IRA, are flourish-
ing on industrial depression. I have been told of young Protestants
being attracted into illegal organisations. Juvenile delinquency is
markedly on the increase and if things go on much longer in the
present way, the situation, already pregnant with possibilities of
trouble, will become alarming. It already gives the greatest concern
to those who care most for the province and its people.[11]

Keir's premonitions left it an open question whether Northern
Ireland was really prepared either psychologically or materially to
withstand a German attack. This came sooner than he could have
anticipated from the sky over Belfast in April and May 1941. With
the amalgamation in 1936 of Harland and Wolff with the aircraft
builders Short Brothers, the city's strategic production potential had
begun to grow and, once war came, orders began to flow again into
the shipyards. This, along with the re-equipment of James Mackie,
the big engineering works on the city's Springfield Road, so that it
could mass produce artillery shells, clearly made Belfast a target. Not
everyone was convinced, however, that the city's preparations of its
defences were adequate. The Air Raid Precautions (ARP) controller,
a Major F. S. Eastwood, was reported telling a public audience in
August 1938 that 'it all looked rather grim and that they were
eighteen months behind'.[12]

They were still behind at the start of 1941 despite the brutal
evidence of what the Luftwaffe could do to English cities. Because of
ministerial inertia and indecision, insufficient representations had
been made to London about Belfast's anti-aircraft gun defences.
Additional batteries were scheduled for transfer to the city but the
Luftwaffe's onslaught came first. A squadron of RAF Hurricane
fighters was moved from Edinburgh to Aldergrove airfield but
without night interceptor equipment. Recruitment to the ARP had
not been easy, with bitter and orchestrated opposition to it in
republican areas. Worst of all, shelter accommodation was adequate
for just one-quarter of the city's population.

The first exploratory attacks came on the night of 7 and 8 April
and intensified the following week. On Easter Tuesday, 15 April, 200
German bombers left their bases in France and the Low Countries to
saturate large areas of Belfast with incendiary bombs and high
explosives as well as parachute mines. By 4 a.m. the next day, much
of the north side of the city was ablaze and the Falls area and the
docks were also severely hit. For a time the fires were beyond the
control of the local fire service and help famously came, with de

Valera's authorisation, from the Dublin fire brigade though not all of their hoses could be fitted to Belfast's hydrants. A British Ministry of Information report described the scene after the bombers had left:

> When morning broke, parts of the city were a gruesome sight. The ruin-fringed roads were blocked by heaps of smoking debris and acrid-smelling craters. Water ran through the rubble, gas mains spouted fountains of flame and where the fire-fighters were still at work every now and again a wall crashed.[13]

Under the rubble were the bodies which the rescue services had to dig for.

The diggers and ambulance crews soon found that the expansion of mortuary space had not rated as a priority with the city authorities prior to the attack. One result of this was that, on the Falls Road, the swimming baths were drained to hold the bodies retrieved in the area until they could be identified. Not far off, many people had taken shelter in the vaults and cellars of Clonard Monastery.[14] Its Redemptorist priests had been targets for Loyalist gunmen from the Shankill twenty years earlier but, as the Luftwaffe attacks reached their height, Protestant families were gladly given sanctuary there.

The Dublin correspondent of Scotland's main Catholic newspaper saw something of the raids and their aftermath, and wrote of how 'numbers of homeless persons took refuge in churches and scores of drum-beaters entered a Catholic place of worship for the first time in their lives and slept in it the sleep of exhaustion, while the gentle murmur of the Mass went on'.[15] He had wrongly claimed in an earlier report that Catholics were deliberately excluded from Northern Ireland's ARP and civil defence services[16] but later seemed to contradict himself by writing of the irony of ARP wardens who were Catholics helping Blitz victims in areas from where their co-religionists had been burned out in the violence of 1935.[17]

A timelessly graphic and terrible image of the Blitz and what it did has been left us by Emma Duffin, a Belfast nursing sister with First World War experience. In 1941 she was in charge of a Voluntary Aid Detachment (VAD) unit of nurses and ambulance crews. After the Easter Tuesday attack she was assigned to St George's Market to help with the identification of the corpses stacked into it. She had seen death before, she wrote in her diary,

> but here it was grotesque, repulsive, horrible. No attendant had soothed the last moment of these victims, no gentle reverend hand

had closed their eyes or crossed their hands. With tangled hair, staring eyes, clutching hands, their grey faces covered in dust, they lay, bundled into coffins, half-shrouded in rugs or blankets, often wearing their dirty, torn, twisted garments. Death should be dignified, pacific. Hitler had even made death grotesque. I should have felt pity, instead feelings of repulsion and disgust assailed me.[18]

The government account of the Blitz referred to earlier did not try to deny that large numbers of Belfast people reacted to air attack by seeking refuge outside the city. Some, it admitted, mostly women and children, had gone as far as Dublin in search of safety.[19] Moya Woodside witnessed the reality of an exodus of panic proportions as people with cars, with mattresses and bedding tied on top, streamed out of Belfast. Not all of them, in her view, had come from bombed areas.[20] Her own mother, who lived in the country, took in a working-class family who had joined the flight only to realise that the children had skin diseases and tuberculosis.[21] For her and many like her the blitz was a stark revelation of how Belfast's poor lived.

Moya Woodside had joined the Northern Ireland Labour Party and had experience of voluntary welfare work in some of Belfast's most impoverished areas. She therefore clutched at the hope that the flight from the city might have a real impact on the comfortably off who, like her mother, took in homeless families.[22] She also resented local press coverage, however, which seemed to her to minimise the reality of what was happening and what it revealed of the huge inequalities which had been allowed to exist in the province.[23]

She admitted in her diaries that she had not taken Air Raid Precautions seriously and had not thought of Belfast as a German target. She was not alone, as Belfast's unpreparedness for the German Blitz made clear. As far back as August 1940, the Stormont Ministry of Public Security had received a detailed report from the London Civil Defence Service on the kind of explosives likely to be used in any attack on the city, the likely scale of fires and the importance of shelter construction.[24] Much of the action needed to implement this report came after and not before the April Blitz. Even so, Sir Wilfrid Spender, the head of the civil service, could still claim immediately after the Easter Tuesday attack that the authorities had come through 'creditably.'[25]

He did at least admit that the resources and organisation were not there to cope with a series of attacks, were the Germans to be capable of them.[26] Others in government became preoccupied with the continuing exodus from the city, especially as night fell and people feared further raids. John MacDermott, the public security minister, wrote a memorandum about it for the Cabinet on 12 May, declaring that 'the morale of the city as a whole is not first class. Indeed it is in some ways definitely disappointing. There is much fear.'[27] The word refugee was used officially for the first time at the end of the month as Spender noted in his diary in response to a Home Affairs ministry report which 'apparently conveyed to the Cabinet an appalling description of the situation in Belfast . . . there was far more panic amongst the people of Belfast than in the cities in Great Britain which had been subjected to worse bombardments.'[28]

The evacuation of target cities by their populations, especially where shelter provision was inadequate and new attacks were feared was, in fact, a common feature of the Blitz in places as far apart as Clydebank and the English Channel ports.[29] Belfast's introduction to what air power could do was the same as theirs, perhaps more brutal, for its loss of 1,100 lives had been worse than any city outside London. Over the long months of 1940 and 1941, when Britain's cities were the front line, morale sometimes bent badly but it never broke and recovered, too, under renewed attack. There is no reason to suppose that Belfast and other places in Northern Ireland would have been different had their ordeal continued.

Stormont reports tended to focus on morale, or the loss of it, in working-class areas but middle-class families, often from unbombed homes, joined the flight out of Belfast, anticipating what they assumed would be renewed attacks by the Luftwaffe. Cardinal MacRory also anticipated this but he took no chances, visiting the German legation in Dublin to seek special protection for Armagh, the seat of his archdiocese.

Hempel, the German minister, was receptive to the cardinal's information that Armagh had no munitions plants or other strategic manufactories and few troops based locally. The cardinal, Hempel stated, was a personal friend of his: 'he was very anti-British and a strong supporter of Irish neutrality and independence as well as having good relations with the Italians'.[30] The safety of Lord Carson's statue in front of the Stormont parliament building would not have been one of the cardinal's priorities but it was for John Andrews, the prime minister. Spender noted how Andrews had phoned him urgently on the need to protect the statue but added: 'I feel sure that Carson himself would not have wished this matter to be regarded as one of major importance in existing conditions.'[31]

The Blitz and its aftermath shook the confidence of a lacklustre administration. The ruling Ulster Unionist party had already lost Lord Craigavon's North Down seat to an independent candidate in a February 1941 by-election. Much worse followed in November of that year. At another Stormont by-election in Willowfield in Belfast, previously a rock-solid Unionist seat, Harry Midgley won a notable victory for the Northern Ireland Labour Party and, on his return to parliament, was quick to call for a thoroughgoing reconstruction of the government. This had to wait until April of 1943, when the Stormont Unionist members finally forced Andrews out in order that Sir Basil Brooke could take over as prime minister.

What gave borrowed time to the Andrews government, and to Unionism more generally, was the fact that the German bombers did not return and that a major increase in employment was brought to Northern Ireland by large war-production contracts. Unemployment had, indeed, been starting to fall before the 1941 Blitz and, in March of that year, 23,500 men, mostly Protestants, were at work in the Harland and Wolff shipyard in Belfast. Months ahead of the Pearl Harbor attack, work was also starting on Lough Foyle to expand docking facilities for the American fleet. This, though meant to be kept secret, created more jobs as did the building and expansion of facilities for the RAF in the province.[32]

The restoration of something approaching full employment brought with it new bargaining power to organised labour and often a hardening of relations between it and management. The official history of Northern Ireland at war devotes just one paragraph to strikes,[33] yet, during the six years of hostilities, the province accounted for 10 per cent of the total working days lost through strikes in Britain though its workforce constituted only 2 per cent of the British total.[34]

This was despite the Conditions of Employment and National Arbitration Order which in August 1940 was applied to the entire United Kingdom. It prohibited strikes and set up a national machinery for resolving disputes. Under it, those involved in work stoppages could be prosecuted and were, famously, in the case of the miners at Betteshanger colliery in Kent in 1944.[35] This prosecution was abandoned but, in Northern Ireland, employers, backed by the Stormont state, made significantly more use of the powers available to them under the 1940 order than was the case in the rest of the United Kingdom.

In an undated document which it compiled late on in the war, the RUC claimed that there had been a total of 260 strikes in Northern Ireland during the war, nearly all of them illegal, it stressed, because of the strikers' refusal to comply with the 1940 order. It listed 6,000 prosecutions arising from this, a much higher figure in proportion to the size of the wartime workforce than in England, Scotland and Wales.[36] This level of police involvement was, in large measure, a product of their belief that strike action could be linked to political subversion but this became harder to prove once the Communist Party, with its membership of around 1,000, came out in full support of the war after the German invasion of the Soviet Union. After this, its shop stewards did their best to oppose strikes and to stress the priority of production for an anti-fascist war over sectional interests. This led the RUC to look for a more familiar enemy within the labour force.

Some Stormont ministers came to feel that the 1940 order might be better repealed if it was failing to deter strike action but this lay outside their jurisdiction. All the same, John MacDermott, the public security minister, raised this with Andrews in November 1942 because of strike action among Short and Harland workers over the management's dismissal of two shop stewards. No representations on the matter were, in fact, made to Churchill who would not have been receptive and was greatly concerned by this strike.[38] MacDermott also revived the issue of conscription which had been talked of after the 1941 Blitz. 'As a people we are not well disciplined to withstand the stress of total war,' he told Andrews during the Short and Harland strike, adding: 'I feel that, taking the long view, conscription should be earnestly sought.'[39]

Conscription would not have halted workplace unrest in Northern Ireland any more than it did in the rest of the United Kingdom. Denunciations of strikes continued to come, and not just from Unionist ministers. Harry Midgley, back as a Stormont member and soon to make a final break with the Northern Ireland Labour Party, described the 1942 Short and Harland strike as 'almost criminal' and declared that: 'Our country is at war against nations which have destroyed trade unions and democratic organisations. In such an hour no stoppage of production is justified.'[40] The reality, however, was that industrial unrest was a product of antagonistic relations between often authoritarian managements and workers with fresh and bitter memories of pre-war hardship and victimisation. As the war dragged on, strikes increased and intensified.

In March 1944, an engineering workers strike for a pay increase at Harland and Wolff and Short Brothers brought 14,000 workers out for over three weeks, and five prominent shop stewards were arrested and imprisoned after police raids on their homes during which they were questioned as to whether or not they were Catholics. Robert Morrow, secretary to Belfast Trades Council, wrote in protest to Sir Basil Brooke and his colleagues declaring that

> as all of you must be aware, whenever industrial trouble breaks
> out in Belfast, the danger of the importation into the dispute of a
> sectarian element is never far away. Some interested party or
> parties was or were sedulously spreading the report that the shop
> stewards movement was manned almost exclusively by persons of
> the Roman Catholic faith who were natives of Éire.[41]

Despite calls from the union's London leadership to end it, the strike escalated in response to rumours that the Shorts plant was going to be closed, with dock workers taking sympathy action. Brooke and Churchill corresponded over the strike, the Stormont leader taking the view that the existing negotiating machinery was too slow with the result that the union leaders had lost control of their members.[42] Churchill replied to him, describing the strike as 'most serious and lamentable'[43] and promised to refer it to the Ministry of Labour but there was no action to expedite a settlement. It required Brooke to act, persuading the shop stewards that, if they accepted bail, their appeal against their sentences would get a sympathetic hearing. This, along with the offer of a wage increase, brought the strike to an end.

This strike was the culmination of wartime industrial unrest in Northern Ireland, and it led Sir Basil Brooke to talk to his Cabinet colleagues of a possible general strike, with his home affairs minister taking a hard line over what he represented as a challenge to the law that would need the full mobilisation of the RUC.[44] It was also a reminder – though one which few trade unionists in Belfast needed – of Stormont's fear of solidarity within the Protestant workforce and of how easily Catholic and anti-partitionist influence could be invoked by the authorities.

One strike participant, Bessie Brown who, with many other women, had been recruited from the linen mills and domestic service to work at Shorts on the production of Sunderland flying boats for RAF Coastal Command, later recalled the strike as a time of excitement, especially when the entire workforce marched on Stormont.

> The march was conducted in an orderly and dignified manner;
> there was no malice or hostile chanting from the crowds . . . you
> were out to fight for your job in a happy sort of way, there was a
> good atmosphere, you just whistled and walked along.[46]

On the march and at strike rallies in the Ulster Hall, she also recalled 'how for the first time, she encountered the old adage 'United We Stand, Divided We Fall'.'[47]

The incidence of strike action and what is claimed to have been the underperformance of Northern Ireland's wartime industry are sometimes treated as integrally related topics. In March of 2000 a venomous letter to the *Irish News* expressed this belief in response to an Ulster Television programme which had lamented the passing of Harland and Wolff as a major shipbuilder and praised its wartime role.

> The reality is that Harland and Wolff's contribution to the British war effort was a disgrace. In the Second World War its productivity was a pathetic half of that of British shipyards. While the men fighting Nazism were dying in their millions at the front, the 'loyal' workers back at the shipyard even went on a strike in 1942, knowing that they had a desperate British government over a barrel and prepared to submit to their selfish demands.[48]

The letter writer, who signed himself as resident in the republican stronghold of Andersonstown in West Belfast, was voicing the still raw resentment within his community of what it had always seen as a Loyalist stronghold but he moved on to wider ground in his concluding paragraph: 'The endless, unfounded, boasting claims by unionists that they supposedly made a significant contribution to Britain's war effort might be just slightly less tiresome if there was any truth to them.'[49]

There is, indeed, well-documented evidence of Harland and Wolff's shortcomings.[50] These included inefficiency, wastage and high levels of absenteeism, as well as reluctance to co-operate with Sir Basil Brooke when he was still commerce minister in 1943 and wanted to talk with the yard's management about raising its output levels. To him it seemed to be a firm that was uninterested in the welfare of its workers and unwilling to make savings by subcontracting some of its operations to other nearby companies. He also began to feel that much of its management was involved in post-war planning at the expense of immediate wartime needs.[51]

Raising output had certainly not been helped by damage to the yard caused by the 1941 Blitz or by the fact that the war on the Atlantic involved the workforce in extensive ship repairs which did not count as productivity. Even so, the British Admiralty would still not have wanted to be without Harland and Wolff, and complaints about low workplace morale went beyond their workforce. On 8 June 1944, a young English-born supervisor at Littlewood's Mail Order Stores in Carrickfergus wrote to Sir Basil Brooke complaining of what she claimed was the poor motivation of the women workers in her charge. Absenteeism and sick notes too readily given were among her complaints: 'I really think the Labour Department of Northern Ireland should be stricter on these female shirkers,'[52] she told the prime minister, adding: 'it makes it very hard for me to see this supposed Loyal Ulster spirit which our sons and husbands are giving their lives for'.[53]

There were also success stories where thoughtful management, which was attentive to its workers' needs and to their self-respect, could create highly productive and strike-free plants. A case in point was James Mackie's huge foundry on West Belfast's Springfield Road. It produced munitions and components for bomber aircraft and flying boats, and its output was so good that, in 1942, the Ministry of Aircraft Production considered assigning to it overall responsibility for all aircraft work in Northern Ireland.[54] As in the rest of Britain, so in Northern Ireland the morale and motivation of the workforce could vary and be influenced by many different factors.

In fact, the overall performance of Northern Ireland's industries improved as the war went on. This applied not just to heavy engineering but also to textile production. The province's many mills, which had been hard hit by a raw material shortage and lost export contracts at the outset of the war, went on to achieve a huge output of clothing and uniforms for the armed forces as well as diversifying to make flax fabric parachutes and harnesses for them.[55] If strikes continued, which they did, they need to be seen as part of a people's war which served to strengthen organised labour's bargaining power. Shop-floor activists in Northern Ireland and elsewhere believed both in victory over Germany and in workers' rights in a democratic workplace. As the historian of the engineering workers has put it, wartime militancy in industry had a dual nature, being 'anti-Fascist and anti-managerial'.[56]

One effect of Northern Ireland's wartime need for labour was a much-increased movement across its border by Éire citizens who may not have relished the longer trip to England or Scotland but who needed work which the north could provide. The official history of Northern Ireland at war is imprecise about the numbers involved[57] but, from early in the war, everyone not resident there had to apply for a permit, renewable every six months if they wanted work. The numbers were never as great as some Unionists imagined but, predictably, the matter soon became an issue both in terms of a threat to 'Ulster' jobs and to national security.[58]

The possibility that Éire citizens living and working across the border could be classified for security reasons as aliens under British legislation was seized upon by Nationalists, and the *Irish News* devoted an editorial to the issue of who should decide 'when an Irishman in his own native land is not an Irishman'.[59] Two years later, Sir Basil Brooke as prime minister was still having to defend in Cabinet the way work permits were being issued[60] and stressed that the scheme had been introduced to secure additional labour and had never been meant to serve as the basis for any sectarian head count.[61]

The Unionist press continued to run scare stories on the issue, along with calls for Stormont to be given full control over cross-border movement. The *Londonderry Sentinel* even argued that it could become a resignation issue for the government. 'We realise all too fully', it told its readers, 'the perils to the security of our Ulster state which are growing about us. These have increased since the war and, strange as it may seem, they are in part due to the Imperial Government.'[62] Abortive talk followed about possible ways of differentiating between loyal and disloyal Éire workers and, in February 1945, there was another Cabinet debate on border control, with Brooke describing it as a 'burning question'.[63]

In February 1942, a Stormont Cabinet subcommittee debated the matter. Its chairman took the view that entry from Éire should be controlled and that the necessary powers to do this should be sought from London. There was disagreement over possible security risks, and it was pointed out that Éire-born workers needed five years' residence to qualify for unemployment benefit and so would be deterred from long-term settlement. The parliamentary secretary to the home affairs ministry was not convinced. He argued that 'certain organisations would make every endeavour to keep them here for political purposes'.[64] It was clearly the republican movement that he had in mind.

Newspapers in Northern Ireland followed up with scare stories on the security issue,[65] and R. Dawson Bates, the home affairs minister, put the case for control of the movement of Éire workers and for those already in Northern Ireland to be required to inform the RUC of any changes of address.[66] Correspondence followed between Bates and Herbert Morrison, the British Home Secretary. His view was that control schemes were unlikely to be wholly effective and that the expulsion of 'undesirables' from Éire on the RUC's recommendation could be ordered by his department under its 1940 emergency powers.[67]

Border control, however, was in the main part of a long and losing battle by both the Northern Ireland and Éire authorities against smuggling. Since partition in 1920, this had centred mainly on livestock and sheep but the war gave it a major stimulus with the shortages it created. Much more tea was available in Northern Ireland than in Éire so people hoarding it for lucrative cross-border sales became the target of numerous investigations and prosecutions. Among the many domestic goods in chronically short supply in Éire by 1943 was electric wiring, and that year a Belfast man, who was arrested and searched at a border railway crossing was found to have 60 yards (55m) of it wrapped round his body. There was also a lively market in high-quality watches and jewellery which reached Éire from neutral Switzerland. and could be sold profitably north of the border.[68]

Alcohol had, of course, a well-established place in cross-border smuggling and, at the height of the war, the RUC's finest were deployed along the border to intercept illegal supplies entering Northern Ireland. The force's review of crime during the war reported one operation which gives the flavour of this work:

> On August 9 1943 a Constable on Customs duty observed a person of well-known smuggling proclivities driving a donkey and cart laden with hay from the direction of the border to Aughnacloy village [in County Tyrone]. This constable discreetly followed the donkey and cart to the rear of McCarroll's licensed premises.[69]

A search revealed the hay to be covering a large consignment of whiskey bottles. The driver of the cart was arrested and charged as was the licensee, McCarroll, whose home was found to be well stocked with contraband spirits and wine from across the border.

Policing the border, however, as the war went on came close to being a sectarian issue rooted within the siege psychology of Protestant Ulster and its fear of infiltration from Éire. This led to a major debate about the province's constitutional position. The debate was driven not just by fear of Éire but by the thought that a post-war Labour government in London would seek to impose its will on a predominantly Unionist electorate. Dominion status was called for by some as an alternative to such an outcome but Brooke steered a careful course despite having seemed to have gone some way to agreeing with his critics on the border issue. He was, as the war neared its end, mindful of how the constitutional status quo would secure for Northern Ireland the full benefits of Labour's promised welfare legislation.[70]

Brooke brought much-needed energy to the business of wartime government in Northern Ireland but, as both the debate on border controls and the strikes of 1944 showed, sectarianism was an issue that was never far from his desk. His administration remained a predominantly Protestant one in its composition and recruitment, though some Catholics could make careers within it. A case in point was Patrick Shea, a Catholic born in County Westmeath whose father had served in the old Royal Irish Constabulary. After partition, he settled in Newry and brought up his family there. Shea, who later became a talented writer, made a successful career in the Northern Ireland Civil Service, finishing up as permanent secretary to the education ministry in the early 1970s.

Even so there were episodes in his career when his religion was used against him. Early in the war, Sir Wilfrid Spender recommended Shea for the important position of private secretary to the new Financial Secretary to the Ministry of Finance. Major Maynard Sinclair, the newly appointed financial secretary, had to report to Spender that his political advisers had warned him strongly against having a Catholic private secretary. It fell to Spender to explain this to Shea, who later recalled that 'Spender made the words 'political advisers' sound unclean',[71] as he offered an apology to him. At this same time, Shea also found that, in fact, he had been transferred to the finance ministry because, at his previous department, the Ministry of Labour, the Unionist minister in charge did not want any Catholics in senior positions.[72]

As the holder of a different ministerial brief, Brooke was not directly involved in any of this. In late March 1944, however, when as prime minister he was preoccupied with strikes at Belfast engineering plants and with the imminence of a second front in Europe, he still had to read a letter which arrived on his desk from a constituent with serious anxieties. These were about the recent appointment of a Tipperary Catholic to the position of temporary chief milk inspector to the Stormont Ministry of Agriculture. 'There appears to be a case for close investigation', his correspondent urged,

as to why people from Southern Ireland are appointed to these positions in Northern Ireland over the heads of our own people and when their outlook and sympathies are opposed to ours. He certainly will not work for the strengthening of our Imperial Connection.[73]

The new appointee may, indeed, not have done that but Northern Ireland's milk supply survived and its prime minister's reply is not on record.

Of more concern to Brooke and his predecessor, John Andrews, was the rabidly anti-Catholic content of a paper called the *Ulster Protestant*. First published in March 1934, it was initially owned by the Ulster Protestant League which sought to put pressure on the Unionist government for tougher measures against what it saw as Ulster's enemy within the gates. One of its speakers told a rally in Armagh in early 1936 that Protestant Ulster was in real danger and that 'the people to blame were the Protestant employers. If they didn't employ Catholics, Catholics would have been unable to exist in Ulster'.[74] Later that year the League made significant gains in local elections in areas which had seen the worst of the previous year's sectarian violence.[75]

The Stormont government took the view that it had not the power on its own to close the paper down though, in 1943, Andrews, while still in office, approached the *Ulster Protestant*'s printers to warn them about continuing to handle it unless its content was modified. There is little evidence of this happening. Brooke, like Andrews, was disinclined to act. This has been called '. . . a disposition consistent with a well-entrenched reluctance on the part of successive Unionist leaderships to come into conflict with sections of its own constituency and thereby to exacerbate tensions within Unionism'.[76] Britain's acquiescence in this inaction, it has also been said, typified the way in which Stormont was allowed 'to act strictly in accordance with its own narrow partisan priorities even in the context of wartime'.[77]

While the paper readily espoused Britain's cause in 1939, its tone and content remained undiluted and, in late 1942, Gray, the American minister in Dublin, complained to London about the offence likely to be given to Catholic American service personnel based in Northern Ireland who might see copies of it. Maffey, Britain's representative in Dublin, agreed. Neither was impressed by the argument that the *Ulster Protestant* had only a small circulation, and Gray took the view that it provided potential material for Irish Nationalist and republican anti-war propaganda. The issue dragged on without being resolved, though the British Home Office and Dominions Office were drawn into the argument.[78]

The *Ulster Protestant* remained in business and continued to be published into the 1950s when it became associated with the National Union of Protestants, one of whose leaders was a young Ian Paisley. Northern Ireland's sectarian fault lines had been left almost untouched by the war and were there before it as even a glance at the mini-state's press makes clear. One clear manifestation of them was the issue of conscription, considered elsewhere in this book. Lord Craigavon's declaration of support for the Chamberlain government's Military Training Bill in April 1939 was accompanied by the words: 'Do not leave Ulster out'[79] calculated to enrage Nationalist opinion and to prompt calls for an all-Ireland campaign against any call-up.[80]

The communal violence of 1935 was still fresh in people's memory as for many was the bloodbath which had followed partition in 1920, and threats to public order were never far away. In October 1938 'heavy concentrations of police'[81] had to be deployed in the Willowfield area of Belfast when the new Catholic church of St Anthony's was opened there. The clergy and congregation were jeered and taunted by a Loyalist protest demonstration and, prior to this, two landmines had been planted within the building in an unsuccessful attempt to destroy it.[82]

Only weeks later, police drew their batons against Nationalist crowds on Belfast's Falls Road as they had done on polling day at the Stormont elections earlier in the year.[84] The New Year 1939 saw tensions rising with the IRA's announcement of its new bombing campaign and, in late January, Sir Basil Brooke departed a little from his brief as agriculture minister to tell Orangemen at Newtonbutler, County Fermanagh, to 'Put your trust in God and keep your powder dry.'[85]

Three months later Brooke was under Nationalist attack for what was claimed to be his failure as chairman of Fermanagh County Council to act over its bias against Catholics in its appointments policy. The Nationalist press was quick to point out that this was the same Sir Basil Brooke who, five years earlier, had openly defended such discrimination, declaring to another Fermanagh audience that Roman Catholics 'were endeavouring to get in everywhere and were out with all their force and might to destroy the power and constitution of Ulster.' This made him feel justified in appealing to Loyalists to 'employ Protestant lads and lassies'.[86] Unionist rule did, however, have its critics within the fold and some went into opposition to the party. One of them, W. J. Stewart, a former Westminster MP, formed his own Progressive Unionist Party to press for a more active and interventionist approach to Northern Ireland's acute housing and employment problems.[87]

Early in 1938 Stewart told a Belfast meeting that 'We have here a government which is perhaps more completely in control of the six counties than either Hitler or Mussolini in their own countries.'[88] Unionist electoral manipulation, inaction on urgent social problems and indifference to the minority community was, he warned, going to lose Northern Ireland the friends it most needed. His party won 43,000 votes in that year's Stormont election but this proved no more of a threat to Unionist rule than the subsequent increase in support for the Northern Ireland Labour Party during the war.

Overt sectarian tension may have gone on hold once the war started but it was never far away, as the bitter scenes at the time of the execution of Tom Williams in 1942 should remind us. Brian Moore remembered Loyalists blaming the Blitz of the previous year on 'Fenian treachery', and this appears in his later fictional account of it.[89] Sectarianism, however, was always a two-way street and, as we have seen (Chapter 4) the Belfast IRA was prepared to attack the emergency services if the Luftwaffe returned to bomb the city, and its readiness to identify with the cause of the Third Reich could only continue to feed Protestant and Unionist fears.

Members of the British forces stationed there did not need long to realise that Northern Ireland was a place apart, not least in its rigid Sabbath observance, regardless of the needs of servicemen and women on leave. Moya Woodside was outraged by this when, on a wet and dismal Belfast Sunday, she saw forlorn troops roaming its empty streets. Those responsible for the city's virtual closure, with neither pubs, cafes nor cinemas open, she thought, probably had no objections to soldiers, sailors and aircrews facing combat and death on Sundays.[90]

Those members of the forces who were either befriended by local people or were willing to talk to them soon became aware of the deep divisions within Northern Ireland. One young sailor, Harry Marlow, found himself on leave in Londonderry just after the war ended and was shocked when two girls in the city told him and his friend of their families' hatred of the Stormont state. He was shocked, too, by the fervour with which the 1945 Twelfth of July was celebrated in the city and how the family who had invited him to their house that day stayed well out of the way because, as they told him, they were Taigs (derogatory term for Catholics), a word he had not, of course, heard before. He pondered, too, his hosts' prediction that 'the top will blow off one day'.[91]

James Maginnis was also in the Royal Navy but he was a Catholic from West Belfast who had gone to the same school at which Gerry Adams would later be a pupil. His extraordinary courage as a crew member of a midget submarine who fitted limpet mines to a Japanese battlecruiser in Singapore harbour earned him the Victoria Cross, the only one awarded in the war to someone from Northern Ireland. Normally, VC winners were awarded the freedom of the city or town from which they came but Belfast corporation's Unionist majority avoided doing this for Maginnis. Instead they held a civic reception for him and launched a monetary appeal, or 'shilling fund' as they called it, on his behalf, to which ordinary citizens contributed rather than the corporation as a body. As a biographer of Maginnis put it: 'they might as well have attended Mass at St. Peter's on the Falls Road as award the Freedom to a Catholic from West Belfast'.[92]

When Maginnis later left the Navy and returned to Belfast, his fame brought resentment from many in the Nationalist community at someone who had joined the Crown forces. He moved to East Belfast but found himself less than welcome there as a Catholic and moved with his family to England, dying in Halifax, Yorkshire, in 1986. The only permanent recognition granted him by civic Belfast was a small photograph of him which was displayed in the city hall. It took until 1999 before a proper memorial, funded from National Lottery money, was raised and dedicated to him in the city hall's gardens. Many councillors attended but Sinn Féin absented itself. One of its spokesmen told the press: 'The current political climate would not allow us to attend the ceremony. He was a member of the British forces.'[93]

Leading Seaman Maginnis returned from his war service to a Northern Ireland where deeply ingrained divisions seemed unchanged.[94] For Brian Moore, whom war work for the British government had taken to North Africa, Italy and France, one brief visit to Belfast in late 1945 was enough[95] though he set several of his novels there. Among those who remained, nearly 126,000 people cast their votes for parties of the left in the July 1945 Stormont elections. This yielded up five parliamentary seats, hardly enough to undermine Unionist power in a chamber of fifty members.

One of the five whose leftist credentials were already being questioned was Harry Midgley. After his break with Labour and his formation of the Commonwealth Labour Party, Brooke brought him into the government as Minister for Public Security in April 1943[96] and later as Minister of Labour. Midgley pressed hard for action on the housing crisis which had been accentuated by the 1941 Blitz. He also argued that, if Éire-born men who had enlisted in the British forces were to be given post-war residence permits in Northern Ireland, these would be granted only with reference to the overall employment situation, and that ex-servicemen from the province should be given priority on the jobs market.

Midgley also joined forces with those Unionists who hoped for the full implementation of the 1942 Beveridge Report in post-war Northern Ireland. Churchill's ministers reacted with little enthusiasm, and Sir Kingsley Wood, the Chancellor of the Exchequer, rejected the concept of the province's right to parity in welfare services with the rest of Britain.[97] It needed a Labour government in London to apply this principle and, indeed, Churchill himself was reluctant to give any undertakings on the rapid enactment of the Beveridge plan in Britain as a whole, never mind Northern Ireland.

At least Brooke's government launched the first-ever official inquiry into Northern Ireland's housing needs. The Blitz and the condition of many of those evacuated after it from Belfast had brought home to many public figures the scale of the problem. One former moderator of the Ulster Presbyterian general assembly had declared, after a tour of bombed areas, that Belfast's housing was mostly unfit to be rebuilt and, on the eve of the Blitz, a Belfast Corporation committee had reported that, in some working-class areas, people were living 'in mere hovels in indescribable filth and squalor'.[98]

A rebuilding programme, with some funding reluctantly granted for it by the Treasury in London, got under way in 1943 and, in July of the next year, a housing trust was set up with statutory powers to speed up and co-ordinate local-authority housing, to build houses itself, and to make sure that all housing was properly allocated on the basis of need. This proved easier said than done and, twenty years later, many of those who had been active in campaigns against the underprovision and sectarian allocation of housing gravitated to the Northern Ireland Civil Rights Association. In August 1969 the trust was replaced by the new Housing Executive with responsibility for all public-sector housing. One result of this, it has been said, was that nearly all paramilitary combatants in the Troubles, Loyalist and republican, lived in accommodation funded in part by British taxpayers.[99]

The Brooke government also acted in 1944 to increase Stormont's funding of the 'controlled', or Catholic, part of the province's school system. At that point almost 40 per cent of those enrolled in education were Catholics so there was a body of opinion within Unionism which took the view that this must be reflected in a substantial funding increase which was incorporated in the government's 1947 Education Act. Patrick Shea, as a senior Catholic civil servant in the education department, was later able to write with pride of the support Stormont gave the minority community's schools.[100]

Not all Unionists shared this view, and funding of the Catholic school system remained an issue. Within Brooke's Cabinet there were those whose tolerance of Catholicism was not something he could take for granted. William Lowry, whom Brooke had appointed home affairs minister in April 1943, remained in the Cabinet despite an outburst by him the following year when he had heard that a former Orange Hall in Portrush was being used temporarily for Catholic soldiers in the American army to hear Mass. Lowry remarked that the premises would need to be fumigated afterwards and then had to apologise to the local bishop for the offence given to the American forces and their Catholic chaplains.[101]

In the longer term, however, Brooke's most significant failure to act was on the issue of the local government franchise. This gave votes to ratepayers, sometimes multiple votes based on the ownership of houses and of business premises. The discrimination integral to it was class based. Many Protestants were excluded from the vote but almost certainly more Catholics were. Assimilating the local franchise to the Westminster system has been described as Unionism's chance 'to take a risk and strike a blow for fairness'.[102] Any such change would have undermined the party's strength on some councils, notably in Londonderry, where Unionists took their control for granted. It was a bridge too far for Brooke to cross but he lived long enough to hear the slogan 'One man, one vote' being chanted on the first civil rights marches.

It was a crucial failure of nerve by a prime minister who, in 1945, showed the will to introduce family allowances in Northern Ireland on the same basis as Churchill's government had agreed to in London. Predictable warnings came of how Catholics would benefit disproportionately and whether it was wise so to reward a disloyal population. Brooke held his ground on this issue at least, recording in private his view that 'the only chance for the political future of Ulster' would be for it to become 'so prosperous that the traditional political attitudes were broken down'.[103]

Achieving that, or even making the attempt, was certainly well beyond the horizons of the London government in 1945. Action on the issue of the local council franchise might have been a start but Churchill had much else on his mind, and the issue passed him by though Britain had the power to intervene under the 1920 Government of Ireland Act. It was a power which had lain dormant since then and would remain so until the onset of the Troubles in 1969.

At the war's end, Nationalist Ireland had little to offer that would have helped to reduce ancient hatreds in the northern counties. The Nationalist community there had nothing at all. At the 1945 Stormont elections, its voters in South Armagh elected as their Nationalist Party member Malachy Conlon, a blood-and-soil cultural fascist and anti-Semite who talked the language of blood sacrifice and visceral hatred of Britain. His victory over a moderate and socially progressive Northern Ireland Labour Party candidate was an ominous signal to the Protestant and Unionist majority and to anyone across the water concerned enough to interpret the result.

In November 1945, Conlon took a leading role in forming the Anti-Partition League whose aim was to bring together in a new campaign for Irish unity constitutional nationalists as well as those of the insurrectionist republican tradition. The League built up a broad body of support and never saw fit to disown or even reprimand Conlon for the increasingly deranged analogies he drew between the position of Catholics in Northern Ireland and those of the Jews in the recently overthrown New Order in Europe.[104]

This example of the malign form which the post-war remobilisation of Nationalist Irish opinion could take, along with a complacent Unionism's slowness to espouse the cause of change and reconciliation, guaranteed the return of conflict to Northern Ireland. When it came, it would take, though over a much longer period, many more lives than Goering's bombers did over Belfast in 1941, and inflict an even greater trauma on Northern Ireland's people.

In 1969, John Hewitt, the Belfast-born poet and socialist, addressed in one of his finest poems, a post-war leadership of Northern Ireland and their supporters who, in his view, had simply coasted along, averting their gaze from the chasm of misunderstanding and prejudice which partition, devolved government and world war had failed to close.

The cloud of infection hangs over the city,
a quick change of wind and it might spill over the leafy suburbs.
You coasted too long.[105]

Notes

1. Daiken (ed.), *They Go, the Irish*, p. 22.
2. Walker, *The Politics of Frustration: Harry Midgley and the Failure of Labour in Northern Ireland*, pp. 114–46.

3. R. Munck and W. Rolston, *Belfast in the Thirties: an Oral History* (Belfast: Blackstaff, 1987), pp. 27–40.
4. *Irish News*, 26 August 1932.
5. Ibid., 5 March 1938.
6. Ibid.
7. Ibid., 29 March 1939.
8. PRONI, Com. 61/440, Board of Trade Report, 2 January 1941.
9. PRONI, Com. 61/440, Churchill to Ernest Bevin, 23 January 1941.
10. PRONI, Com. 61/440, Bevin to John Andrews, 28 January 1941.
11. PRONI, Com. 61/440, Sir David Lindsay Keir to Harold Wilson, 27 February 1941.
12. *Irish News*, 30 August 1939.
13. *Front Line 1940–1941: the Official Story of the Civil Defence of Britain* (London: His Majesty's Stationery Office, 1942), p. 123.
14. J. Gardiner, *Wartime: Britain 1939–1945* (London: Headline Publishing, 2004), p. 395.
15. *Glasgow Observer and Scottish Catholic Herald*, 16 May 1941.
16. Ibid, 25 April 1941.
17. Ibid., 16 May 1941.
18. PRONI, D/21/09/18/9, Emma Duffin Diary; see also B. Barton, *Northern Ireland in the Second World War* (Belfast: Ulster Historical Foundation, 1995), p. 46.
19. *Front Line, 1940–1941*, p. 123.
20. M. Woodside Diaries, 17 April 1941.
21. Ibid.
22. Ibid., 20 April 1941.
23. Ibid., 5 May 1941.
24. PRONI MPS 1/3/7 Ministry of Public Security file, 16 August 1940.
25. PRONI D. 559, Spender diaries 15/16 April 1941.
26. Ibid.
27. PRONI, Cab. 4/473/10, MacDermott to the Cabinet, 12 May 1941.
28. PRONI D. 559, Spender diaries, 30 May 1941.
29. A. Calder, *The Myth of the Blitz* (London: Jonathan Cape, 1991), pp. 130–3; also T. Harrison, *Living through the Blitz* (London: Collins, 1976), pp. 182–3, 230, 260–1.
30. J. P. Duggan, *Herr Hempel at the German Legation in Dublin 1937–1945* (Dublin: Irish Academic Press, 2003), p. 134.
31. PRONI D. 559, Spender diaries, 8 May 1941.
32. Ibid., 18 June 1941.
33. J. W. Blake, *Northern Ireland in the Second World War* (Belfast: Her Majesty's Stationery Office, 1956), pp. 425–6.
34. PRONI, Cab 9C/22/2, R. R. Bowman to the Cabinet Secretary, 6 April 1945.
35. Gardiner, *Wartime: Britain 1939–1945*, pp. 516–17.
36. PRONI, Cab 3A/78B, RUC History of the War: Crime Branch.
37. PRONI, Cab 9C/22/1, MacDermott to Andrews, 2 November 1942.
38. PRONI, Com 61/440, Churchill to Andrews, 2 October 1942.
39. PRONI, Cab 9C/22/1, MacDermott to Andrews, 2 November 1942.
40. *News Letter*, 17 October 1942.
41. PRONI, Cab 9C/22/2 Robert Morrow to Sir Basil Brooke, 1 May 1944.
42. PRONI, Cab 9C/22/2, Brooke to Churchill, 9 March 1944.
43. PRONI, Cab 9C/22/2, Churchill to Brooke, 15 March 1944; see also Fisk, *In Time of War*, p. 467.
44. PRONI, Cab 9C/22/2, Brooke to the Cabinet, 5 April 1944.

45. Ibid.
46. K. Ford, 'Thy Sons Shall Come from Afar; Thy Daughters Shall Rise Up By Thy Side', *New Ulster: Journal of the Ulster Society*, No. 22, 1994, pp. 12–17.
47. Ibid.
48. *Irish News*, 16 March 2000.
49. Ibid.
50. Fisk, *In Time of War*, p. 465.
51. Barton, *Northern Ireland in the Second World War*, pp. 19–20.
52. PRONI, Cab 9C/22/2, letter to Sir Basil Brooke, 8 June 1944.
53. Ibid.
54. Barton, *Northern Ireland in the Second World War*, p. 21.
55. Ibid., pp. 78–82.
56. Croucher, *Engineers at War 1939–1945*, p. 375.
57. Blake, *Northern Ireland in the Second World War*, p. 177.
58. Delaney, *Demography, State and Society: Irish Migration to Britain 1921–1971*, pp. 128–9.
59. *Irish News*, 19 June 1942.
60. PRONI, Cab 9C/47/2, Cabinet Review of Resident Permits, 10 July 1944.
61. Ibid.
62. *Londonderry Sentinel*, 6 July 1944.
63. PRONI, Cab 4/615, Cabinet Conclusions, 15 February 1945.
64. PRONI, Fin 18/22/37, Cabinet subcommittee, 5 February 1942.
65. *News Letter*, 24 March 1942.
66. PRONI, Fin 18/22/37, Cabinet minute, 15 March 1942.
67. Ibid., Morrison to Bates, 18 April 1942.
68. Gray, *The Lost Years: the Emergency in Ireland 1939–45*, pp. 210–12.
69. PRONI, Cab 3A/76B, RUC Crime Branch History of the War.
70. Walker, *A History of the Ulster Unionist Party: Protest, pragmatism and pessimism*, pp. 105–6.
71. P Shea, *Voices and the Sound of Drums: an Irish Autobiography* (Belfast: Blackstaff, 1981), pp. 142–3.
72. Ibid.
73. PRONI, Cab 9C 47/2, letter to Brooke, 23 March 1944.
74. *Irish News*, 28 January 1936.
75. Walker, *A History of the Ulster Unionist Party: Protest, pragmatism and pessimism*, p. 73.
76. Ibid.
77. Ibid.
78. G Walker, 'Northern Ireland, British–Irish Relations and American Concerns 1942–1956', *Twentieth Century British History*, Vol. 18, No. 2, 2007, pp. 194–218.
79. *Irish News*, 29 April 1939.
80. Ibid.
81. Ibid., 17 October 1938.
82. Ibid., 7 September 1938.
83. Ibid., 28 November 1938.
84. Ibid., 9 February 1938.
85. Ibid., 24 January 1938.
86. J. D. Brewer and G. I. Higgins, *Anti-Catholicism in Northern Ireland, 1600–1998: the Mote and the Beam*, (Basingstoke: Macmillan, 1998), p. 98.
87. Walker, *A History of the Ulster Unionist Party: Protest, pragmatism and pessimism*, pp. 74–5.
88. *Irish News*, 19 February 1938.

89. Moore, *The Emperor of Ice-Cream*, pp. 206–7.
90. M. Woodside, Diary, 8 December 1940.
91. *Irish News*, 22 February 1999.
92. Ibid., 2 June 2004.
93. Ibid., 9 October 1999. For an excellent study of Leading Seaman Maginnis, see G. Fleming, *Maginnis VC: the Story of Northern Ireland's Only Winner of the Victoria Cross* (Dublin: History Ireland, 1998).
94. M. Goldring, *Belfast – from Loyalty to Rebellion* (London: Lawrence and Wishart, 1991), pp. 90-7.
95. P. Craig, *Brian Moore: a Biography* (London: Bloomsbury, 2002), p. 95.
96. Walker, *A History of the Ulster Unionist Party: Protest, pragmatism and pessimism*, pp. 164–5.
97. Barton, *Northern Ireland in the Second World War*, pp. 59–61.
98. B. Barton, *The Blitz: Belfast in the War Years* (Belfast: Blackstaff, 1989), pp. 156–7.
99. K. Myers, *Watching the Door: Cheating Death in 1970s Belfast* (Dublin: Lilliput Press, 2006), p. 156.
100. Shea, Voices and the Sound of Drums: an Irish Autobiography, pp. 161 and 179.
101. O. P. Rafferty, *Catholicism in Ulster 1603–1983: an Interpretative History* (London: Hurst and Company, 1994), p. 243.
102. Walker, *A History of the Ulster Unionist Party: Protest, pragmatism and pessimism*, p. 163.
103. PRONI, D 3004, Sir Basil Brooke Diaries, 5 September 1944; also B Barton, *Northern Ireland in the Second World War*, p. 130 .
104. Walker, A History of the Ulster Unionist Party: Protest, pragmatism and pessimism, pp. 100–2.
105. M. Longley and F. Ormsby, *John Hewitt: Selected Poems* (Belfast: Blackstaff, 2007), p. 73.

8

Emergency, War and their Aftermath

Germany's surrender and the end of the war in Europe prompted huge celebrations in the centre of Belfast on Tuesday, 8 May. As one newspaper put it, 'all the spirit of the Twelfth was there, doubled and re-doubled'.[1] Outside the City Hall the biggest crowd seen there since the signing of the Ulster Covenant in September 1912 gathered to cheer Churchill's broadcast, relayed through loudspeakers. Away from the centre, street parties were held, though mainly in Loyalist areas where flags and bunting were readily available, having been set aside for the Boyne celebrations that were still two months away.

At Enniskillen, close to Lough Erne, which had played a vital part in RAF Coastal Command's operations in the Atlantic, there were also celebrations. These included High Mass in St Michael's Catholic church A dual message was offered there, of thanksgiving for peace but also for Ireland's preservation from the awfulness of war.[2] In predominantly nationalist Londonderry, victory celebrations were muted. Some wartime contracts, which had provided work in the city's mills, were already ending and there was uncertainty about the future, there and elsewhere in Northern Ireland. Its prime minister privately echoed this mood: 'I find that I have no feelings of elation, only thankfulness that others will not have to endure the losses that we have suffered. One realises also the vast and difficult problems which lie ahead.'[3]

In Dublin, as described in an earlier chapter, the Irish Times celebrated the victory of Britain and its allies with a front-page design intended to mock and defy a censorship whose role was already redundant.[4] At Trinity College, the mainly Anglo-Irish student body flew the flags of the allies from the roof of the building and also set fire to an Irish tricolour which they hurled down into the street. This incensed Nationalist students from the city's University College and there were street clashes with Trinity students. Two UCD undergraduates set alight a Union flag in College Green as a reprisal. One of them was Charles Haughey who later became a controversial and almost indestructible figure in the politics of the Irish state.[5]

Only six days earlier, de Valera had famously paid his visit to Hempel, still German minister in Dublin, to offer his condolences on Hitler's death. The storm of criticism which this unleashed in Britain, the United States and elsewhere was not matched by a similar reaction in Éire. There, it has been said, majority opinion was not shocked by the Taoiseach's action after six years of a censorship designed to inoculate Irish people against any temptation to believe in the moral superiority of the cause of Britain and its allies.[6] Even with hostilities in Europe at an end, de Valera felt no need to bring to the population's attention the reality of the Third Reich's barbarism.

Sir John Maffey, Britain's Dublin representative who could seldom resist a witticism, wrote of the visit to Hempel as 'an act of conspicuous neutrality in the field'[7] and, in a sense, that is exactly what it was, given de Valera's preoccupation with protocol. Soon afterwards he wrote to Robert Brennan, Éire's ambassador in Washington, insisting that such a formal act as his visit implied no judgement of any kind on the late Führer. Not to have gone, he argued, 'would have been an act of unpardonable discourtesy to the German nation and Dr Hempel himself'.[8]

It could as well be argued that, given what de Valera already knew about the mass murder of Jews and the brutality of Germany's 'New Order' in Europe,[9] any discourtesy to Hitler's Dublin spokesman would have been entirely pardonable. Those close to de Valera had advised him against the visit, and John Dulanty, Éire's high Commissioner in London, found that he had a hopeless task on his hands trying to explain the Taoiseach's action.[10] Only Falangist Spain commended him for his 'brave, human and Christian attitude to Hitler's death'.[11] Alone among neutral states, Spain and Portugal under the neo-fascist Salazar regime, paid official respects to Hitler on his demise.

This was sinister company for a democratic Irish state to keep. A propaganda gift had been presented to the Stormont government in Belfast and the condemnation from Irish America as well as from the British press was a bitter blow to Éire citizens who had made their

choice to serve with the British forces. One of them wrote to de
Valera in order to tell him that 'by your unforgivable act you have
alienated any remaining sympathy or friendship for Éire. We are now
a nation exiled from the world.'[12] De Valera, however, still has his
defenders over this episode[13] and, in any event, the fallout from it
was quickly dissipated by Churchill's ill-judged victory broadcast on
13 May 1945 and de Valera's reply to it.

Churchill paid generous tribute to Northern Ireland but was
unable to resist a final condemnation of Éire's neutrality, though
he did acknowledge the thousands of Éire men and women who had
enlisted in the British forces. De Valera's stance, he declared, had
imperilled Britain and, had it not been for Northern Ireland, he went
on,

> we should have been forced to come to close quarters with Mr de
> Valera or perish from the earth. However, with a restraint and
> poise to which, I say, history will find few parallels, His Majesty's
> Government never laid a violent hand upon them, though at times
> it would have been quite easy and natural, and we left the de
> Valera Government to frolic with the Germans and later with the
> Japanese representatives to their heart's content.'[14]

Three days later de Valera broadcast an eagerly awaited reply to
Churchill which has been described as the most effective speech of
his entire career. It was both low key and statesman-like. He made
allowances for Churchill but tackled the central inference to be
drawn from his broadcast that Britain might have seen fit for its own
purposes to violate Éire's neutrality. 'It seems strange to me', de
Valera added, 'that Mr Churchill does not see that this, if accepted,
would mean that Britain's necessity would become a moral code.'[15]
He went on to applaud Churchill for not yielding to the temptation of
invading Éire and thus 'adding another horrid chapter to the already
bloodstained record of relations between England and this country.'[16]

Sir John Maffey in Dublin had not been consulted about the
content of Churchill's broadcast and admitted to his frustration at
the way it had swung opinion towards de Valera again after what he
called 'the smear of moral turpitude' that some had associated with
his visit to Hempel. De Valera's speech, Maffey wrote, 'is acclaimed in
all quarters, even in TCD [Trinity College Dublin] and by the 'Irish
Times''.[17] Churchill had played into the hands of de Valera and, as
one of his biographers has put it, the Taoiseach 'unquestionably

spoke for a united people of the twenty-six counties. For once, the ice melted in support behind him.'[18]

By the time of these broadcasts, Irish cinemas, free from the wartime censorship, had begun to show newsreel and British army film footage of the recently liberated death camps such as Belsen. Irish audiences were ill-prepared for this. Press coverage was limited and some of it shamefully sceptical. The *Irish Times* carried more readers' letters on the VE Day disturbances at Trinity College than on either Belsen or Auschwitz[19] and, in Kilkenny, the local newspaper printed several letters from readers claiming that the film footage of Belsen had been faked for British propaganda's always devious purposes.[20]

On 11 June 1945 the *Irish Press,* which had a national circulation, carried an article entitled 'Buchenwald becomes Box-Office'. It was the work of the paper's film critic whose concern was clearly to implant questions in the minds of audiences about the awful footage they saw: 'doubt comes creeping, not with regard to what the camera shows, but as to what was behind what the camera shows'.[21] A week later the same critic was deploring the fact that the end of the Emergency censorship was exposing filmgoers to pro-Allied propaganda in which he seemed to include footage from the German death camps.[22]

The emotional response in Éire, indeed, was much greater to the destruction of Hiroshima and Nagasaki in August 1945 by atomic bombs. This was, of course, something in which Britain could be directly implicated because of its endorsement of President Truman's decision to use the new weapons. It would also be seen as the culmination of a decade of air war, starting in China, Abyssinia and Spain and, therefore, at one level more comprehensible than the German state's years of methodical, premeditated mass murder of innocent millions.[23]

Some have seen this muted and morally ambivalent Irish reaction to the first revelations of the Holocaust as a product not just of censorship but also of the state's ungenerous policy to Jews who had sought sanctuary in Éire before and during the war. Their chance to secure this depended upon Ireland's nationality law. This was codified in the Dáil's 1935 Citizenship and Nationality Act and also in an Aliens Act which laid down strict conditions for anyone other than a British citizen entering the state. These included an immigration officer's authorisation, a work permit from an Irish employer, proper identification and proof that, without a work permit, applicants for entry could support themselves and their families.

A small staff in the Justice Department had to administer this law. Even as Nazi persecution of Jews and political opponents worsened, the way the department did this was 'not liberal'[24] in the words of one of its employees talking to an interviewer about its role between 1935 and 1939. The following year, 1936, saw the League of Nations convening a conference on the legal status of refugees leaving Germany. The Justice Department was represented but opposed the Dublin government signing up to any measures which would place 'such refugees in a more favourable position than other aliens'.[25] It also remained silent about the new Reich's viciously discriminatory Nuremberg laws.

The result of this was near enough to a closed door. There was to be no 'Ireland of the welcomes' for Europe's Jews and no counterpart in pre-war Éire to Britain's admission of more than 10,000 Jewish children who escaped the Nazis on special trains, or *kindertransport*, organised, and in part funded, by campaigners who also provided homes for them.[26] A closed door was, in fact, what the Justice Department in Dublin wanted. In the early weeks of the war it gave temporary entry rights to a few Jews but, in December 1939, its senior secretary, S. A. Roche, minuted to colleagues about a new order under the state's emergency legislation which authorised him to sign deportations: 'The main purpose of this order is to deal with the Jews and other undesireables [sic] who came here in August and September.'[27]

Roche's view had support within G2, the army's intelligence service and, in late July, Colonel Liam Archer wrote to ministers about the case of Marcus Witztum, a Jewish businessman resident in Éire since before the war. Witztum was already under surveillance because of the influence it was feared he might use to secure entry for other Jews as much of Europe fell under German rule. Archer drew wider conclusions from this case:

> On the question generally of admitting aliens to this country my point of view is that no others of the fraternity [i.e., Jews] should be allowed to enter under any circumstances as we have more than enough to do to control and supervise the number of aliens already here.[28]

This was almost certainly what Roche wanted to hear.

Six years later Roche had not altered his view. Éire had probably admitted no more than sixty Jews during the Emergency period. He felt able to write to a colleague that

Our practice has been to discourage any substantial increase in the Jewish population. They do not assimilate with other people but remain a sort of colony of a world-wide Jewish community. This makes them a potential irritant in the body politic and has led to disastrous results from time to time in other countries.[29]

The Irish state was also loyally served in these years by men of conscience who had no illusions about the German Reich and its exterminationist racial policy. One of them was Con Cremin who, in 1943, was made head of the Éire Foreign Service's Berlin mission. There he worked tirelessly, though with tragically little success, to secure German agreement to the issuing of Irish passports and visas to Jews in occupied France, especially children, liable for deportation to the death camps. German officials cynically strung him along with ambivalent and mendacious responses. He later recalled one of them pointing out the implications of what he was trying to do for Éire and how the Reich 'would gladly save us the inconvenience of having so many Jews'.[30] Cremin at least confronted the regime over the deportations and, it has been said, 'bore witness to the Holocaust, even in the last days of the Third Reich'.[31]

Nationalist Ireland as a whole, and the republican movement in particular, preferred to avert its gaze and avoid awkward questions about the naked aggression and barbarism of Nazi Germany. On 1 April 1943 an *Irish News* letter writer could even inimitably declare: 'There is no kind of oppression visited on any minority in Europe which the six-county Nationalists have not also endured.'[32] At the time this appeared, the remaining Jews in the Warsaw ghetto were still holding out against the monstrously superior firepower of the *Wehrmacht* and the SS. The insight of the *Irish News* contributor, Professor Joseph Lee has pointed out, 'would no doubt have helped the victims lining up for the Auschwitz gas chambers place their plight in consoling comparative perspective'.[33]

As pointed out already in this book, there were Irish people who accepted Éire's neutrality without ever wanting, or trying, to justify it in their own minds as any sort of moral stance. This set them far apart from the Belsen and Auschwitz sceptics who clung longer than they ever should have to the notion of a moral equivalence between the war's major combatants. Denis Johnston, the Dublin-born writer and dramatist, worked for the BBC during the war, like his friend the poet Louis MacNeice. He became a front-line reporter and saw Buchenwald after its liberation. His wartime diaries and journals show a growing irritation with the attempts of Irish politicians, as well as senior clerics, to endow the state's neutrality with a moral status which his experiences made it impossible for him to accept.[34]

Samuel Beckett (1906–89) was living in Paris at the time of the fall of France in 1940. He could have returned to Éire but he knew what he wanted to do and that was to join the French Resistance. The cell in which he became active did important intelligence gathering work to help Britain but it was broken up by Gestapo infiltration and he had to go on the run and into hiding. He returned briefly to Éire after the war but was uncomfortable with the atmosphere there and went back to France to work for the Red Cross.[35]

Had the war's outcome been different, many, or indeed most, of Éire's Jews would have taken their places in Auschwitz's gas chambers. At Wannsee in Berlin, where leading Nazi bureaucrats and SS officers agreed to adopt the 'Final Solution' to the 'Jewish Question', Jewish populations across Europe, including still-neutral states, were carefully quantified. Éire was listed as having 4,000 Jews.[36] It is well documented what the fate of Jews in neutral states would have been had the Nazis' New Order prevailed across Europe as a whole. Irish republicans would have accepted Ireland's unification as a gift from a victorious Reich, and how far an Irish state would then have been able, or willing, to protect its Jewish citizens has to remain problematic.

Ireland, Mr Deasy declared to Stephen Daedalus in James Joyce's *Ulysses*, could claim the honour of never having persecuted Jews, and he put the question to him and others in Barney Kiernan's pub in Dublin as to why this was. His clinching answer to his own question was that Ireland had never admitted Jews. This, of course, was not wholly true because, at the time of the Emergency, the Irish state had a well-settled but small community of Jewish people. On occasions, however, they had come under attack, as in Limerick in 1904 when the local Jewish population was subjected to an economic boycott which, for a time, became violent.

A local priest bore much of the responsibility for what happened but Sinn Féin's founder, Arthur Griffith, a virulent anti-Semite, supported the boycott and wrote of Jews as 'vultures'.[37] He was rightly denounced for this in a letter to the *Irish Times*,[38] written many years later by the son of a victim of a pogrom which served to break up and permanently disperse Limerick's Jewish community.[39] Though Joyce captured some of Dublin's casual anti-Semitism in *Ulysses*, there was no comparable event there to what happened in Limerick, and its Jewish population has been described as a well-integrated one.

Before and after he became Taoiseach, de Valera was on good terms with Ireland's Chief Rabbi, Dr Isaac Herzog. Herzog moved to Palestine in 1936 but was a major source of private information for de Valera on the murderous evolution of the Nazi state's policy towards Jews in Germany itself and in occupied Europe.[40] De Valera was also friendly with a Jewish TD, Robert Briscoe, who had settled in Dublin in the early years of the century. His loyalty to de Valera's government was unswerving but his links to the Zionist movement and to organisations helping Jewish refugees from Europe made him suspect to G2, the Irish army's intelligence service.

Like the defence forces as a whole, they were wary of recruiting Jews and also of Briscoe's urging them to join the Local Security Force, broadly an equivalent to Britain's Home Guard, which later became known in Éire as the Local Defence Force. In June 1940, G2 reported that 'certain responsible citizens, on finding a large number of young Jews in the local Security Body – one said he thought he had wandered by accident into a synagogue rather than a Garda station – immediately abandoned their intention of serving in that body'.[41] The document also referred to 'persons of only 50 per cent loyalty' and to how Jewish entry could be a 'grave danger to recruitment'.[42]

Earlier on in this report, G2 also alluded to 'the present widespread objection in the civil population to the Jewish community, recently much swollen in numbers'.[43] Neither assertion was sustainable but G2 used it to back its case for a 'period of residence' clause to be incorporated in the conditions of service for the Local Security Force. This mindset clearly lay behind the degree of surveillance which was applied to Briscoe and his contacts[44] though it was never justified because, although he identified himself passionately with his fellow Jews in their darkest hour, he missed no chance in his travels outside Éire to uphold the state's right to its neutrality.[45]

G2's concern with Briscoe was only part of a much larger operation by it, and also by the Garda's Special Branch, to document and monitor the activity of Europe's smallest Jewish community. G2's files in the Irish Military Archive are a reminder to this day of the assiduous way in which this work was carried out. The files are extensive, and some of the brown folders holding them are simply marked 'Jewry'. Surveillance continued until late on in the war, with some files running to thirty pages of carefully compiled details on the Jewish community and its political sympathies and possible Zionist links.[46]

At some points, it should be added, the G2 files do provide evidence that the Irish state was also monitoring active and political anti-Semitism. G2 was being briefed on this by the Garda even before the Emergency[47] and, after September 1939, the state censors often passed on to it for filing anti-Semitic material which it required newspapers and other publications to delete.[48] In September 1944, G2 received from the censors a copy of a letter from Dublin which it had intercepted for the London-based *Catholic Times*. The letter was viciously anti-Semitic and praised the work of Father Denis Fahey of the order of the Holy Ghost Fathers. He was also active in an organisation called Maria Duce whose concern was to expose what it claimed was Jewish power in Ireland.[49]

Ten years after the war's end, guilt in the Irish state over what became known as the Holocaust, if there was ever much of it, proved no impediment to a renewed anti-Semitic campaign once more in Limerick. Among its targets were local cinemas which were picketed and leafleted for allegedly corrupting audiences with the output of a Jewish-controlled Hollywood. The leader of this campaign was Father Fahey, and one of his protégés was Seán Sabhat, or Seán South, as he is better known. He, it has been said, apart from being a member of Maria Duce, 'held anti-Semitic views, was an opponent of trade unions and an admirer of Senator Joseph McCarthy'.[50] None of this stopped him from being allowed to serve in an army reserve unit or from being recruited by the IRA and, in January 1957, he was killed in a raid across the Fermanagh border. Ever since, he has been 'Seán South of Garryowen' and a heroic song and IRA hagiography have edited out of the record his political views and his role in trying to protect Limerick from the worldwide Jewish conspiracy.

It took many years for official Ireland to render proper tribute to Jewish victims of Nazi genocide. The way was finally cleared for this by events across the border when the IRA announced a ceasefire at the end of August 1994. In Dublin seven months later, on the occasion of the reopening and rededication of the city's Islandbridge memorial to the Irish who gave their lives on Britain's side in two world wars, the then Taoiseach, John Bruton, spoke eloquently of the Holocaust and made an unscripted reference to countries 'which closed their doors and their ports'[51] to refugees from it. Everyone present, including even Sinn Féin's representative, must have known what he meant.

Whether the moral compromises involved in neutrality influenced the post-war Irish state in its policy on asylum and rights of residence to those who had either collaborated with, or been active in, support of the German Reich is an issue which has been raised intermittently over the years. Robert Fisk did so though his focus was on such people being allowed to buy property in Éire[52] and, in January 2007, a two-part RTE documentary reopened the issue.

Near the end of the war, David Gray, the United States minister in Dublin, demanded that no 'war criminal' be given asylum in Éire. It was a demand to which de Valera, given his tense wartime relationship with Gray, was never going to agree to publicly. He was ready, it has been said, 'to sacrifice good relations with the Allies in the short term in order to assert Irish sovereignty'.[53] What doing this meant in practice was admitting to Éire some members of the Breton Nationalist movement who feared reprisals from the French Resistance which had regarded their wartime autonomism as treason to France. Some Bretons had collaborated with the Germans and one of them, who settled in Éire, Yann Goulet, was sentenced to death in France in 1947.

Others who had been involved in ethnic separatist politics in the Flemish area of Belgium and in Croatia also gravitated to Ireland. One of them, Andrija Artuković, had been a wartime minister in the collaborationist and anti-Semitic wartime Ustashi-run Croatian puppet state which did much vile work for the Germans. Papers relating to him and the year he spent in Éire, after being released from British custody, remain closed to access. He later made his way safely to the United States.[54] Post-war anti-Communism and the crude imperatives of the Cold War soon gave a role to many of those who had compromised themselves politically by apparent sympathy for the Axis cause. Britain itself gave post-war asylum to many Ukrainian and other collaborators, some of whom much later would stand trial on war crimes charges.

When it mattered during the war the Irish state and its intelligence and security forces took a tough line against a few extreme Scottish nationalists who arrived in Éire hoping to make contacts with the IRA,[55] and as already shown, an even tougher one with German agents and any who sought to aid them. After the war, as during it, the state's primary concern was the protection and exercise of its sovereignty, and de Valera and his ministers saw entry and asylum policy as vital to it.

Twelve years after the war, the issue took on new life when an exclusive country club party near Dublin was attended by Otto Skorzeny, the scar-faced Waffen SS officer famous for his part in the airborne raid to rescue Mussolini from captivity in 1943 after the Italian armistice. Since he was forbidden entry into Britain, rumours that he might settle in Ireland were of concern to the Dublin government. He was, in fact, given visas for one or two brief visits and, in June 1959, bought a substantial property in County Kildare. Between then and 1969, Skorzeny and his wife spent a few weeks every year at Martinstown House, working at tree clearing and sheep farming on its adjoining 165 acres (67 ha). Rumours continued to be rife about his alleged contacts with both Adolf Eichmann and Leon Degrelle, the Belgian Nazi leader who had found sanctuary in Madrid.[56]

Irish intelligence services kept a close watch on his movements. Another of his possible contacts was thought to be Oswald Mosley, the disgraced leader of the British Union of Fascists who also bought property in Ireland, in his case at Clonfert in County Galway. This was after the Irish Justice Department had advised him against seeking permanent residence. Mosley and his wife Diana spent what she later recalled in a crass and self-serving volume of memoirs as an idyllic period there. They rode with the East Galway hounds and employed servants and private tutors for their children. Everything, she wrote, 'reminded one of how little Ireland had changed since the eighteenth century'.[57]

One unrepentant Nazi who believed he could resume residence in post-war Ireland and restart his career in its museum service was Dr Adolf Mahr. He had abused the career preferment given him by a democratic Irish state to serve the cause of Nazi Germany and, when war came, he worked willingly for its propaganda service. In late 1947, after a period in British detention in Germany, he wrote a begging letter to de Valera disclaiming any personal guilt and asking for reinstatement in the work he had done before the war. He received no reply either from the Taoiseach or from his staff.[58]

Problems lay ahead for German legation staff who had spent the war in Dublin. Gray, the American minister, demanded the legation's closure and, on 10 May 1945, its keys were handed over to the Americans. Its contents, including the famous book of condolences for Hitler's death, were later sold off by auction in Belfast. For Hempel and his colleagues, bereft of the Reich which had employed them, financial hardship followed. Hempel may have received some help from de Valera and Sir John Maffey, and his wife, a talented baker, was able to make and sell German cakes to shops and to friends. It was not until 1949 that Hempel and his wife finally returned to their homeland.[59]

There were also German internees, Luftwaffe and U-boat crew members in the main, whom the British government wanted for questioning. De Valera agreed to this with the proviso that no capital charges be brought against them and that none of them should be forced back to the area of Germany which had fallen under Soviet control. Washington was uneasy over this, feeling that the Taoiseach's conditions would be resented by the Soviet government at a time when maintaining the western states' alliance with it still seemed a priority.

When the war in Europe ended, there were 266 German Luftwaffe and navy men interned at the Curragh army camp in County Kildare. Only 138 of them elected to return to Germany when given the choice. The camp's increasingly relaxed day, and latterly, weekend parole system had allowed them in many cases to relate very well to the local community, playing golf, swimming, shopping and visiting pubs and family homes and, in some cases, taking degree courses at University College Dublin.[60] Their rather bizarre 'war' is amply documented in the Irish Military Archives in which the camp commandant can be found observing that, in reality, the German internees had little incentive to escape compared to the British and Allied servicemen interned close by in their own compound.[61]

If the British and Allied internees escaped, they could hope to reach Northern Ireland, as did quite a few aircrew men who survived crashes close to the border. They could do this without obstruction from the Irish state forces provided they had not broken their paroles. One escaper, an American who had volunteered for the RAF only to crash in Éire, made it to Belfast in 1942 but was returned to the Curragh by the authorities there in the belief that he had broken his parole.[62] Although the Irish army personnel who ran the camp had on occasions to deal with fights between German and Allied internees at local pubs and dances, as well as some of the internees' exploits with local women,[63] the camp could be called 'a showcase for Irish neutrality. The Allied prisoners in it were on show for German spies in Ireland',[64] and Sir John Maffey himself visited it to impress this upon British officers there.

In 1999 the internees' experience inspired a feature film, *The Brylcreem Boys*, and fifteen years earlier, a novel, *Broken Wings*, written by John Clive. The latter puts its central dramatic emphasis on an escape attempt by Allied aircrew men. The author also drew what he thought was the necessary distinction between the German and Allied internees. The Germans organised a system of lectures and, at one point, took delivery at their compound of forty volumes of the writings of Goethe. 'Our boys', one fictional RAF officer says, 'rightly or wrongly, feel that if they organise classes it might be interpreted as acquiescence in their lot, whereas they want it known that they are doing all they can to re-join their units.'[65] Perhaps, indeed, even with the pubs and other attractions of Naas, Newbridge and Dublin rather closer to hand than those of Berlin, something of the spirit of Colditz and Stalag Luft 3 existed at the Curragh.

In 1945 de Valera's position seemed secure, especially after the huge success of his response to the charges made by Churchill in his victory broadcast. The country's wartime isolation had, it has been argued, suited de Valera and had let him rule 'as the philosopher king of Irish pastoralism and frugal comfort'.[66] There were, however, those among his colleagues, such as Seán Lemass, who questioned how realistic was the vision of Ireland that de Valera had set out in his 1943 St Patrick's Day radio address. Accelerating post-war emigration[67] suggested to Lemass and others that only a real change in state policy could reverse this and bring needed economic growth.

No such change came with the 1948 election defeat of de Valera and his party. A loose coalition of Fine Gael, led by John Costello, Labour and Clann na Poblachta, formed by a one-time IRA chief of staff, Seán MacBride, managed to win a Dáil majority. They took over from their predecessors a scheme drawn up in outline to tackle the Irish state's unacceptable level of child mortality. This involved the phasing in of free ante- and post-natal care and advice for mothers, as well as free health treatment without a family means test for all children under sixteen. Dr Noel Browne, a talented political maverick, threw his weight as health minister behind legislation to enact these measures but he seriously underestimated the power of the medical profession and a Church hierarchy who feared the scheme would open the way to family planning.

The 'mother and child' legislation was abandoned in April 1951 before the fall of the coalition, and Browne later wrote his own angry indictment of what he saw as a dismal failure by Irish politicians to act for the common good.[68] It would take another two decades for the Irish state to see any movement on issues like this. If anything, the years of the Emergency had aborted the possibility of it, and 1945 saw no swing in Ireland to the democratic left or to any consensus on welfare policy: Browne's treatment by his own colleagues and by the Church was proof of that.

Apart from this failure, the Costello government's major claim to fame was its decision to repeal de Valera's 1936 External Relations Act. This, enacted at speed during the crisis caused by Edward VIII's abdication, left the British Crown with a residual role in the Irish state's external affairs for so long as it was still in association with other Commonwealth countries. The decision to repeal the act was announced by Costello while on a visit to Canada, and it was followed by the formal creation of an Irish republic at Easter 1949.

Some saw the hand of MacBride, as external affairs minister, behind the move, which was a powerfully symbolic name change. The new republic's constitution was still that drawn up by de Valera in 1937 but nonetheless, the political initiative had been seized from him and his party because, after sixteen years in power, they had not moved from rhetoric to the actual declaration of a republic. Ulster Unionism was hardly surprised but its leaders reacted with outrage and, in response, the Attlee government in London presented to parliament legislation copper-fastening Northern Ireland's continued membership of the United Kingdom until the Stormont parliament decided otherwise.

This, in turn, brought a storm of protest from the newly proclaimed republic. The coalition in Dublin had already formed an all-party anti-partition group known as the Mansion House Committee. Fianna Fáil joined it, although de Valera himself had no real enthusiasm for any anti-partition campaign which he did not control himself. He much preferred speaking tours of Britain, Australia, New Zealand and North America, which he had embarked upon after losing office in 1948.

To American audiences in particular de Valera addressed some eloquent attacks on partition, never losing the chance to defend Irish neutrality in the recent war. To a Detroit meeting in March 1948 he declared: 'Our territory was still occupied by Britain, and the injustice continued. You cannot ask a small nation to fight with you for justice when you are inflicting an injustice on that small nation.'[69] To a Boston audience, he compared partition to the brutality of the Soviet Union's control of Eastern Europe: 'If what is happening in partitioned Ireland today were being done in Eastern Europe by Russia, the people to whom it was being done would be entitled to ask assistance, and many who talk of democracy now would cry out against the injustice.'[70]

The British Labour government's 1949 legislation, securing, as it seemed to do, Britain's veto on Irish unity by transferring it to the custody of the Ulster Unionists, added to the anger of de Valera's oratory. Yet, on his return to office with Fianna Fáil in 1951, he had little to offer in terms of actual policy initiatives on the border question, and the Mansion House anti-partition committee was allowed to languish. Yet Fianna Fáil went on with its ritual condemnations of partition when it met for its annual Ard Fheis or conference.[71]

There was little comfort in any of this for northern Nationalists. Stagnant and ritualistic though Irish political discourse was in the post-1945 period, however, expectations on the national question were still fuelled, although by 1950 the Anti-Partition League's campaign was losing momentum. These were expectations which, if not met, could lead to renewed violence. The republican movement began to regroup as its wartime internees were released. Sinn Féin re-formed as a party, and the *United Irishman* was relaunched to support it. At the 1949 Bodenstown commemoration of Wolfe Tone, a resolution was carried pledging Sinn Féin and the IRA to expelling 'the invader' from Irish soil and a 'military campaign' to achieve this was promised.[72] A new generation of activists and some 'forties men' would soon demonstrate their readiness to be part of it.

That partition still had an integral relationship to the Irish state's foreign policy was clear when the 1948–51 coalition government made it known in 1949 that it would not be joining the new North Atlantic Treaty Organisation (NATO). Initial post-war defence planning by Britain clung to the hope that Éire, still within the Commonwealth, would play some part in the West's military response to the growing power of the Soviet bloc but the fear was always that Dublin would continue to link the partition issue to any abridgement of Irish neutrality.[73] So it proved, and external affairs minister MacBride told both London and Washington that partition was still an historic wrong which must be addressed before Irish membership of NATO could be considered.

This was, however, a shift in policy. After all, in the 1940–41 period, all de Valera had been prepared to offer in return for Churchill's talk of Irish unity was an affirmation of the state's benevolent neutrality.[74] Neither the United States nor Britain pursued the issue. The latter, while strongly committed to the NATO treaty, was not going to use it to call into question Northern Ireland's constitutional future. There was also the fact that the recent war had shown that shipping in the eastern Atlantic could be protected without recourse to the Irish Treaty Ports.

It is not an exaggeration to say that, for de Valera, neutrality as a policy had been set in stone by his own experience and that, indeed, it had become part of the Irish state's self-image. In 1939 many, if not most, European states had opted for neutrality as a policy but Éire was one of just five which were able to sustain it. In 1953, two years after de Valera returned to office, the *Irish Press*, which he and his family owned, launched a lengthy series of articles in defence of the state's policy during the years of the Emergency.

These were written by T. Desmond Williams who had held a history chair at University College Dublin before the war but had served with British intelligence during it. The series made legal history because of the way in which Williams chose to interpret the wartime role of Leopold Kerney, de Valera's minister in Madrid, who had played a part in securing Frank Ryan's release from captivity in Spain. Kerney has had his critics among historians. One referred to him as a 'monumental fool'[75] but Williams accused him of compromising Éire's neutrality by meeting Edmund Veesenmayer, a sinister figure in the German Foreign Office.[76] Kerney had, in fact, done nothing more than give him a non-committal hearing, and he took a successful libel action against Williams.[77]

Despite this episode, de Valera and his ministers were happy with the way Williams explained and justified neutrality as a policy which followed on from the Irish state's pre-war stance at the League of Nations.[78] Securing control of the Treaty Ports in 1938 was, Williams argued, 'a necessary antecedent to the prosecution of neutrality'.[79] De Valera's view of Britain's cause and that of its allies was, he stressed, always a benign one but that it was also a view constrained by the continuing reality of Ireland's partition.[80]

Churchill's apparent readiness in the summer of 1940 to move on the issue of partition was not, as we have seen, enough to bring Éire into the war, whatever the degree of sympathy for Britain de Valera may have had. Ten years later, as the dividing lines of the Cold War hardened, the Irish state's anti-communism and support for the West were in equally little doubt, yet partition was still invoked as the main basis for neutrality and for continuing to stay out of NATO.

The Rome Treaty of 1957 and the formation of the European Common Market had attractions for Ireland as well as the potential both to enlarge its membership and ultimately to develop its own defensive arrangements distinct from those of NATO. Arguments for the 'decoupling of neutrality and partition'[81] however, began to be cautiously aired behind the scenes after Seán Lemass succeeded de Valera as Taoiseach in 1959. These came to little after the Irish state's application to join the United Nations was finally accepted in December 1955. After all, this offered a politically non-controversial role for the defence forces in the organisation's worldwide peace-keeping operations.

What other role the defence forces could have played in the post-1945 period must remain problematic. As the war in Europe neared its end, General Dan McKenna, chief of staff of the Irish defence forces, saw the need for a longer-term policy which would at least give military credibility to neutrality. In a paper presented to the government on 31 March 1945, he even made the case for some form of call-up to maintain adequate force levels.[82] He need not have bothered, for politicians had no wish to learn any lessons from the war about the fate of so many small nations or the potential for Éire's defence to be co-ordinated on an all-Ireland basis.

The decision had already been made to cut back the defence forces to pre-1939 levels but these were not implemented before some splendid ceremonial parades were held to mark the phasing out of the Emergency and to celebrate the state's deliverance from danger. One of the biggest of these was mounted by the garrison of the renamed Michael Collins barracks in Cork. A history of this establishment recalled that 'after a number of years in training the troops were highly skilled and a superb performance was put on for the people of Cork'.[83] Most of the troops on parade, in fact, would be demobilised within a few months.

Independent defence on the cheap is always a contradiction in terms but not, it seems, to the parties who have exercised power in the Irish state since 1945. The leaders of its defence forces have tried, and largely failed, to challenge this, even when they have pointed to the example of other neutral states. To say this is not to decry what Irish troops have done for the United Nations nor, indeed, the work the state and its representatives have done for human rights on a world stage, notably when the former president, Mary Robinson, joined the United Nations as one of its human rights commissioners. Yet, when any new departure in the politics of the European Union carries with it even the hint of an enlarged military role for the Irish republic, alarm bells will ring for its electorate. This has been clear, at the time of writing, in the outcome of the June 2008 referendum on the Lisbon treaty.[84]

Whether Irish neutrality has been really compatible with western democratic values either in the war against Hitler or in the much longer Cold War with the Soviet bloc which followed, it is likely to engage historians for a long time yet. Where the struggle to crush Hitler is concerned, there is little doubt that the Irish state's neutrality or non-belligerency was benign to Britain and its allies, increasingly so as their cause became certain to prevail. This tempts some historians to ask what de Valera had to lose by joining the war in its later stages on the side of the allies when there was no German invasion threat to Éire. Its role would not have been a major combatant one but its anchorages could have aided the 1944 Normandy invasion, helped its supply lines and taken pressure off the English Channel ports.

Short of this, de Valera, his critics still argue, could at least have gone public at the war's end with an expression of Éire's relief at its outcome. With Hitler dead and his Reich in ruins, this would have carried no threat to the state. It would also have run with the grain of most Irish opinion, even among those who had been strong in their support for neutrality. Instead, he settled for the macabre and unnecessary protocol of his visit to Hempel to offer his condolences for the death of an evil racist and warmonger.

Britain by then had learned to live reluctantly with the neutrality of its near neighbour and continued to do so under alternating governments in the post-war era. For Northern Ireland, the neutrality of its even nearer neighbour served to raise higher the walls of misunderstanding rooted in the partition of 1920 and events long pre-dating it. These grew higher still with the onset of the Troubles in 1969 but have now begun to crumble as part of the process of their slow resolution.

Positions on international issues taken by Éire, or the republic which it became in 1949, could still bring tensions to the surface. This happened in 1982 when the Thatcher government went to war with Argentina over the Falkland Islands. Robert Fisk called it a miniature conflict which 're-awoke all the ghosts of Anglo-Irish distrustfulness'.[85] Charles Haughey, the Taoiseach, incurred Margaret Thatcher's fury by his reluctance to support an economic boycott of Argentina and by his insistence that the Falkland Islands' status was a quarrel which should be resolved at the United Nations.

Haughey liked to think of himself as a Fianna Fáil leader cast in the mould of de Valera, and invoking the Irish republic's right to be neutral came easily to him during this short-lived crisis. It was a crisis which cost lives, and there were young Irishmen once more enlisted in Britain's armed forces.[86] Some were killed but there was no likelihood of their bodies being returned to Irish soil for military burial and, indeed, the following year Haughey's party, by then in opposition, strongly criticised the new Fine Gael government for its participation in ceremonies in Dublin to commemorate those from Ireland who had fallen in the two world wars.

The defence minister was confronted by demonstrators as he left a memorial service in Dublin's Church of Ireland cathedral, and one of them called him a traitor to his face. Fianna Fáil's defence spokesman, Sylvester Barrett, issued a statement to the media calling for the government to withdraw army participation in the ceremonies. He described them as 'offensive and divisive' as well as being 'totally inconsistent with our national honour and independence'.[87] The defence forces had been represented before at such events, and the rancour of 1983 had arguably been fuelled by Haughey's clash with the Thatcher government eighteen months earlier.

Twenty years later much had changed. An uneasy peace, painfully achieved, remained intact in Northern Ireland. In Dublin, the Island-bridge memorial to those who had fallen in the world wars had been rededicated in the presence of the state's party leaders and with units of the defence forces on parade. Even Sinn Féin was represented[88] but, in 2003, British forces were at war in Iraq, and Irish regiments were there with them. On 6 April, Lance Corporal Ian Malone of the Irish Guards was killed by sniper fire near Basra.

Long before his death Thomas Davis had famously written of how

> On far foreign fields from Dunkirk to Belgrade.
> Lie the soldiers and chiefs of the Irish brigade.

Ian Malone had been born in Dublin and the army brought him back there to be buried. For the first time since the handover of the Treaty Ports in 1938, soldiers of the Crown paraded in uniform on Irish soil, and it was the first British military funeral agreed to in the Irish state since 1922. In the working-class suburb of Ballyfermot people on the streets heard a piper from the Irish army play the march of the Irish Guards, *Let Erin Remember*. He also played a lament at the Catholic Church of the Assumption as the coffin was carried from it by comrades of Lance Corporal Malone and by soldiers of the Irish army.[89]

The parish priest who conducted the Requiem Mass declared to a congregation of more than a thousand people how unique an event this young soldier's funeral was for the modern Irish state. He added that its symbolism would 'not be lost on people on both sides of the Irish sea'.[90] Ireland has seen more than its fair share of funerals that have been charged with political symbolism. This one, however, served to draw together many strands of a long and troubled relationship which, sixty years earlier, in a time of war and emergency, had faced one of its most severe tests.

Notes

1. Barton, *Northern Ireland in the Second World War*, p. 135.
2. Ibid., p. 138.
3. PRONI, D3004, Sir Basil Brooke Diaries, 7 May 1945.
4. See Chapter 3.

5. Fisk, *In Time of War*, p. 537.
6. Duggan, *Neutral Ireland and the Third Reich*, pp. 242–4.
7. Hillier, *John Betjeman: New Fame, New Love*, p. 198.
8. D. Ferriter, *Judging Dev: a reassessment of the life and legacy of Eamon de Valera* (Dublin: Royal Irish Academy, 2007), p. 263.
9. D. Keogh, *Jews in Twentieth Century Ireland: Refugees, Anti-Semitism and the Holocaust* (Cork: Cork University Press, 1998), p. 174.
10. D. Keogh, 'De Valera, Hitler and the Visit of Condolence, May 1945', *History Ireland*, autumn 1997, Vol. 5, No. 3, pp. 58–61.
11. Ibid.
12. G. Lucy, ' 'I Do What I think is Right': de Valera and the death of Hitler', *New Ulster*, No. 31, March 1997, pp. 10–13.
13. Ferriter, *Judging Dev*, p. 263; also Ryle Dwyer, *Eamon de Valera*, p. 126.
14. Fisk, *In Time of War*, p. 538.
15. Ryle Dwyer, *Eamon de Valera*, pp. 127–8.
16. Ibid.
17. Kenny, *Sir John Maffey and Anglo-Irish Relations During the Second World War*, p. 40.
18. O. D. Edwards, *Eamon de Valera* (Cardiff: GPC Books, 1987), p. 146.
19. Wills, *That Neutral Island*, pp. 400–3.
20. Fisk, *In Time of War*, pp. 549–50.
21. Wills, *That Neutral Island*, pp. 408–9.
22. Ibid.
23. Ibid., pp. 418–21.
24. Keogh, *Jews in Twentieth Century Ireland*, p. 117.
25. Ibid., pp. 116–19; also M. R. Marrus, *The Unwanted: European Refugees in the Twentieth Century* (Oxford: Oxford University Press, 1985), pp. 164–5.
26. M. J. Harris and D. Oppenheimer, *Into the Arms of Strangers: Stories of the Kindertransport* (London: Bloomsbury, 2000).
27. Keogh, *Jews in Twentieth Century Ireland*, p. 160.
28. IMA, G2/2631, 23 July 1940.
29. Keogh, *Jews in Twentieth Century Ireland*, p. 161.
30. D. Keogh, 'Con Cremin, Berlin and "Die Billige Gesandschaft" ', in D. Keogh and M. O'Driscoll (eds), *Ireland in World War II: Diplomacy and Survival* (Cork: Mercier Press, 2004), p. 168.
31. Ibid., p. 170.
32. Bew, *Ireland: the Politics of Enmity 1789–2006*, p. 473.
33. Lee, *Ireland 1912–1985*, pp. 266–7.
34. Wills, *That Neutral Island*, pp. 403–8.
35. Ibid., pp. 413–14.
36. M. Gilbert, *Atlas of the Holocaust: a Complete History* (London: Michael Joseph, 1982), p. 86.
37. Bew, *Ireland: the Politics of Enmity 1789–2006*, p. 364.
38. *Irish Times*, 13 August 1984.
39. D. Keogh and A. McCarty, *Limerick Boycott: Anti-Semitism in Ireland* (Cork: Mercier Press, 2005), p. 102. See also *A Great Hatred*, Channel 4 documentary, 15 October 1997.
40. Keogh, *Jews in Twentieth-Century Ireland: Refugees*, pp. 184 and 190.
41. IMA, G2/X/0040, Minute No. 2, 19 June 1940.
42. Ibid.
43. Ibid.
44. IMA, G2/2631, 21 May 1941, also G2/X/0040, 13 and 14 February 1945.

45. O'Halpin, *Defending Ireland*, pp. 220–1.
46. IMA, G2/X/0040, 11 December 1944 and 21 January 1945; also 1 March 1945.
47. G2/X/0040, 25 May 1939.
48. Ibid., 15 March 1943.
49. Ibid., 28 September 1944.
50. D. Staunton, *The Nationalists of Northern Ireland* (Blackrock, Co. Dublin: Columba Press, 2001), p. 366.
51. *Irish Times*, 29 April 1995.
52. Fisk, *In Time of War*, pp. 549–50.
53. P Leach, 'Irish Post-War Asylum: Nazi Sympathy, pan-Celticism or raisons d'etat', *History Ireland*, May/June 2007, Vol. 15, No. 3, pp. 36–41.
54. Ibid.
55. Ibid.
56. O'Halpin, *Defending Ireland*, pp. 289–90; also O'Reilly, *Hitler's Irishmen*, pp. 281–300.
57. D. Mosley, *A Life of Contrasts: an Autobiography* (London: Hamish Hamilton, 1977), p. 237.
58. Mullins, *Dublin Nazi No 1*, pp. 193–6.
59. Duggan, *Neutral Ireland and the Third Reich*, p. 244.
60. IMA, File 733/P, undated; see also T. Ryle Dwyer, 'Guests of the State', in Keogh and O'Driscoll (eds), *Ireland in World War II: Neutrality and Survival*, pp. 106–25.
61. Ibid., File 733/P.5/231, 25 November 1942.
62. *Guardian*, 21 April 1999.
63. IMA, File 2C/3/45, 27 June 1945; also File C/229.A, 27 March 1942.
64. *Guardian*, 21 April 1999.
65. IMA, C229/P, 5 March 1942; also J. Clive, *Broken Wings* (London: Granada, 1983), p. 413.
66. Bew, *Ireland: the Politics of Enmity 1789–2006*, p. 474.
67. Delaney, *Demography, State and Security: Irish Migration to Britain 1921–1971*, Ch. 4, pp. 160–266.
68. Browne, *Against the Tide*, pp. 156–88.
69. Coogan, *De Valera: Long Fellow, Long Shadow*, p. 639.
70. Ryle Dwyer, *Eamon de Valera*, p. 132.
71. Bowman, *De Valera and the Ulster Question*, p. 205.
72. Coogan, *The IRA*, pp. 255–7.
73. L. Campbell, 'Britain's Changing Attitude to Irish Neutrality 1938 to 1950', *Oglaigh na hEireann, Defence Forces Review*, 2003, pp. 29–33.
74. O'Halpin, *Defending Ireland*, pp. 260–1.
75. Ibid., p. 197.
76. See Chapter 4.
77. M. O'Riordan, 'Leopold H. Kerney, Irish Minister in Spain, 1935–1946', *History Ireland*, Vol. 15, No. 2, March/April 2007, pp. 60–1; also E. Kerney (ed.), www.leopoldkerney.com.
78. *Irish Press*, 18 July 1953.
79. Ibid., 27 June 1953.
80. Ibid., 29 June 1953.
81. O'Halpin, *Defending Ireland*, p. 263.
82. Ibid., p. 258.
83. D. Harvey and G. White, *The Barracks: a History of Victoria/Collins Barracks, Cork* (Cork: Mercier Press, 1997), p. 159.
84. *Guardian*, 12 June 2008; *Irish News*, 14 and 19 June 2008; also *Am Phoblacht/ Sinn Féin Weekly*, 5, 12, 19, 26 June 2008.

85. Fisk, *In Time of War*, pp. 555–6.
86. Ibid.
87. *Irish Times*, 12 November 1983.
88. *Guardian*, 29 April 1995; also *Sunday Times*, 4 June 1995.
89. *Irish News*, 25 April 2003.
90. Ibid.

Bibliography

M. Adams, *Censorship: the Irish Experience* (Tuscaloosa: University of Alabama, 1968).

P. Addison, *Churchill on the Home Front 1900–1955* (London: Jonathan Cape, 1992).

P. Addison and A. Calder (eds), *Time to Kill: the Soldier's Experience of War in the West* (London: Pimlico, 1997).

P. Alter, *Nationalism* (London: Arnold, 1989).

M. Anderson and E. Bort (eds), *The Irish Border: History, Politics, Culture* (Liverpool: Liverpool University Press, 1999).

B. Barrington (ed.) *The Wartime Broadcasts of Francis Stuart* (Dublin: Lilliput Press, 2000).

T. S. Bartlett and K. Jeffrey, *A Military History of Ireland* (Cambridge: Cambridge University Press, 1996).

B. Barton, *The Blitz: Belfast in the War Years* (Belfast: Blackstaff, 1989).

B. Barton, *Northern Ireland in the Second World War* (Belfast: Ulster Historical Foundation, 1995).

B. Behan, *Borstal Boy* (London: Hutchinson, 1958).

B. Behan, *Confessions of an Irish Rebel* (London: Hutchinson, 1965).

J. B. Bell, *The Secret Army: the IRA 1916–1979* (Swords: Poolbeg Books, 1989).

J. W. Blake, *Northern Ireland in the Second World War* (Belfast: HMSO, 1956).

J. Bowman, *De Valera and the Ulster Question 1917–1973* (Oxford: Oxford University Press, 1982).

T. Bowman, *The Ulster Volunteer Force and the Formation of the 36th Ulster Division* (Irish Historical Studies XXXII, No. 125, May 2000).

T. Bowman, 'The Ulster Volunteers 1913–14: Force or Farce?', *History Ireland*, Vol. 10, No. 1, spring 2002.

D. George Boyce and A. O'Day, *The Ulster Crisis* (London/Basingstoke: Palgrave Macmillan, 2005).

A. E. C. Bredin, *A History of the Irish Soldier* (Belfast: Century Books, 1978).

J. D. Brewer and G. I. Higgins (eds), *Anti-Catholicism in Northern Ireland 1600–1998: the Mote and the Beam* (Basingstoke: Macmillan, 1998).

S. Brown, '"Outside the Covenant": Scottish Presbyterian Churches and Irish Immigration 1922–1938' (*Innes Review*, Vol. XLII, Spring 1991).

N. Browne, *Against the Tide* (Dublin: Gill and Macmillan, 1986).

P. Buckland and K. Lunn (eds), *The Irish in British Labour History* (Liverpool University, Institute of Irish Studies, 1992).

A. Calder, *The Myth of the Blitz* (London: Jonathan Cape, 1991).

L. Campbell, 'Britain's Changing Attitude to Irish Neutrality 1938 to 1950', *Oglaigh na hEireann/Defence Forces Review*, 2003.

P. Campbell, *My Life and Easy Times* (London: Anthony Blond, 1967).

J. T. Carroll, *Ireland in the War Years* (Newton Abbot: David and Charles, 1975).

W. A. Carson, *Ulster and the Irish Republic* (Belfast: William Cleland, 1956).

R. Cathcart, *The Most Contrary Region: the BBC in Northern Ireland 1924–1984* (Belfast: Blackstaff, 1984).

J. Charmley, *Churchill: the End of Glory – a Political Biography* (London: Hodder and Stoughton, 1993).

R. S. Churchill, *Young Statesman: Winston S. Churchill 1901–1914* (London: Heinemann, 1967).

W. S. Churchill, *The Second World War, Vol I: The Gathering Storm* (London: Cassell, 1948).

W. S. Churchill, *The Second World War, Vol II: Their Finest Hour* (London: Cassell, 1949).

W. S. Churchill, *The Second World War, Vol III: The Grand Alliance* (London: Cassell, 1950).

W. S. Churchill, *The Second World War, Vol IV: The Hinge of Fate* (London: Cassell, 1951).

W. S. Churchill, *War Speeches*, ed. C. Eade (London: Cassell, 1951).

J. Clive, *Broken Wings* (London: Granada, 1983).

R. Cole, *Propaganda, Censorship and Irish Neutrality in the Second World War* (Edinburgh: Edinburgh University Press, 2006).

J. Colville, *The Fringes of Power: Downing Street Diaries 1939–1955* (London: Cassell, 1985).

T. P. Coogan, *Michael Collins: a Biography* (London: Arrow Books, 1991).

T. P. Coogan, *De Valera: Long Fellow, Long Shadow* (London: Hutchinson, 1993).

T. P. Coogan, *The IRA* (London: HarperCollins, 1995).

P. Craig, *Brian Moore: a Biography* (London: Bloomsbury, 2002).

M. Cronin, *The Blueshirts and Irish Politics* (Dublin: Four Courts Press, 1997).

R. Croucher, *Engineers at War* (London: Merlin, 1982).

L. Daiken (ed.), *They Go, the Irish* (London: Nicholson and Watson, 1944).

A. Danchev and D. Todman (eds), *War Diaries 1939–1945: Field Marshal Alanbrooke* (London: Weidenfeld and Nicolson, 2001).

J. Deeny, *To Cure and to Care: Memoirs of a Chief Medical Officer* (Dublin: Glendale Press, 1989).

E. Delaney, *Demography, State and Security: Irish Migration to Britain 1921– 1971* (Liverpool: Liverpool University Press, 2000).

F. Delaney, *Betjeman Country* (London: Paladin, 1983).

P. Devlin, *Straight Left: an Autobiography* (Belfast: Blackstaff, 1993).

A. V. Dicey, *A Fool's Paradise: Being a Constitutionalist's Criticism of the Home Rule Bill of 1912* (London: John Murray, 1912).

R. Doherty, *Clear the Way: A History of the 38th (Irish) Brigade 1941– 47* (Dublin: Irish Academic Press, 1993).

R. Doherty, *Irish Men and Women in the Second World War* (Dublin: Four Courts Press, 1999).

P. Dollan, *Unpublished Memoirs* (Glasgow: Michell Library, undated).

P. Dooley, *The Irish in Britain* (Watford: Connolly Association, 1943).

E. Doyle, 'Soldier and Officer: the Army in Two Perspectives in the 1930s', (*Irish Sword*, Vol. XVIII, No. 72, winter 1991.

E. Duffin, *Unpublished Diary* (Belfast: Public Record Office of Northern Ireland).

J. P. Duggan, *Neutral Island and the Third Reich* (Dublin: Gill and Macmillan, 1975).

J. P. Duggan, *Herr Hempel and the German Legation in Dublin 1937– 1945* (Dublin and Portland, OR: Irish Academic Press, 2003).

T. Ryle Dwyer, *Eamon de Valera* (Dublin: Gill and Macmillan, 1980).

T. Ryle Dwyer, *Strained Relations: Ireland at Peace and the USA at War 1941–45* (Dublin: Gill and Macmillan, 1988).

O. D. Edwards, *Eamon de Valera* (Cardiff: GPC, 1987).

R. English, *Ernie O'Malley: IRA Intellectual* (Oxford: Clarendon Press, 1998).

R. English, *Armed Struggle: the History of the IRA* (London: Macmillan, 2003).

R. Fanning, *Independent Ireland* (Dublin: Helicon, 1983).

D. Ferriter, *Judging Dev: a reassessment of the life and legacy of Eamon de Valera* (Dublin: Royal Irish Academy, 2007).

R. Findlay, 'Nationalism, Race, Religion and the Irish Question in inter-war Scotland', *Innes Review*, Vol. XLII, spring 1991.

R. Fisk, *In Time of War: Ireland, Ulster and the Price of Neutrality* (London: Paladin, 1983).

D. J. L. Fitzgerald, *A History of the Irish Guards* (Aldershot: Gale and Polden, 1949).

G. Fleming, *Magennis VC: the Story of Northern Ireland's Only Winner of the Victoria Cross* (Dublin: History Ireland, 1998).

C. Foley, *Legion of the Rearguard: the IRA and the Modern Irish State* (London: Pluto, 1992).

K. Ford, 'Thy Sons Shall Come From Afar: Thy Daughters Shall Rise Up By Thy Side', *New Ulster: Journal of the Ulster Society*, No. 22, 1994.

R. F. Foster, *Paddy and Mr Punch: Connections in Irish and English History* (London: Penguin, 1993).

R. F. Foster, *W. B. Yeats: the Apprentice Mage* (Oxford: Oxford University Press, 1998).

R. F. Foster, *The Irish Story: Telling Tales and Making it Up* (London: Penguin, 2001).

A. Gailey, 'King Carson: an Essay on the Invention of Leadership', *Irish Historical Studies* XXX, No. 117, May 1996.

T. Gallagher, *Glasgow, the Uneasy Peace: Religious Tension in Modern Scotland* (Manchester: Manchester University Press, 1987).

J. Gardiner, *Wartime: Britain 1939–1945* (London: Headline Books, 2004).

G. Gelborn, *Francis Stuart: a Life* (Dublin: Raven Arts, 1990).

M. Gilbert, *World in Torment: Winston S. Churchill 1916–1922* (London: Heinemann, 1975).

M. Gilbert, *Atlas of the Holocaust: a Complete History* (London: Michael Joseph, 1982).

B. Girvin and G. Roberts (eds), *Ireland and the Second World War: Politics, Society and Remembrance* (Dublin: Four Courts Press, 2000).

V. Glendinning, *Elizabeth Bowen: Portrait of a Writer* (London: Phoenix Books, 1977).

M. Goldring, *Belfast: from Loyalty to Rebellion* (London: Lawrence and Wishart, 1991).

T. Gray, *Mr Smyllie, Sir* (Dublin: Gill and Macmillan, 1991).

T. Gray, *The Lost Years: the Emergency in Ireland* (London: Little, Brown and Co., 1997).

F. L. Green, *Odd Man Out* (London: Michael Joseph, 1945, also Sphere Books, 1991).

B. Hanley, *The Impossible Victory: a Personal Account of the Battle for the River Po* (London: William Kimber, 1980).

B. Hanley, *The IRA 1926–1936* (Dublin: Four Courts Press, 2002).

M. J. Harris and D. Oppenheimer, *Into the Arms of Strangers: Stories of the Kindertransport* (London: Bloomsbury, 2000).

T. Harrison, *Living Through the Blitz* (London: Collins, 1976).

D. Harvey and G. White, *The Barracks: a History of Victoria/Collins Barracks, Cork* (Cork: Mercier Press, 1997).

M. Hastings, *Armageddon: the Battle for Germany 1944–45* (Basingstoke and Oxford: Macmillan, 2004).

A. G. Hepburn, *Communism in Scotland* (Glasgow: John S. Burns, 1941).

R. Herzstein, *The War that Hitler Won: the Most Infamous Propaganda Campaign in History* (London: Hamish Hamilton, 1979).

J. R. Hill (ed.), *A New History of Ireland*, Vol. VI: *Ireland 1921–1984* (Oxford: Oxford University Press, 2003).

B. Hillier, *John Betjeman: New Fame, New Love* (London: John Murray, 2002).

F. H. Hinsley and C. A. G. Simkins, *British Intelligence in the Second World War*, Vol. 4: *Security and Counter-Intelligence* (London: HMSO, 1990).

A. Hoar, *In Green and Red: the Lives of Frank Ryan* (Dingle, Co. Kerry: Brandon Press, 2004).

J. L. Hodson, *Towards the Morning* (London: Victor Gollancz, 1941).

J. Horgan, 'Fianna Fail and Arms Decommissioning', *History Ireland*, Vol. 5, No. 4, winter 1997.

J. Houston (ed.), *Brian Faulkner: Memoirs of a Statesman* (London: Weidenfeld and Nicolson, 1978).

C. Hull, *Memoirs*, Volume Two (London: Hodder and Stoughton, 1948).

M. M. Hull, *Irish Secrets: German Espionage in Wartime Ireland 1939–1945* (Dublin and Portland, OR: Irish Academic Press, 2003).

J. Hutchinson, *The Dynamics of Cultural Nationalism: the Gaelic Revival and the Creation of the Irish Nation State* (London: Allen and Unwin, 1987).

H. Montgomery Hyde, *The Life of Sir Edward Carson, Lord Carson of Duncairn* (London: Heinemann, 1953).

B. Inglis, *West Briton* (London: Faber and Faber, 1962).

P. Inman, *Labour in the Munitions Industries* (London: HMSO and Longman Green, 1957).

A. Jackson, 'Unionist Myths 1912–1985', *Past and Present*, 136, August 1962.

A. Jackson, *Sir Edward Carson* (Dublin: Historical Association of Ireland/Dundalgan Press, 1993).

A. Jackson, *Ireland 1798–1998: Politics and War* (Oxford: Blackwell, 1999).

H. Jordan, *Milestones in Murder: Defining Moments in Ulster's Terror War* (Edinburgh: Mainstream, 2002).

D. L. Keir, *A Constitutional History of Modern Britain* (London: Adam and Charles Black, 1938).

S. Kennedy (ed.), *One Million Poor? the Challenge of Irish Inequality* (Dublin: Turoe Press, 1981).

K. Kenny, *Sir John Maffey and Anglo-Irish Relations During the Second World War* (Edinburgh University, Centre for Second World War Studies, MSc Dissertation, 1998).

D. Keogh, *Twentieth Century Ireland: Nation and State* (Dublin: Gill and Macmillan, 1994).

D. Keogh, 'De Valera, Hitler and the Visit of Condolence, May 1945', *History Ireland*, Vol. 5, No. 3, autumn 1997.

D. Keogh, *Jews in Twentieth Century Ireland: Refugees, anti-Semitism and the Holocaust* (Cork: Cork University Press, 1998).

D. Keogh and M. O'Driscoll, *Ireland in World War Two: Neutrality and Survival* (Cork: Mercier Press, 2004).

D. Keogh and A. McCarty, *The Limerick Boycott: Anti-Semitism in Ireland* (Cork: Mercier Press, 2005).

E. Kerney (ed.), www.leopoldkerney.com.

W. K. Kimball (ed.), *Churchill and Roosevelt: an Alliance Forged* Vol. II (Princeton: Princeton University Press, 1984).

D. Leach, 'Irish Post-war Asylum: Nazi Sympathy, Pan-Celticism or Raisons d'Etat?', *History Ireland* Vol. 15, No. 3, May/June 2007.

R. N. Lebow, *White Britain, Black Ireland: the Influence of Stereotypes on Colonial Policy* (Philadelphia: Institute for the Study of Human Issues, 1976).

J. J. Lee, *Ireland 1912–1985: Politics and Society* (Cambridge: Cambridge University Press, 1989).

M. Lennon, M. McAdam and J. O'Brien (eds), *Across the Water: Irish Women's Lives in Britain* (London: Virago, 1988).

Earl of Longford and T. P. O'Neill, *Eamon de Valera* (Dublin: Gill and Macmillan, 1970).

M. Longley and F. Ormsby, *John Hewitt: the Selected Poems of John Hewitt* (Belfast: Blackstaff, 2007).

G. Lucy, 'I do what I think is right': de Valera and the Death of Hitler', *New Ulster*, No. 31, March 1997.

F. S. L. Lyons, *Ireland Since the Famine* (London: Weidenfeld and Nicolson, 1971).

S. McAughtry, *McAughtrey's War* (Belfast: Blackstaff, 1985).

M. MacDonald, *Titans and Others* (London: Collins, 1972).

U. MacEoin, *The IRA in the Twilight Years* (Dublin: Argenta Books, 1997).

Y. McEwen, 'Deaths in Irish Regiments and the Extent of Irish Volunteering for the British Army', *Irish Sword*, Vol. XXIV, No. 95, summer 2004.

Y. McEwen, What Have You Done for Ireland? The 36th Ulster Division in the Great War: Politics, Propaganda and the Demography of Deaths', *Irish Sword*, Vol. XXIV, No. 95, winter 2004).

F. McGarry, *Eoin O'Duffy: a Self-made Hero* (Oxford: Oxford University Press, 2005).

J. R. B. McMinn (ed.), *Against the Tide: a Calendar of the Papers of the Reverend J. B. Armour, Irish Presbyterian and Home Ruler* (Belfast: Public Record Office of Northern Ireland, 1985).

T. Magee, *Northern Ireland: Crisis and Conflict* (London: Routledge, 1974).

M. Manning, *The Blueshirts* (Dublin: Gill and Macmillan, 1970).

N. Mansergh, The *Unsolved Question: the Anglo-Irish Settlement and its Undoing 1917–1972* (New Haven and London: Yale University Press, 1991).

M. Marrus, *The Unwanted: European Refugees in the Twentieth Century* (Oxford: Oxford University Press, 1985).

E. Meehan, *Free Movement between Ireland and the UK: from the 'common travel area' to the Common Travel Area* (Dublin: Trinity College Policy Institute, 2000).

R. Menzies, *Afternoon Light: Some Memories of Men and Events* (London: Cassell, 1967).

M. Milotte, *Communism in Modern Ireland* (Dublin: Gill and Macmillan, 1984).

E. Moloney, *A Secret History of the IRA* (London: Penguin/Allen Lane, 2002).

R. Monck and W. Rolston, *Belfast in the Thirties: an Oral History* (Belfast: Blackstaff, 1987).

N. Monsarrat, *The Cruel Sea* (London: Cassell, 1951).

B. Montgomery, *Memoirs of Field Marshal the Viscount Montgomery of Alamein* (London: Collins, 1958).

B. Moore, *The Emperor of Ice-Cream* (London: Andre Deutsch, 1965).

Lord Moran, *Winston Churchill: the Struggle for Survival* (London: Constable, 1966).

D. Mosley, *A Life of Contrasts: an autobiography* (London: Hamish Hamilton, 1977).

G. Mullins, Dublin Nazi No. 1: the Life of Adolf Mahr (Dublin: Liberties Press, 2007).

D. Murphy, *A Place Apart* (London: John Murray, 1978).

K. Myers, *Watching the Door: Cheating Death in 1970s Belfast* (Dublin: Lilliput Press, 2006).

H. Nicolson, *Diaries and Letters 1939–1945* (London: Collins, 1967).

C. C. O'Brien, 'Yeats and Fascism: What Rough Beast', *New Statesman*, 26 February 1965, Vol. LXIX, No. 1772.

C. C. O'Brien, *Ancestral Voices: Religion and Nationalism in Ireland* (Dublin: Poolbeg, 1994).

C. C. O'Brien, *Memoir: My Life and Themes* (London: Profile Books, 1998).

E. O'Connor, *Reds and the Green: Ireland, Russia and the Communist International 1919–1943* (Dublin: UCD Press 2004).

D. O'Donoghue, *Hitler's Irish Voices: the Story of German Rado's Wartime Irish Service* (Belfast: Beyond the Pale Publications, 1998).

D. O'Donoghue, 'A State Within a State: the Nazis in Neutral Ireland', *History Ireland*, Vol. 14, No. 6, November/December 2006.

D. O'Driscoll, *Censorship in Ireland 1939–1945: Neutrality, Politics and Society* (Cork: Cork University Press, 1996).

E. O'Halpin, *Defending Ireland: the Irish State and its Enemies Since 1922* (Oxford: Oxford University Press, 1991).

E. O'Halpin, 'Aspects of Intelligence', *Irish Sword* 1993–94, Vol. XIX.

E. O'Halpin, *MI5 in Ireland 1939–1945: the Official History* (Dublin: Irish Academic Press, 2003).

J. O'Neill, *The Blood-Dark Track: a Family History* (London: Granta, 2000).

T. O'Reilly, *Hitler's Irishmen* (Dublin: Mercier Press, 2008).

M. O'Riordan, 'Leopold Kerney, Irish Minister in Spain 1939–1946', (*History Ireland*, Vol. 15, No. 2, March/April 2007).

S. Orwell and I. Angus, *The Collected Essays, Journalism and Letters of George Orwell*, Volume 2: *My Country Right or Left 1940-1943* (London: Penguin, 1968).

B. O'Shea, *Myth and Reality: Propaganda, Censorship and the Creation of the Irish Free State, January 1919–June 1922* (Unpublished Ph.D. thesis, Open University, 2002).

D. Parsons, 'Mobilization and Expansion 1939–40', *Irish Sword* 1993–94, Vol. XIX.

H. Patterson, *Ireland Since 1939: the Persistence of Conflict* (Dublin: Penguin, 2006).

C. Ponting, *1940: Myth and Reality* (London: Cardinal, 1990).

J. B. Priestley, *English Journey* (London: Heinemann and Gollancz, 1933).

O. P. Rafferty, *Catholicism in Ulster 1603–1983: an Interpretative History* (London: Hurst and Company, 1994).

J. Richards, *Visions of Yesterday* (London: Routledge and Kegan Paul, 1973).

S. W. Roskill, *The War at Sea 1939–1945*, Vol. 1 (London: HMSO, 1954).

A. Roth, *Mr Bewley in Berlin: Aspects of the Career of an Irish Diplomat 1933–1939* (Dublin, Four Courts Press, 2000).

M. Ryan, *Tom Barry, Freedom Fighter* (Cork: Mercier Press, 2003).

T. Salmon, *Unneutral Ireland: an Ambivalent and Unique Security Policy* (Oxford: Clarendon Press, 1989).

R. C. Sanger, *Malcolm MacDonald: Bringing an End to Empire* (Liverpool: Liverpool University Press, 1995).

B. Share, *The Emergency: Neutral Ireland 1939–1945* (Dublin: Gill and Macmillan, 1978).

D. Sharrock and M. Devenport, *Man of War, Man of Peace: the Unauthorised Biography of Gerry Adams* (London and Basingstoke: Macmillan, 1997).

P. Shea, *Voices and the Sound of Drums: an Irish Autobiography* (Belfast: Blackstaff, 1981).

D. Sheridan (ed.), *Wartime Women: a Mass Observation Anthology: the Experience of Women at War* (London: Mandarin, 1990).

A. Slide, *The Cinema and Ireland* (Jefferson, NC and London: McFarland and Co., 1988).

G. R. Sloan, *The Geo-Politics of Anglo-Irish Relations in the Twentieth Century* (Leicester University Press, 1997).

E. Staunton, 'The Boundary Commission Debacle 1925: Aftermath and Implications', *History Ireland*, Vol. 4, No. 2, 1996.

E. Staunton, *The Nationalists of Northern Ireland* (Blackrock, Co. Dublin: Columba Press, 2001).

E. Staunton, 'Frank Ryan and Collaboration: a Reassessment', *History Ireland*, Vol. 5, No. 3, autumn 1997.

A. T. Q. Stewart, *Edward Carson* (Dublin: Gill and Macmillan, 1981).

C. Townshend, *Political Violence in Ireland: Government and Resistance Since 1948* (Oxford: Clarendon Press, 1983).

P. Verney, *The Micks: the Story of the Irish Guards* (London: Peter Davies, 1970).

B. Loring Villa, *Unauthorised Action: Mountbatten and the Dieppe Raid, 1942* (Don Mills, ON and Oxford University Press, 1989).

G. Walker, *The Politics of Frustration: Harry Midgley and the Failure of Labour in Northern Ireland* (Manchester: Manchester University Press, 1985).

G. Walker, *A History of the Ulster Unionist Party: Protest, Pragmatism, Pessimism* (Manchester: Manchester University Press, 2004).

G. Walker, 'Northern Ireland, British/Irish Relations and American Concerns, 1942–1956', *Twentieth Century British History*, Vol. 18, No. 2, 2007.

N. West (ed.), *The Guy Liddell Diaries, Vol 1 1939–1942* (Abingdon: Routledge, 1997).

T. De Vere White, *Kevin O'Higgins* (Kerry: Anvil Books, 1988).

C. Wills, *That Neutral Island: a Cultural History of Ireland During the Second World War* (London: Faber and Faber, 2007).

J. Winant, *A Letter from Grosvenor Square* (London: Hodder and Stoughton, 1947).

I. S. Wood, *Churchill* (Basingstoke: Macmillan, 2000).

F. Wright, *Two Lands on One Soil: Ulster Politics Before Home Rule* (Dublin: Gill and Macmillan, 1996).

P. Young, 'Defence and the New Irish State', *Irish Sword*, 1993–94, Vol. XIX.

Newspapers and Journals Consulted

An Phoblacht/Republican News
Daily Mail
Éire-Ireland
Glasgow Observer and Scottish Catholic Herald
Guardian
History Ireland
Historical Journal
Innes Review: Journal of the Scottish Catholic Historical Association
Irish Historical Studies
Irish Independent
Irish News

Irish Press
Irish Sword: Journal of the Military History Society of Ireland
Irish Times
Londonderry Sentinel
New Statesman
New Ulster: Journal of the Ulster Society
News Letter
Northern Whig
Observer
Oglaigh na hEireann: Defence Forces Review
Sunday Times
Sunday World
Twentieth Century British History

Manuscript Sources

Public Record Office of Northern Ireland, Belfast

Sir Wilfrid Spender Diaries D559
Sir Basil Brooke Diaries D3004
Cabinet Papers: Cab 3A/78/B
Cab 4/61/5
Cab 4/622
Cab 4473/10
Cab 9C/22/1
Cab 9C/22/2
Cab 9C/47/2
Cab 9CD/85/8
Ministry of Home Affairs HA 9/2/650
HA 20A/1/24
Ministry of Commerce Com 6/1/440
Ministry of Finance Fin 18/22/37
Ministry of Public Security MPS 51/3/7
Emma Duffin Diary D/21/09/18/9

Irish Military Archive, Dublin

G2 – Army Intelligence G2X/0040
G2X/0093
G2X/0257

G2X/2631
G2 2C3
G2/ C/229 A
G2 C/229 P

Other Sources

Tom Harrisson Mass Observation Archive, University of Sussex, Brighton.
Files relating to Northern Ireland, Moya Woodside Diary.
Front Line 1940–41: Official History of the Civil Defence of Britain. (London: His Majesty's Stationery Office, 1942).

Index